Broke In Boston

A Guide to Living Cheap in the City

2007
Edition

Editor-in-Chief
Primary Author
Andrew Brett Einhorn

Contributing Authors
Lindsay Holst
Joelle Hobeika
Kevin Collins
Rebecca Dreilinger

Editorial Assistants
Rebecca Dreilinger
Amanda Byers

Copy Editor
Lisa Gerry

Cover
Michelle Cormier
www.michillustrator.com

Library of Congress Control Number: 2006906486

Although we strive for perfection, the authors and publisher accept no responsibility for loss, injury, or other consequences sustained from using this book.

Please report any errors or problems with the book to us via our website www.brokeinboston.com.

ISBN 0-9787917-0-3

This book is dedicated in loving memory to Sidney Einhorn and to his two beautiful, great-granddaughters Brooke Sidney Einhorn and Payton Rachel Einhorn

A special thanks to Mr. Googins, Mrs. Hansen, and Mrs. Hartigan of the Kingswood-Oxford School for teaching me how to write, and to my family for all of their love and support.

Table of Contents

Getting There and Away

BY CAR

If you're driving, keep in mind Massachusetts drivers are notoriously aggressive, and routes in downtown Boston may be marked differently than on maps—especially older maps—due to the Big Dig: a huge road construction project that has spanned nearly two decades. The major interstates servicing Boston are I-90, which runs East/West, and I-93, which runs North/South. I-90 is a toll road. The two interstates meet in downtown Boston, and much of Boston's traffic originates at that intersection. Expect big delays during rush hour and Sunday evenings when droves of Bostonians return from weekend getaways.

BY PLANE

If you fly into or out of Boston, you'll be using **Logan International Airport**, located on a bed of tidal flats across the Boston Harbor from South Boston. Logan Airport is accessible via the **Blue Line** of the **"T"** (metro system—see "Transportation" section). A shuttle bus connects the Blue Line Airport T stop to the Airport terminal. Stops for the shuttle service are marked with an encircled T and are numerous. It takes about 10-15 minutes to get to Government Center (downtown) from the Airport T stop.

The Silver Line of the T connects the South Station T and Rail station to the airport as well. Costs per ride on the T vary depending on the distance to the final destination, but most rides cost $1.25. Consult the T staff window for the exact cost and to get a token valid for a single, one-way ride. If you're in a rush, **taxis** wait outside the airport. Bear in mind, though, Boston traffic may slow you down.

Water taxis also service the airport from various points along the waterfront in downtown Boston (Rowes Wharf, Long Wharf, Anthony's Pier 4, etc.). Rides cost $10 one-way, $17 round trip and take approximately seven minutes to downtown. Board the water transportation (#66) bus at the curb outside of the arrivals area at each airport terminal to get to the water taxis. Call ahead for a ride or ask your bus driver to do it for you. Tickets are sold on board the boat. For more information, call 617-422-0392, or visit *www.citywatertaxi.com*.

A variety of **discount airlines** service Logan Airport including JetBlue, America West, Midwest, United Express, and AirTran Airlines. While internet search engines like Orbitz and Expedia make locating cheap tickets easier, they do not list discount carriers like JetBlue. Go directly to the websites of these airlines and search for fares as needed, or signup for email notifications of special flight deals.

If you're a student, the Student Travel Agency (STA) often provides excellent flight deals in and out of Boston. Visit their website *www.statravel.com* or one of their three offices in Boston:

Boston University	Downtown Boston	Northeastern University
738 Comm Ave Boston, MA 02215	297 Newbury St, Boston, MA 02115	Curry Student Center Rm 144 Boston, MA 02115
617-264-2030	617-266-6014	617-373-7900
Hours: 10-6 M-Sa closed Sunday	Hours: 10-7 M-F, 10-6 Sa, 10-5 Su	Hours: 9-6 M-F
T (Green B): BU Central	T (Green B/C/D): Hynes	T (Green E): Northeastern

Flight costs are posted in shop windows daily. Travel may also be booked online. One drawback to STA is that they often require you to purchase an international student ID card if traveling overseas. However, their agents are extremely helpful.

OTHER METHODS FOR LANDING A CHEAP FLIGHT:

- Fly into or out of **Providence's (Green) Airport** instead of Boston's (Logan) Airport—flights are almost always cheaper and Providence is only an hour's drive from Boston. Try flying Southwest for great deals (*www.southwest.com   800-435-9792*). To get there, take I-93 South from downtown to I-95 South and get off at Exit 13. Rates for long-term parking are $11/day, $56/week.

- It will always be cheaper to fly to a cold place during winter than to fly to a warm place during winter, unless the cold destination is host to ski areas. So if you're looking to make spring break plans, think about heading to Seattle, Vancouver, or Montreal instead of Cancun. The same holds true during the summer, when serious deals abound for flights or vacation packages to Florida, Mexico, and the Caribbean.
- Internet booking is cheaper than speaking to an agent.
- Flying on Saturdays, weekdays, holidays (e.g. Christmas Day), and on overnight flights will save you lots of money, as will departing very early or very late in the day.
- Fares will increase significantly once the two week advance purchase threshold has been breached, so try booking well in advance. However, **last-minute travelers** may be rewarded with specials if flights do not fill up; so check the websites of low fare carriers frequently for last-minute deals.
- Great deals may be found on Hotwire.com and by naming your own price on Priceline.com. For success with Priceline bidding, find the lowest price available via Orbitz or Hotwire online, and submit a bid for tickets that is 10-20 percent lower than that price.   Both Hotwire and Priceline offer last-minute travel deals.

BY TRAIN

There are three train stations serviced by **Amtrak** (*www.amtrak.com 800-872-7245*) in Boston: South Station, Back Bay Station, and North Station. Trains coming from the north of Boston empty out at North Station. Trains originating from parts south of Boston come into South Station. Trains originating from the west empty at Back Bay Station. All stations are serviced by public transit (the T—see map in back). Taxis also wait outside each station.

LODGING

Hotels are expensive but you'll get the best deals on Hotwire.com, or by bidding for a hotel on Priceline.com. Generally, the further you stay from downtown, the cheaper the hotel will be. If you're willing to learn to use the T (metro), you can shave big sums of money off your lodging costs. If you're looking for a **hostel** or very cheap accommodations, your best bet is to visit *www.hostels.co*

Transportation

The entire public transit system for Boston is called the Massachusetts Bay Transportation Agency (**MBTA**). The MBTA is composed of buses, commuter trains, trolleys and subways (the "T"), and water taxis or ferries. Information about the MBTA may be found on its website: *www.mbta.com*.

DISCOUNTED FARES

- Up to 2 children **under 5** years old ride for FREE when accompanied by an adult.
- **Children 5-11** need only pay 60¢ per ride on the T, 45¢ for bus rides.
- **Junior high and high school students** need only pay 60¢ per T ride or 45¢ per bus ride if they show an MBTA student ID badge—available at participating junior high and high schools. Fare reduction is only valid to and from school on days that school is in session and only until 8pm.
- **Senior Citizens** pay a reduced fare on all MBTA service with a Senior Citizen ID Card. These cards may be obtained for 50¢ from the Senior & Access Pass Program Office located at Back Bay Station. Open 8:30-5:00, M-F. For more information, call 617-222-5438. Subway service at most stations is 35¢ and regular local bus service is 25¢.
- **Persons with disabilities**: Reduced fare on all MBTA service with a Transportation Access Program (TAP) card. Application available by calling 617-222-5438 or at Back Bay Station, open 8:30-5:00, M-F. Medicare Card holders are automatically eligible.
- **Blind** persons travel FREE.

MONTHLY PASSES

Monthly passes for travel on the various components of the MBTA may be purchased online via the MBTA website (*www.mbta.com*) or at Government Center Station, Harvard Station, Downtown Crossing Station, and South Station.

    Monthly subway passes—valid for unlimited use on the T (subway)—cost $44 while **monthly bus passes** for unlimited travel on all local bus routes costs $31. $71 will get you a **monthly combo pass** good for unlimited travel on the T, regular bus routes, commuter rail (zones 1A and 1B), as well as a $2.20 discount on express bus routes. Additional fares may be added for Red Line riders originating at the Quincy Adams and Braintree stops. Add $8 for a **Monthly Combo Pass Plus**, which gets you unlimited travel on Inner Harbor Ferries as well ($79/month total). For **monthly commuter passes outside zones 1 and 2** (immediate suburbs), costs vary from $106-198.

    Monthly pass holders of any kind may travel with one companion for FREE on Sundays. Additionally, pass holders receive 10 percent off collision and property damage auto insurance (up to $75.00) when they turn in 11 out of 12 passes per policy year to their insurance carrier.

    For a complete list of pass sales locations, visit: *www.mbta.com/traveling_t/sales_locs.asp*. PASSES ARE NOT REPLACEABLE IF LOST OR STOLEN.

THE "T"

    The city's metro system or subway is lovingly referred to as "**the T**"— short for trolley. (Maps of the T may be found at the end of this book.) Fare costs for the T vary with distance traveled but are normally $1.25 per ride. Each station has a booth where MBTA staff sells tokens for rides. Trains are marked *Inbound* (toward downtown) and *Outbound* (away from downtown). To indicate which direction a trolley is traveling, the last stop in the direction the trolley is headed is posted on the front of the train and on various signs around stations.

TIPS:

    If you know you will be making many trips on the T in the same day, it may make more economic sense to pick up a one-day **visitor's pass** for $7.50, a three-day pass for $18, or a seven-day pass for $35 at any T station. Day passes allow riders to travel as much as they want on the T, buses, commuter rail, and Inner Harbor Ferries for one cost instead of having to buy tokens for each ride.

6 Transportation

WARNINGS:

"Express" trains head directly to one stop without stopping at the normally scheduled stops before it. If you accidentally stay on a train headed express to somewhere, you may end up blowing right by your stop. So pay attention to any announcements from the drivers.

There are four Green Line trains (B, C, D, and E) that use the same track downtown. Make sure you note which of the four you are getting on if headed Outbound, so you don't end up in a different part of town than you wanted to go. A red line through the letter on a sign means that the train goes only part way on that route. (Ask the driver what the end point is if concerned.)

T HOURS:

Generally speaking, the T runs from 5am-1am M-Sa, and 6am-1am on Sundays. However, schedules vary slightly by line and station origin. For detailed schedules, consult the schedule charts in the back of this book on page 196.

PETS:

Certified service animals and guide dogs are always allowed on the T. During rush hours (*6-10am Inbound & 3-7pm Outbound*), small animals may be carried in lap-sized containers. During off-peak hours (*10am-2pm & 7pm-1am*), non-service dogs are allowed on at the discretion of operators. Dogs must be leashed and are not allowed to annoy riders or take up a seat.   *–Courtesy of www.MBTA.com*

BIKES:

Conventional bicycles are not allowed on the Green Line or the Mattapan Trolley at any time. Bikes are allowed on the Blue, Red, and Orange Lines only. On weekdays, bikes are allowed during off-peak periods: before 7am, 10am-4pm, and after 7pm. Bikes are permitted all day on weekends. Bikes are not allowed on buses that substitute for rail service (e.g. Silver Line). Bikes are allowed at all stations **except** Park Street, Downtown Crossing (except to transfer), or Government Center. Folding bikes are allowed on the subway at any time when folded in the most compact position and carried in a pouch or carrying case intended for that purpose. Due to train crowding often associated with special events, bikes are not allowed on the T on St. Patrick's Day, Patriot's Day and July 4th. *–Courtesy of www.MBTA.com*

OVERVIEW:

Bostonians will quickly and sometimes curtly correct you for calling the T a subway or metro. While this practice may seem strange, there is one major distinguishing feature of the T which sets it apart from the metros or subways of other cities: it runs aboveground and underground. Predominately though, the T runs aboveground— allowing riders to gaze out of train car windows and gain a greater understanding of the city's layout.

A major drawback of this system lay in that the T is subject to the same traffic laws as cars and makes frequent stops for red lights. Additionally, since turning lanes must cross T tracks, inconsiderate or oblivious drivers cause frequent delays for T riders by hovering over T tracks for too long while attempting to turn. As expected, cars and Ts do collide occasionally.

The **Green Line** of the T is the major aboveground line and is composed of the B, C, D, and E lines. The Green Line runs East and West, and can easily be understood by looking at your own hand. If you extend all of your fingers out as far as possible and eliminate your thumb, you have a scaled down model of the four Green Lines (B,C,D,E) where your wrist represents downtown, the eastern point where all lines meet.

Generally speaking, the *B Line* services Boston University, the neighborhood of Brighton, and Boston College; the *C and D lines* service the town of Brookline; and the *E Line* services Northeastern University and the neighborhood of Jamaica Plain. **All outbound trains on the B, C, and D lines originating after Kenmore are FREE.** The same is true of outbound trains on the E line originating after the Symphony stop.

The **Red Line** connects the towns of Somerville and Cambridge—the location of Harvard University—to downtown and South Boston. The **Blue Line** services Government Center, the airport, the famed Boston Aquarium, and the town of Revere. The **Orange Line** services the neighborhoods of Jamaica Plain, Back Bay, Chinatown, and Charlestown.

Finally, the **Silver Line**—a recent edition to the T system—is actually a high-speed bus that runs both above and below ground. It connects the Red, Orange, and Green Lines to the commuter rail, intercity buses, and Amtrak. The Silver Line also connects South Station to Logan Airport, and the waterfront to other parts of downtown.

8 Transportation

USEFUL NUMBERS:

MBTA Main Switchboard:	617-222-5000
Traveler's Information Center:	617-222-3200
or	800-392-6100
LOST & FOUND (T/Bus, 8:30am- 5pm M-F):	617-222-5000
MBTA Police: 617-222-1000 Emergency:	617-222-1212

COMMUTER RAIL

A network of aboveground trains—referred to as the lightrail—brings suburban-dwelling passengers without access to the T to and from Boston daily. Costs vary according to distance traveled, but do not exceed $6 each way. Tickets can be purchases on the trains for an additional charge of $2 during rush hour, $1 otherwise.

Frequent riders may purchase monthly combo passes: see "monthly passes" above under "Transportation." A map of all commuter rail stops and routes may be found in the back of this book on page 205. Visit the MBTA website for a detailed schedule: *www.mbta.com*.

USEFUL NUMBERS
Lost & Found

North Station (*7am-11pm daily*):	617-222-3600
South Station (*7:30am- 4:30pm M-F*):	617-222-8120
MBTA Police: 617-222-1000 Emergency:	617-222-1212

BUSES

A large system of **buses** provides transportation to parts of Boston both serviced and not serviced by the T. Visit the MBTA website (*www.mbta.com*) for a complete set of maps and stops. The destination sign above the windshield shows the bus' **route number** and **destination**.

Bus fares are typically 90¢ per ride. Long and express bus routes cost between $1.55 and $3.75. Frequent riders may purchase weekly or monthly combo passes: see "monthly passes" above and *www.mbta.com/traveling_t/passes_index.asp* for more information.

If you need to ride on more than one route, ask for a transfer while paying your fare. It can get you on another local route for FREE. The same is true if transferring from T to bus. To travel from bus to T, add 35¢ to the transfer. **HOURS** vary drastically by route and day; check the MBTA website for details.

FERRIES

Two types of boats bring passengers through the Boston Harbor: MBTA **Commuter Ferries** and the **Inner Harbor Ferries**. Commuter ferries shuttle passengers from Boston suburbs like Quincy, Hingham, and Hull into Long Wharf downtown. Rides cost $6 each way. Visit the MBTA website or call the Long Wharf station (*617-222-6999*) for exact schedules.

Inner Harbor Ferries only cost $1.50 and shuttle passengers between Charlestown, Long Wharf, Lovejoy Wharf, World Trade Center and Courthouse. A Combo Plus Pass is good for unlimited rides. These ferries can be a fabulous way to get around Boston on a nice day as the views of the city are spectacular. Crossing times are 10-15 minutes; ferries leave about every 15 minutes.

Half-fares apply to children aged 5-11, senior citizens, and persons with disabilities. Children under 5 and blind persons ride for free.

DRIVING

Driving into and around Boston can prove extremely frustrating and difficult due to certain obstacles (laid out below), and the fact that drivers from this area drive aggressively and fast. These characteristics have earned them the name "Massholes."

Thanks to the Big Dig—a large highway construction project mentioned in more depth later on—roads in downtown Boston may be difficult to predict using older maps (or any maps for that matter). Moreover, in the oldest parts of the city (those furthest East), streets are narrow, frequently one way, and do not adhere to any pattern. Finally, since the T is an aboveground fixture around much of Boston, it creates an additional obstacle to keep track of while turning.

Stay away from I-90 to avoid paying tolls and use Storrow Drive instead to reach points West and East. Avoid driving to the airport as a hefty toll ($4.50) is imposed on vehicles returning to Boston.

10 Transportation

PARKING

      Parking in Boston can also be very difficult as street parking is often restricted to residents of that neighborhood, scheduled street cleanings may require you to move your car once parked, and parking restrictions apply during periods of heavy snowfall to make room for snow piles. Read all parking signs carefully, or your car may end up towed or buried in snow.

      Bluntly: don't park in No Parking Zones; you will be towed, as there are many different towing companies and what seems like an unlimited supply of tow trucks. If you are towed, it will cost you around $100 to get your car back that day, and towing companies also charge big bucks for daily lot storage fees. To find out if your car was towed, call the local police department of the town/neighborhood you are in. Drivers must first call in to a city tow line and log the tow into a database the police can access. We've listed the numbers of all local police departments on page 29 for your convenience.

      If you see your car being towed, you have two options: You can try to bribe the driver into letting your car down—this requires $40 to make it worth his while; or if you are an attractive woman, you can try to show some good cleavage while pouting and pleading with the driver to let your car down. We recommend the first option. However, option two could at the very least earn you a ride to the towing facility so you don't have to pay for a cab.

      If you recently moved to Boston or just want to get a **permit** to park in your neighborhood, you'll have to register your vehicle with the neighborhood's town hall. (This assumes you've already become a Massachusetts resident by registering with the MA Registry of Motor Vehicles — called the RMV, though most states call it the DMV — and have obtained a valid MA driver's license.) To find out how to get a MA license, go to the MA RMV website: *www.mass.gov/rmv*.

      To register for a residential parking permit, bring your MA license, a current utility bill or bank statement denoting your local address, and your vehicle registration to the appropriate location below:

BOSTON NEIGHBORHOODS:
Boston City Hall, Government Center, 1 City Hall Square: 2nd Floor, Rm. 224, Boston, MA 02215, 617-635-4000
Hours: M-F 9am-4:30pm

SOMERVILLE:
Somerville Office of Traffic and Parking
133 Holland Street, Somerville, MA, 617-625-6600
Hours: M-W 9am-4pm, Th 9am-7pm, F 9am-12pm

BROOKLINE: Does not issue street parking permits. An overnight ban exists on all streets. However, you may rent a space ($100/month) from the town or get a temporary parking permit. Visit the website for more details: *www.townofbrooklinemass.com*.

CAMBRIDGE:
Traffic, Parking & Transportation, City of Cambridge
344 Broadway, Cambridge, MA 02139, 617-349-4700
Hours: M 8:30am-8pm, T-Th 8:30am-5pm, F 8:30am-Noon
$8 fee charged. Applications accepted online:
www.cambridgema.gov/traffic/permits.cfm.

ZIPCAR

Zipcar rents cars by the hour for about $9/hour (insurance and gas included). Cars are parked strategically throughout the city, and renters simply reserve a car online then use a coded badge to unlock the vehicle they reserved. Zipcar can save you lots of money if you need a car from time to time but don't want to pay for one of your own, or if you simply don't want the hassle of figuring out parking for your vehicle.

To rent a car, fill out an online application to become a member. Members must be over 21 years old. The most basic plan requires a $25 one-time membership application fee and a $50 annual fee. Other plans are available for more frequent renters. Visit *www.zipcar.com* for more information.

CAB NUMBERS

Checker Cab Boston	617-536-7500
Checker Cab Cambridge	617-536-7500
Town Taxi	617-536-5000
Yellow Taxi	617-876-5000
City Cab	617-536-5100
ITOA	617-825-4000
Metro Cab	617-782-5500

A Very Brief History of Boston

First settled in 1624 by European Puritans escaping persecution, it wasn't long before Boston grew into the main trading post of the American Colonies. This growth stemmed from the accessibility of the Boston Harbor, which granted ships easy access to Boston's shores, and from the area's exceptional fishing.

Puritans emphasized academics and possessed a strong work ethic, which many historians believe attributed to the successful colonial growth of the 17th and 18th centuries.   This emphasis on knowledge and education led to the founding of the Boston Public Latin School in 1635 and the famed Harvard College in 1636. As Boston grew, so too did its academic sphere. To date, 60 colleges and universities—including Harvard, Boston University, Boston College, Tufts University, and MIT—reside within a 60 square mile radius of Boston, making the city the irrefutable intellectual breeding ground of the world.

During the 1770's, excessive British taxation of its American colonies created a sea of anger among the colonists. These tensions, coupled with the heavy British military presence in Boston, led to brawls between soldiers and civilians.   One confrontation ended with British troops firing their muskets into a rowdy crowd. The event, known as the **Boston Massacre**, took place in the winter of 1770 just outside the **Old State House** on the corner of Devonshire and State Street, and set the seeds for the American Revolution.

Additional taxes levied against colonists led to the first colonial demonstration of outrage known as the **Boston Tea Party** in 1773. Demonstrators, led by Samuel Adams, dumped British Tea Shipments overboard, and the British responded by closing the shipping ports, demanding repayment for the lost tea, and bringing in more troops—many of whom were placed in the homes of Bostonians against their will.

When a British General learned that colonial troops—or minutemen as they were called—had been storing arms in Concord, he ordered his soldiers there to seize the weapons and arrest Samuel

Adams and John Hancock in Lexington for treason. On April 18, 1775, the night before the arrival of British soldiers, Paul Revere completed his famous "midnight ride" to alert the minutemen in Lexington and Concord the British were coming. The following morning in Lexington, British forces collided with minutemen to mark the beginning of the American Revolution. Depictions of these events—including paintings of secret meetings of the leaders of the revolution—reside on the walls of many old restaurants and bars in downtown Boston to date.

Following the American Revolution, Boston's trade and industry grew even faster, and the city became a leading international trading port for rum, fish, tobacco, and salt. As Boston grew, it continued to draw settlers and colonists to the area. The rapid growth created a need to expand housing and build more roads.

To increase the city's size to make room for residents and businesses, this hilly city was leveled. Land from the hilltops was used to fill in wetlands and estuaries in order to create the areas known today as Back Bay, Charlestown, and parts of the South End, South Boston, the Financial District, and Chinatown. The organization of these neighborhoods, given their relative youth, is much more reflective of modern urban planning methods than the city's older neighborhoods, i.e. streets are wider and gridded.

Today, Boston occupies 48.4 square miles of land—a small amount for a city with a population of 590,000 (as of 2005) and a metropolitan population of roughly 6 million (as of 2000). Given its compact size, Boston is known as "**America's walking city**." Indeed, residents and tourists can walk from end to end through the historic and often cobblestoned streets with little difficulty (so long as the weather permits).

Neighborhood Descriptions

Boston is composed of a number of different burros, neighborhoods, and towns, many of which vary dramatically given the age of the area. We've outlined and described the major areas of the city below, and have divided the city maps in the back of the book similarly. Each description is intended to be an overview of the character and flavor of an area and should not be read as in-depth report.

Allston

Located North of Brighton neighborhood and Brighton Avenue, Allston is undeniably Boston's student and young professional Mecca. Nestled in between Boston University, Boston College, and Harvard University, Allston attracts the young and restless, as can be heard at any hour of the night. The dense collection of cheaper bars, restaurants, and retailers around the intersection of Harvard Ave and Brighton Ave caters to this young demographic and provides a fun, urban buzz.   Allston residents enjoy affordable housing and great entertainment at the expense of having to use the T's unforgivably slow Green B Line, which services the area.

Back Bay

Comprising areas east of Massachusetts Avenue, west of Arlington Street, and north of Stuart Street, Back Bay is arguably the most fashionable area of the city. Restaurants and cafes are stacked with energetic parties year round; well-dressed after-work and weekend crowds pack the bars along Boylston Street; tourists snap off picture after picture of the Prudential and John Hancock skyscrapers; and everyone seems to meander down streets, hang out in Copley Square, and pick up the latest fashions in the Prudential Center Mall or Newbury Street.

While it may be every Bostonian's dream to live in Back Bay and have access to the area's fine dining, shopping, and the shores of the Charles River, it is rarely in anyone's budget to do so. But even if you're not rich enough to live here, it's easy enough to get to via the Green and Orange line T stops that service the area.

Beacon Hill

Bordered by Cambridge Street to the North, Government Center to the West, Beacon Street and the Boston Commons to the South, and the Charles River to the East, Beacon Hill— one of Boston's oldest neighborhoods—remains a pinnacle of Boston's heritage. Tree-lined, illuminated by gas lamps, and cobblestone in parts, Beacon Hill is one of the most historic and beautiful neighborhoods in all of Boston. Take a stroll down Charles Street, the business heart of Beacon Hill, for antique shopping, pub crawling, eating, people watching, or just taking in the well-preserved 19th-century architecture.

Brighton

Located West of Allston and bordered by Newtown to the West, Cambridge to the North, and Brookline to the South, Brighton, like Allston, is home to predominately students, young professionals, and families. Washington Street and Commonwealth Avenue compose the neighborhood's main thoroughfares. Though only part of Brighton is serviced by the Green T Line, Brighton's myriad of streets are lined with apartment complexes and homes. Businesses, restaurants, and pubs are scattered throughout the area, the largest collection of which sits in Oak Square—situated at the intersection of Washington Street and Chestnut Hill Avenue.

Brookline

Sitting just outside of metropolitan Boston and centered around Beacon Street, Brookline—one of Boston's most affluent and beautiful neighborhoods—has been home to many famous faces including John F. Kennedy, the poet Amy Lowell, and even *20/20*'s Barbara Walters. Even today, big name coaches and owners like Terry Francona of the Red Sox and Bob Kraft of the Patriots call Brookline home. What does that mean for the rest of us who can't afford multi-million dollar homes and $100,000 sports cars? It means that the area caters to an upbeat, upper class crowd—making it a superb place to eat, drink, and be merry.

Despite its wealth, the independent district of Brookline holds treasures for those less well off—especially the many college students and young professionals who live within its still-affordable fringes and take advantage of the neighborhood's many parks, tree-lined streets, and brownstone domiciles services by the Green C and D lines.

Cambridge

Cambridge residents like to think of themselves as Boston's free-thinking, altruistic, and alternative neighbor across the Charles River—and they aren't too far off the mark. The 100,000+ person city of Cambridge incorporates two of the most prestigious and widely known institutes of higher education in the world: Harvard University and the Massachusetts Institute of Technology (MIT). These institutes exert a tremendous influence on the area as many MIT and Harvard students and professors reside there. Consequently, Cambridge boasts a higher median household income and average annual wage than its neighbor Boston.

Though in area Cambridge is quite large (6.5 square miles) and incorporates many suburban housing developments, there are three main urban centers serviced by the Red Line that give the city its character and reputation: Harvard Square, Central Square, and Kendall Square.

Harvard Square used to be an eclectic collection of unique, artsy and alternative bars, restaurants, and shops. Much of that originality is gone, though the influence still remains. Street performers and bands still entertain crowds in the cement square at all hours while alternative-styles are showcased in windows (though usually in chain stores—some of which originated in Cambridge). There are scattered bistros and interesting bars as well, though much of the area is dominated by corporate chains e.g. Au Bon Pain, Barnes & Nobles, Starbucks, John Harvard's Brewery (a notable exception as this one is the original). Despite the corporate takeover, the square remains a fun neighborhood with an old-town feel that's adjacent to the country's oldest and most notorious university for which the square is named.

Central Square more closely mirrors the independent, alternative influence Harvard Square once showcased. Though small in area, the formerly seedy Central Square is home to a nice variety of cool bars, music venues, cafes, and a myriad of ethnic restaurants.

Kendall Square is definitely the most modern of the squares, as evidenced by the new constructions that house pool halls, bars, a movie theatre, and restaurants. Nearby, biotech companies like Genzyme Corporation—which operates in a highly innovative and energy efficient green building—serve as reminders of Kendall's nearness to MIT. Though smaller, less populated, and less hip than

Central or Harvard Square, Kendall's closer proximity to downtown Boston and younger residences make it a very attractive place to live.

Chinatown

While Boston's Chinatown pales in comparison to the Chinatown in New York or San Francisco, it does exist and provides the city with a great cultural infusion in the form of markets, shops, restaurants, and language. Chinatown is sandwiched between Boylston Street and the Financial District to the North, Washington Street and the Theatre District to the West, I-90 and the South End to the South, and I-93 and the Waterfront to the East, and is serviced by the Orange Line T. Though the area is run-down and a bit on the dirty side, a walk through or evening in Chinatown can be very rewarding. Just don't try to get an apartment here if you mind tight spaces, steep steps, and old buildings.

Downtown

Realistically, the downtown area incorporates the Financial District, Downtown Crossing, Government Center, Faneuil Hall and Quincy Market, the Waterfront, and the areas around the Park Street and Boylston Street T stops. However, for the purposes of this book, we have divided up those areas to make things easier to find. We refer to Downtown as just the areas immediately surrounding the Boylston, Park, and Government Center T stops, including the city's prettiest and most famous green spaces: the Boston Common and Public Gardens.

Downtown Crossing refers to the areas surrounding the intersection of Washington Street and Summer Street, with most of the places of interest situated along Washington Street. Downtown Crossing holds Boston's most affordable shopping inside the walls of H&M, Macy's, Filene's Basement, and a myriad of boutiques. In between Downtown Crossing and **South Station** lay a number of cheap eateries, restaurants, and a handful of bars.

If you walked through Downtown Crossing on Washington Street to the East, you would eventually run into **Government Center**—a huge concrete and brick plaza where the massive and hideous City Hall sits. In the summer, many concerts, demonstrations, religious events, and rallies take place here.

Walk across Government Center to the East to reach two of Boston's oldest tourist attractions: **Faneuil Hall Marketplace**—a collection of independent retailers housed along cobblestone streets—and **Quincy Market**—an enormous building filled with dozens of different food vendors. The entire area is referred to as Faneuil Hall, including the large chain retailers surrounding these 250+ year old relics of Boston's past.

Just as one would expect, most of Boston's big business takes place inside the **Financial District**—situated to the East of Downtown Crossing and South of Government Center. **State Street** divides Government Center from the Financial District to its South. There are a number of bars and clubs along and off of State Street—making the area a mentionable nightlife spot. If you continued along State Street East past the Financial District's skyscrapers, you would reach the Boston Harbor **Waterfront**, where the Aquarium, whale watching vessels, and ferries to points along the Boston Harbor and Massachusetts coast reside.

Fenway

The Fenway, home to Fenway Park (Red Sox stadium), is an urban neighborhood that's densely populated with a hodge-podge of students and professionals. The large area is bordered by Northeastern University and Huntington Avenue to the South, Brookline and Brighton to the West, the Charles River and Boston University to the North, and Back Bay and Massachusetts Avenue to the East. Within these boundaries lay Kenmore Square—where the B, C, and D Green Lines meet, Lansdowne Street—Boston's premier club and concert area, and a quaint collection of parks and water bodies.

Jamaica Plain

JP, as it is known to locals, is the "melting pot" of Boston as it is home to a diverse and alternative population. Over the past few years, there has been a cultural Big Bang along Centre Street, JP's main drag. That explosion birthed a number of unique restaurants and hangouts. Lesser-known to college students because only part of it is serviced by T lines (Green E and Orange Lines), JP is worth the extra effort it takes to get there.

Two of the areas biggest draws to residents are the 76-acre, salmon-stocked, tree-lined JP Pond and the 265-acre Arnold Arboretum, composed of a huge variety of exotic and domestic flora that are used for education, research, and aesthetic enjoyment. The number of quality ethnic restaurants reflects the multicultural influence of the area.

North End

The quintessential Italian section of Boston occupies the very Northeastern corner of the city. The area's narrow, winding streets, tiny buildings, and neighborhood feel are beautiful remnants of an era past. Boston's oldest and most European-like neighborhood has been home to immigrant Irish, Jewish, and Italian populations since it was first settled in 1630 and continues to be home to Italians now. For decades, the North End was cut off from the rest of Boston by the raised Interstate-93, which was recently rerouted underneath the city, allowing the North End to rejoin the rest of the Boston. However, upon entering the North End, you'll still feel as though you've stepped into a different city and time period as you stroll past the neighborhood's rows of café's, markets, and exceptional Italian restaurants.

Northeastern/Mission Hill

The area surrounding the 16,000 student-strong Northeastern University on and around Huntington Avenue is home to some of the most talented artists in Boston. With renowned institutions such as the Museum of Fine Arts (MFA), the Massachusetts College of Art (MassART), and Symphony Hall just to the East, it is no surprise Huntington Ave is called Avenue of the Arts. Galleries open to the public so students and well-known artists may display experiments in classic styles as well as innovative, cutting-edge exhibitions.

The area lacks the number of venues located in other parts of Boston and can be a bit seedy in parts. However, its proximity to Downtown, accessibility by T (Green E), cultural offerings, and lower rental prices make the area attractive to many.

South Boston

"Southie" is situated south of the Financial District and the Fort Point Channel which flows off of the Boston Harbor. The area is predominately a working-class, Irish neighborhood. Given its close proximity to Boston, the area's Northern section is becoming increasing retrofitted with upscale apartments and lofts. The area's revival or gentrification is partly fueled by the arrival of the recent Silver Line, which connects the waterfront areas within Southie to Downtown Boston.

South of this area, within the densely populated lower income neighborhoods, drug use and crime may be problematic at times. However, Southie residents would convince you otherwise as the neighborhood's beautiful views of the Harbor and rich history (battles of the American Revolution and War of 1812 were fought there) are sources of tremendous pride among residents.   Indeed, the area around Broadway Street—a Red Line T stop—holds a number of bars and decent restaurants.

South End

The South End, Boston's most cultural neighborhood, lays Southeast of Downtown bordered by Back Bay and Huntington Ave to the Northwest, I-90 to the North, I-93 to the West, and South Boston to the Southeast.   Like much of Boston, charming 3-5 story red brick domiciles, known as brownstones, provide much of the neighborhood's appeal. The strong presence of the South End's residing artists, young professionals, and gay and lesbian community is reflected in the area's multitude of stylish and exceptional restaurants, bars, and performance centers.   Moreover, the presence of the Boston University Medical Center draws many medical professionals to the area.   Although increasingly expensive, affordable housing may still be found here, as can access to the Orange and Silver T Lines.

Somerville

Somerville is a small, densely-populated, 78,000-person city located just north of Boston and Cambridge. Residents of Somerville vary from blue-collar families to young professionals and college students to recent immigrants. The squares listed below compose the majority of Somerville's places of interest.

Davis Square today is what Harvard Square was in the 70s—a character-packed assemblage of independent businesses and funky realtors. One of Boston's hippest places to live, you don't have to reside in Davis to enjoy its many pleasures or mingle with its young, earthy-but-urbanite populace. A Saturday afternoon and evening are more than enough to cover the half-mile territory. Browse the thrift stores, catch a movie at the Somerville theater, play a game of candlepin at Sacco's, grab an ice cream at JP Licks, or jump on the Red Line and be in Boston in 10 minutes.

Teele Square is just a ten-minute walk from Davis Square and a small crossroads filled with charming and inexpensive eateries. The few bars and restaurants of Teele Square—a well-kept secret among locals and Tufts students—remain full but never packed.

A small collection of shops, specialty stores, and restaurants with a kind of back-alley charm, **Union Square** is somewhere between tacky/ funky and up-and-coming. While not as pedestrian-friendly as

Davis Square, this small intersection is a fun place to visit and hang out. The abundance of ethnic restaurants is ironic given Union Square's thoroughly American name and history—the first flag of the Union was raised just steps away.

Theatre District

Not surprisingly, the Theatre District is called such because it contains a number of major Boston performance arts centers including the Wang Theatre, The Charles Playhouse, and the Shubert Theatre, to name just a few. Parts of the Theatre District—a small area centered around the intersection of Stuart (Kneeland) Street and Tremont Street just to the south of the Boston Common—used to suffer from gang violence. Now the area hosts a number of the city's most upscale night clubs and bars, although the presence of strip clubs serve as remnant's of the red light district's seedy past.

Apartment Hunting

High demand for apartments in Boston coupled with a supply of older units and high rent costs make apartment hunting in Boston a real challenge. There are a number of things to keep in mind, look for, and inquire about when attempting to land an apartment. As far as finding a cheap place goes, the best advice we can give you is to look into the areas of town listed below which provide safe housing at more affordable prices.

Three general rules of thumb to finding a cheap place are:

1)   The further you are willing to live from a T stop, the cheaper the apartment will be.

2)   Apartments become more expensive in the summer and early fall — especially around early September when university enrollment begins — and less expensive during the winter (when no one wants to move) and early spring.

3)   The more roommates you have, the cheaper the apartment will be, as bigger places are tougher for landlords to fill. The reverse is also true. The fewer the roommates, the more expensive the place will be proportionally.

If you plan to stay in Boston for an extended period of time, it may pay off to spend a little more per month as a tenant-at-will (paying month to month with no lease) so you can **get off of the summer/September lease cycle** and ultimately pay less each month.

If you do plan to move into your place in late August or early September, try to **move at night** as the roads are jam-packed with other movers during this time. Be sure to **reserve a rental truck** or van from Budget, U-haul, or Ryder way in advance as reservations for these vehicles are tough to get when the whole city seems to be moving. Budget receives fewer calls than U-haul or Ryder, so start with them. Use the business' websites to locate an office nearest your destination.

CHEAP AREAS TO LIVE (IN SAFE NEIGHBORHOODS)

Brighton is always a safe bet to find a reasonably priced place to live. The drawbacks are parts of the area are loud at night, and the Green B Line is very slow: It takes 30 minutes to get downtown. However, its proximity to Boston University, Boston College, the river, and a plethora of bars makes it attractive to many. **Somerville** is always a safe bet to find a place, especially if you're looking for a group house. **Cambridge** is a great place to live given the area's feel and proximity to downtown (about 10 minutes by T). Avoid Harvard Square altogether, and find a place in Central, Porter, or Kendall Square. The Apartments in Porter Square run larger and cheaper.

If you like upscale surroundings, you'll love **Brookline**, though it's difficult to find anything cheap there. Deals may be found in some of the three to four-person apartments west of Washington St (**Washington Sq**) along Beacon St and the Green C Line.

If you're looking for value though, turn to **Jamaica Plain**. While you may not be able to locate something on the doorstep of the T, most places are within walking distance or serviced by bus #39, which goes straight down Huntington Avenue into downtown (Copley Square).

Many enjoy living in the **South End**. While the area has become more expensive over the years, deals may still be found depending upon your willingness to walk to the T or take the bus. If you don't mind the bus and enjoy saving rent money, consider living in **Chelsea**—located on the opposite side of the Harbor. This former uber-industrial zone is an up and coming neighborhood situated right on the water. A number of buses can have you downtown (Haymarket T Stop) in 15 minutes (excluding rush hour).

WHERE TO FIND AN APARTMENT OR ROOMMATE

- *boston.craigslist.org* →The BEST SOURCE
- Boston Globe (online or classifieds)
- Real estate agents
- Word of mouth – send emails out to find out who's moving
- Postings on community boards
- Exteriors of buildings with availability
- *www.roommates.com*

QUESTIONS TO POSE
WHEN APARTMENT HUNTING

GENERAL INFO

- Does the apartment have good natural **light** or lighting?
- Is there adequate closet space?
- Is there **storage** available elsewhere in the building?
- Are there **water stains** on the walls or the ceiling? [This is an indication of building problems and a potentially hazardous mold problem]
- Is there a cable television hookup?
- Is there high speed **internet** access?
- Do doors and locks work? Is there a deadbolt?
- Can you have pets in the apartment?
- Will the apartment be painted for you?
- Are there any businesses in the building that could generate unusual **smells or noises**? [Being above a bar may sound cool, but the live bands playing every Tuesday until 2am might get annoying. Ask the neighbors or check with the business owners]
- Were **pets** ever allowed here? [for those with allergies]

WINDOWS

- If it's a ground floor apartment; are there **grates** on the windows for security?
- Do the windows open? [They are often painted shut]
- Is there a cross breeze? [A lifesaver in the summer]
- Are there screens and storm windows? [Screens prevent bugs. Storm windows prevent heat from escaping]
- Is the apartment air-conditioned? If not, how many air-conditioners can be used at once before the **fuses** are blown (good question for previous tenants or neighbors)?

THE KITCHEN & BATHROOM

- How is the **water pressure**? [Test the shower]
- Is there a dishwasher?
- Are there toilet and bathroom fixtures or somewhere to store towels and items?
- Is there enough counter space in the kitchen?

- Are the large appliances (refrigerator) in good shape?

THINGS TO LOOK FOR

- If there are a lot of **bug or mouse traps** lying around (check corners and under the sink) it is a good bet the place has a problem.
- How **loud** is the public transportation outside? [Buses can rattle the entire apartment. Don't buckle to pressure to leave; linger long enough to find out]
- Is there any way to **control the heat**? Do the knobs on the radiators turn on/off? [Test them. If they don't turn, you may have to keep the windows open in winter to eliminate extra heat which can allow unwanted noise into your place]
- Are there enough **outlets**? [Many old places have one per room]
- Is the elevator big enough to fit your big furniture? Is the **staircase wide enough** if it isn't?
- Do you have roof access? [Can be a very cool amenity during nice weather]
- Does the super live in the building? [If he does, he will fix building problems faster]
- How old are your immediate **neighbors**? [Gives an idea of how loud or tolerant they will be]
- How sound proof are the walls/floors?
- Are there **laundry** facilities available in the building? If not where is the closest Laundromat?
- How far is it from the nearest **T or bus stop**?
- How long is the **commute** to work/school?

THINGS TO KNOW

- **Bring two checks with you when you look at a place**; one for deposit and one for the first/last month's rent. This is standard practice and unavoidable. Apartments go really quickly in Boston. Having to go get your checks and come back may mean losing the apartment to someone else. The general rule is, if you can live there, and the area is right, sign for it.
- If you have no income, you will need someone (usually a parent) to **cosign** the apartment for you. This can slow the process of getting a place down so have your cosigner near a fax machine.

26 Apartment Hunting

- You will be asked a lot of **personal information** to verify your credit history. This is normal; don't panic.
- Avoid using a **real estate agent** to find a place if they charge a fee [although it can save you time]. Typical fees are a month's rent (may be negotiable). Definitely avoid using them if they make you sign an agreement to be your sole agent.
- First floor and basement apartments get broken into the most.
- The higher your apartment is in a complex, the hotter it is going to be both in summer and in winter.
- Stay away from carpeted places if you have **allergies**. Same is true of basement apartments.
- **English Basement** apartments are part underground, part aboveground so there will only be light coming in on one side.
- A **One-bedroom split** has a long hallway separating the bedroom from the living room/den, so both rooms can be used as bedrooms and the one bedroom can be split. It is a good way to save on rent.
- Meet the landlord if possible beforehand to find out if he/she is a world-class prick.
- In apartment descriptions: **Charming** means small, as does **quaint** and **cozy**.
- **Unique** means odd layout.
- You should know the landlord's address and phone number.
- You should know the telephone number and address of a repairperson.
- There are excellent **tenant's rights** in Massachusetts, making it much tougher to evict a tenant than it is for a tenant to withhold rent for services not supplied by the landlord. **Only a judge can evict you.**
- You are entitled to interest on your security **deposit** and last month's rent if paid in advance. Don't hold your breath for it, but it is the law. For more information: *www.mass.gov/courts/courtsandjudges/courts/housingcourt/housingquestions.html*
- Renter's **insurance** is a good idea and not expensive.

ASK THE PREVIOUS TENANTS OR NEIGHBORS

- How is the landlord? How fast do things get fixed?
- How noisy is it?
- What are the building's big problems?
- Does the elevator ever work or is it just a death trap as most in Boston are?
- What is the fastest and closest form of public transit available?
- What are your monthly utility bills (if they pay them)?

LEASE DETAILS

- Exactly when will the apartment be **available** for you to move in?
- When is rent due? Whom do you send it to?
- What is the penalty for paying late?
- You should try to get at least a one-year option to renew at the same **rent** or an assurance that rent will only be raised a small amount in the lease language.
- How much of a security deposit is required?
- Do you have to sign a **one year lease** (standard)? [Some leases are month to month]
- Are there penalties for **breaking the lease** early?
- Can you rent the place to someone else (sublet)?
- What is included in the rent (e.g., electricity, steam heat/hot water, parking)?
- What are the approximate **utility costs** if they are not covered by the rent? [Good question for previous tenants]
- Is there **parking**?
- Is each **roommate** individually responsible for rent and upkeep of the premises or are they jointly responsible (most cases)? [If jointly responsible, damage or lack of payment by one roommate may result is action being taken to evict/penalize all roommates]

Safety

Given the enormity of Boston's student population, no matter what day of the week, there always seems to be people out and about. This can be a tremendous comfort to the individual coming home alone late at night as it makes the likelihood of a crime occurring less likely. Consequently, Boston is a relatively safe city. But like any city, crimes do occur and people in Boston should take the usual precautions:

- keep track of possessions & be wary of pickpockets
- keep your eye on your drink at all times to prevent someone from drugging it
- walk and use ATMs in lighted and heavily-trafficked areas
- walk in groups
- keep window shades lowered to prevent prying eyes
- avoid looking distracted (e.g. rooting through your purse or talking on a cell phone at night in desolate areas)
- jog during daytime hours only
- don't flash large sums of money in public
- avoid riotous groups, especially on the T
- keep your keys in your hand so they are ready for use instead of fumbling for them later
- carry mace or pepper spray
- avoid empty T cars late at night

At night, the areas around Fenway, Chinatown, and Downtown Crossing can get a bit shady or seedy, as can the Boston Common and Public Gardens. If you are headed there, go with a group of guys. There is a lot of violent crime in Mission Hill, Dorchester, and Roxbury in comparison to other parts of the city, so it is best to steer clear of those areas as much as possible.

Large numbers of mentally disturbed individuals tend to congregate around the Longwood medical area (**Hospital Hill**) in Brookline, as they receive care there. For the most part, they are harmless, but their mental states make them unpredictable and at times violent.

Emergency Numbers

All Emergencies: 911

Police Departments

Brighton	301 Washington St	617-343-4260
Brookline	350 Washington St	617-730-2222
Cambridge	5 Western Ave	617-349-3300
East Boston	69 Paris St	617-343-4220
Jamaica Plain	3345 Washington St	617-343-5630
North End	40 New Sudbury St	617-343-4240
Roxbury	135 Dudley St	617-343-4270
Somerville	220 Washington St	617-625-1600
South Boston	101 W Broadway	617-343-4730
South Boston	650 Harrison Ave	617-343-4250
State Police		617-523-1212
Newton	1321 Washington St	617-796-1000
Waltham	155 Lexington St	781-314-3600

Hospitals

Beth Israel Deaconess (Brookline)	330 Brookline Ave	617-667-7000
Boston University Medical Center (South End)	715 Albany St	617-639-8000
Brigham & Women's (Brookline)	75 Francis St	617-732-5500
Cambridge Hospital	1493 Cambridge St	617-665-1000
Children's Hospital (Brookline)	300 Longwood Ave	617-335-6000
Franciscan Children's Hospital (Brighton)	30 Warren St	617-254-3800
MA General Hospital (Beacon Hill)	55 Fruit St	617-726-2000
Mount Auburn Hospital (Cambridge)	330 Mt Auburn St	617-492-3500
Somerville Hospital	230 Highland St	617-591-4500
St. Elizabeth's Med Center (Brighton)	736 Cambridge St	617-789-3000
Tufts-NE Medical Center (Chinatown)	750 Washington St	617-636-5000

Getting Acclimated

UTILITIES

NSTAR ELECTRIC	800-592-2000
NSTAR GAS	800-592-2000
Keyspan Gas	617-469-2300
VERIZON (Phone/Internet)	800-870-9999
COMCAST (Cable/Internet)	888-633-4266
RCN (Cable/Internet)	800-RING-RCN

Verizon *(www.verizon.com)* offers a pretty good local/long distance package as well as DSL service. Deals vary with the winds so check the latest and greatest offers by calling or visiting their website. However, if AT&T/Yahoo Broadband *(www.sbc.com)* provides service in your area, the package for DSL and phone will almost always be the cheapest.

Comcast *(www.comcast.com)* offers cable TV, cable modem, and calling deals that are pricier than DSL providers but worth it if you like the unmatched speed of a cable modem. RCN *(www.rcn.com)* provides the same service as Comcast. Visit the websites or call the numbers above to determine if either or both service your area, and to compare plans.

Call NSTAR *(www.nstaronline.com)* or Keyspan to have your gas hooked up/billed. Call NSTAR to get your electricity turned on. If you move into an apartment that has these services, you will need to change the name on the bills and pay for the services or they will cut off your services. Sure, it may take them six months to figure it out, but once they do they will charge you for those six months anyway. Better to just be honest and get the bills coming to you right away than have to swim through them later.

BANKS

Below are some of the major banks in the Boston area. Check the Yellow Pages for a more comprehensive list. The numbers are for customer service or general information.

BANK OF AMERICA (800-841-4000) is Boston's largest bank since it acquired Fleet. Having an ATM on every corner has its advantages but you pay big fees for not using one of theirs. Checking fees are charged unless a minimum balance (which varies) is maintained.

CAMBRIDGE SAVINGS BANK (617-864-8700), with branches in Harvard, Porter, and Central Squares, offers FREE checking. Part of the SUM network (almost all Boston banks except for Bank of America are members) which means that it will not charge you a fee for using another SUM bank's ATM.

CAMBRIDGEPORT BANK (800-401-2626). Offers totally free checking, but has few branches. So, it sucks unless you live in Harvard or Central Square.

CITIZENS BANK (800-922-9999) is another large chain. There are several account options, many branches, and lots of ATMs inside T stops.

SOVEREIGN BANK (877-SOV-BANK) offers FREE checking and there are a good amount of branches and ATMs throughout the city.

GROCERY DELIVERY SERVICE

That's right, get your groceries delivered right to your door through Stop & Shop's PEAPOD program. Go to *www.peapod.com*, set up an account, pick out your groceries in the online aisles, schedule a delivery time and you're food will be delivered to your door. It is really a fantastic service that only costs an extra $7 for orders over $100, $10 otherwise. (The minimum order is $50.) Plus, they give you a ton of coupons every time you order.

WEBSITES FOR CHEAP TEXTBOOKS

www.campusbooks.com   *www.Getcheapbooks.com*

www.cheapesttextbooks.com   *www.ecampus.com*

www.half.com   *www.amazon.com*

FREE WIRELESS INTERNET ACCESS

Name	Nearest T Stop	Neighborhood
Herrell's Café *155 Brighton Ave*	Harvard Ave	Allston
Whit Horse Tavern *116 Brighton Ave*	Harvard Ave	Allston
Armani Cafe *241 Newbury St*	Hynes	Back bay
Boston Public Library *700 Boylston Street*	Copley	Back Bay
Espresso Royale *286 Newbury Street*	Hynes	Back Bay
French Press Coffee *2201 Comm Ave*	Cleveland Circle	Brighton
Public Library *361 Washington St*	Washington Sq	Brookline
Café Zing	Porter Sq	Cambridge
Cambridge Brewing Co *1 Kendall Sq*	Kendall	Cambridge
Middle East *480 Mass Ave*	Central Sq	Cambridge
Middlesex Lounge *315 Mass Ave*	Central Sq	Cambridge
News 24/7 *150 Kneeland St*	South Station	Chinatown
Emack and Bolio's *736 Centre Street*	Green St	Jamaica Plain
True Grounds 717 Broadway	Davis	Somerville

Boston Facts

BEANTOWN

Boston is commonly referred to as Beantown because in colonial days, a favorite Boston food was beans baked in molasses for several hours.

WEATHER

As you may expect from a New England City, Boston's winter can be rough. While the average temperature during winter (December to March) falls around freezing (32 degrees Fahrenheit), temperatures fall into the teens and single digits with some frequency. Winds also make the outside temperature seem lower and waiting for the T outside excruciating. Finally, large amounts of snow and sleet— a mix of freezing rain and snow—fall upon Boston each winter, making the sidewalks and roadways quite a mess.

The upside to Boston's tough winter and cold fall is its pleasant spring and temperate summers, punctuated by rare heat spells. We've included a table below to help you predict the seasons a bit.

	Jan	Feb	Mar	Apr	May	Jun	Jul	Aug	Sep	Oct	Nov	Dec
Avg. High	35°	37°	45°	55°	66°	76°	81°	78°	72°	62°	52°	40°
Avg. Low	21°	24°	31°	40°	48°	58°	65°	64°	56°	46°	38°	26°
Mean	28°	30°	38°	48°	58°	68°	74°	72°	65°	55°	45°	34°

CITY HOURS

Unlike New York City, Boston gets its fair share of sleep. By 2am, every bar and club is closed so residents typically head out to places much earlier than they do in other cities. This is important to note, as lines for bars and clubs will also form earlier—by 10:30pm in fact—and even earlier for events.

Last call happens at 1:45pm in Boston proper (includes downtown neighborhoods, Brighton, Allston, and Charlestown) and sometimes earlier for places with bigger crowds. You'll know it's last call when the lights come on and the bouncers start yelling at everybody to get out.

Restaurants typically stop serving food by 10pm or 11pm and close at 12am, but they may stay open later if they have a busy bar. There are a handful of places that serve food after hours. Some of these places stay open after last call as well but do not serve alcohol past then. We've listed these places in the **Midnight Munchies** section on page 137.

Cambridge's hours mirror Boston hours while Somerville and Brookline bars and clubs close at 1am weekends, 12am weeknights.

SMOKING

Smoking has been banned at all workplaces indoors in Metropolitan Boston. Smoking is allowed outside and on balconies. Often times in Boston, what look like discouraging lines outside bars and clubs are just a collection of smokers. Cigar bars still allow smoking inside since they depend on smoking for revenue.

THE SCENE

Given Boston's huge student population, the nightlife is terrific. The city, including its neighborhoods and neighboring towns, are teaming with restaurants, bars, and clubs. There is something for everyone's taste.

If you're into electronic dance music aka techno, you'll want to hit the major clubs: Avalon, Axis, The Roxy, Venu, and Aria. Different nights of the week are host to different types of music so check out the club websites for details. Note: these are some of the most expensive venues so pre-party before heading out the door.

If you're just looking for an average bar, Faneuil Hall and State Street is a safe bet, as is Brighton Ave in Allston. There you'll find much cheaper drinks and a down-home atmosphere host to tons of students. On weekend nights, especially during nice weather, Faneuil Hall can get crazy. The atmosphere is electric, but stay far away if you can't take crowded places.

If you want to view or mingle with a wealthier crowd, stroll along Newbury Street or Boylston Street in Back Bay. The area is host to the city's best shopping and a great place to walk around during the day. At night, the restaurants and bars pack in well-dressed and primped professionals and some students.

Prefer an alternative scene? Head to either Harvard Square or Central Square in Cambridge—home to much more eclectic venues. The areas are also superb for seeing good, local bands.

For quieter locales, head to Washington Square in Brookline (Green (C) line: Washington Square) at the intersection of Washington and Beacon Street.

WHAT'S HOT?	WHAT'S NOT?
Faneuil Hall at night	Chinatown anytime
Newbury Street	South Boston
Red Sox games	Yankee fans
The Patriots	The Celtics
Dive bars	Smoking
Harvard Square	Drink specials
Gay club nights	Lesbian bars
Binge drinking	Late nights
House parties	Strip clubs
Irish Pride	Wealthy Europeans
August	Any other month
BU Girls	MIT Girls
Duck tours	The Big Dig

ANNUAL FESTIVALS & HOLIDAYS

December 31 - "First night" - a collection of theatre, film, music, and dance festivities happening throughout the city. *www.firstnight.org*

Chinese New Year - Late January/Early February - fireworks lit in Chinatown

St. Patrick's Day - March 17th - A huge drinking holiday

St. Patrick's Day Parade - Sunday after March 17th - The country's 2nd largest parade (600,000 spectators) taking place in South Boston along Broadway Street

Red Sox Opening Day - Early April - A very big deal in Boston *www.redsox.mlb.com*

Boston Marathon/Patriot's Day - 3rd Monday in April - One of the country's biggest, oldest, and most watched marathons held on Patriot's Day—the anniversary of the beginning of the American Revolution. *www.bostonmarathon.org*

Chowderfest - June 6th at Government Center - chowder cook-off

Boston Gay Pride Parade - June 14th - Hysterical parade begins at Copley Square and ends at the Public Gardens *www.bostonpride.com*

Harborfest - June 28 through July 4, 2006 - Seven days of celebrations in the form of music and food in City Hall Plaza (Government Center) *www.bostonharborfest.com*

July 3rd - FREE Boston pops concerts at 8pm on the Esplanade

July 4th - FREE Concerts on the Esplanade and fireworks in the harbor to commemorate America's liberation from British rule.

Shakespeare on the Boston Common - Late July to Mid August - FREE Shakespeare performances *www.freeshakespeare.com*

Boston Film Festival - Sept 8-15th - 50 films screened at Lowes Boston Common (T (Green): Boylston   *www.bostonfilmfestival.org*

Oktoberfest - Late Sept/early Oct - Music, beer, and German food at the Harpoon Brewery   *www.harpoonbrewery.com/events/octoberfest*

Head of the Charles - 3rd week in October - the world's largest 2-day rowing event and competition which attracts up to 300,000 spectators   *www.hocr.org*

Boston Common Menorah Lighting - December - Jewish Menorah lit on first day of Hanukkah on the Boston Common *www.cityofboston.gov*

Prudential Center Christmas Tree Lighting - 1st Saturday in December

Boston Idiosyncrasies

ACCENTS

There are a few things you'll need to become acquainted with in order to feel comfortable in Boston—most notably are the heavy Boston accents. A's are pronounced as "ahs," and any word ending in "er" or "or" is pronounced "uh." Here are a few common terms and pronunciations for you:

WORD	PRONOUNCED
Boston Harbor	Bah-ston Hah-buh
Car	Cah
Park	Pahk
Drawers	Drahs
Red Sox	Red Sahx
Chowder	Chowdah
Wicked Awesome	Wikkid ahw-sum (means very cool)

In addition to the accents, Bostonians have a few unique terms for things. For example: jimmies are sprinkles; grinders are subs; **Southie** refers to South Boston; **the Pru** refers to the Prudential Tower, Boston's 2nd tallest building at 750 feet; and of course Fenway refers to **Fenway Park**—Red Sox stadium.

Editor's note: When I first moved to Boston, my girlfriend Sarah asked me: "When was the last time someone saw that monster in the harbor?" Her question completely perplexed me and I asked her what the hell she was talking about.

She responded: "That **Green Monster**; when was the last time someone saw it? Everyone keeps talking about it."

I fell to the floor laughing at her innocence, as all Bostonians know that the incredibly high left field wall of Fenway Park has been called the "Green Monstah (Monster)" as long as anyone can remember. Such is the case due to **Red Sox fever**—a highly contagious disease in which all those around anyone who has Red Sox fever find themselves uncontrollably passionate about the success of the team.

Red Sox fever is usually transmitted after a person has resided in Boston for two years. Symptoms of the fever include: excessive shouting, a refusal to go anywhere without a television, frequent feelings of disgust, depression, and a fixation with statistics. Red Sox fever has no cure and may be latent or active in individuals residing outside city limits.

Individuals with Red Sox fever will often blame some of their emotional symptoms on **The Curse of the Bambino**. According to popular Boston myth, Babe Ruth—one of baseball's greatest heroes— laid a curse on the Red Sox after the team's owner traded him to their arch rivals the New York Yankees to fund a terrible Broadway musical (which flopped). This curse has allegedly caused Red Sox players to bumble plays at the most crucial moments, preventing the Sox from achieving their destiny of becoming Baseball's greatest organization and World Champions.

For 86 years, the curse stopped the team from winning a World Series. In October, 2004, the curse was miraculously broken, allowing the Red Sox to beat the St. Louis Cardinals in four straight games and become World Series Champions. Following the victory, Principal Red Sox owner John Henry traded many of the team's best players. Fans fear additional curses.

THE BIG DIG

Another Boston anomaly is The Big Dig. The Big Dig is the unofficial name of the Central Artery/Tunnel Project, a massive construction project to bury Interstate 93—Boston's major thoroughfare—under the center of the city. Previously, I-93 was an elevated highway that crossed over downtown. The downtown section was a major blight on the landscape, divided the city centre, and clogged downtown roadways with merging traffic.

The Big Dig aims to literally dig a 3.5 mile tunnel under downtown Boston to replace the elevated part of I-93, thereby eliminating the aesthetic blight, opening up green space, and relieving traffic. The project also included construction of the **Ted Williams Tunnel**—which connects I-90 to Logan Airport through a tunnel under the Boston Harbor—and the **Zakim Bunker Hill Bridge,** the widest cable-stayed bridge in the world, which serves as Boston's northern entrance and exit over the **Charles River**.

40   Boston Idiosyncrasies

The Big Dig is the most expensive highway project in American history. The project was estimated to cost $2.5 billion in 1985, six years before construction began. By 2005, estimates were reconfigured to $14.625 billion.

Over its 15-year span, the Big Dig was inundated with delays, embezzlement scandals, skyrocketing costs, leaks, and mismanagement. For a decade and a half, acres of plastic orange construction fence lines and seemingly hundreds of detour signs littered the city while Bostonians patiently awaited an end to the money pit known as the Big Dig.

To date, 98 percent of the project has been completed. The old, elevated I-93 segment has been removed, creating some 27 acres of free space downtown. All connecting tunnels and bridges have been finished.

Living Cheap in Boston

There's no getting around it, Boston is expensive—the 3rd most expensive place to live in the country next to New York City and San Francisco. This is largely due to real estate costs where the laws of supply and demand rule. With 60 colleges and universities located within a 60 mile radius around Boston, the city retains an extremely high occupancy rate within apartments: around 99 percent most years. The high demand and lack of rent control gives landowners the ability to charge as much as they can for real estate rentals and sales. In addition, the compact nature of the city makes real estate rare and more expensive. So real estate owners can charge more for commercial space as well. Retailers inflate the prices of goods to compensate for the expense of rent, and that is one important reason your martini ends up costing $11 when an entire bottle of good vodka only retails for $28.

There are, of course, ways to control spending without sacrificing your lifestyle—this book was written to show you exactly how to do that. Generally, if you want to eat out a lot but still save money, your best bet is to go out for lunch instead of dinner, as prices are often decreased to as much as half of dinner prices. Similarly, cheap lunch buffet options are available from nearly every Indian restaurant in the city.

If you must do **dinner out**, go Monday through Thursday before 7pm, as many places offer specials and deep discounts for happy hour (4-7pm) or just for going out during the week. If you have to eat weekend nights, we've listed plenty of places that will provide you a great atmosphere without bankrupting you.

If you're on a **date** and want to save money, try taking your date for a stroll through part of the city. Too cold for a walk? Try just meeting for drinks and/or appetizers. This is easy to do if you set your date early or late in the evening to avoid dinner time. Restaurants often reserve tables for diners, so make sure you say you're there for dinner when you arrive to get a table and be ready to order at least one appetizer.

To get around paying **cover charges**—which most upscale clubs and live music venues collect—get to the venue before 10pm. Often times, these same venues will dispense coupons on their websites for FREE admission if you check with the site a few days before you plan to head there. Signing up for newsletter emails from venues is another easy way to get around paying cover charges.

For entertainment, parks and private art galleries are abundant and always fun. Even better, they're always FREE. The parks compose many of Boston's most beautiful and historic sights. Just because you live in/around Boston doesn't mean you can't act like a tourist. It's far too easy not to take advantage of a city's sights and sounds when you live there, because you know you can do it anytime. **Resist the urge to be lazy**, and explore the city every time you can because in the blink of an eye your window of opportunity to do so will have disappeared.

Top Ten Ways to Save $

1. Eat lunch out instead of dinner
2. Get to clubs before 10pm
3. Go on walking dates
4. Look for weekday specials
5. Pre-party
6. Live in areas serviced only by bus
7. Take advantage of city events & attractions
8. Make a meal of appetizers and bread
9. Sign up for restaurant email newsletters
10. Use *Craigslist.org* for everything

Excursions

**CRANE BEACH, MA

About an hour's drive from Boston, Crane Beach is one place you'll want to hit year-round. Not only is it fit for beach volleyball and tanning, this beautiful, white-sand coastline is a habitat for wildlife and a natural barrier protecting the Essex River Estuary. More than five miles of designated trails lie in surrounding dunes and maritime forest—a haven for nature enthusiasts.

Be prepared to split the cost of parking among your group ($7-22 depending on the season). Take I-93N to Rt 128N. Take exit 20A (Route 1A N) for 8 miles to Ipswich, R onto Rt 133E for 1.5 miles, L onto Northgate Rd for .5 miles, R onto Argilla Rd to Beach gatehouse.

REVERE BEACH, MA

Just a few miles north of Boston, Revere Beach is one of the easiest getaways. The Wonderland and Revere Beach T stops (Blue Line) let off directly across from the crescent-shaped beach. While the beach was a center of social life in the early 1900s, a quieter spot remains today. Only a few restaurants and bars will give shade and fuel to your day, but Kelley's Roast Beef (410 Revere Beach Blvd)—a hole in the wall with a diehard following—is almost worth the trip itself.

BOSTON HARBOR ISLANDS

The Boston Harbor Islands are one of Boston's best kept secrets. Eleven of the Harbor's 34 islands are open to the public for camping, hiking, picnicking, berry picking, and guided walks. They are all within an hour's ferry ride away, and offer not only natural beauty but also historic landscapes and incredible panoramic views of the Boston skyline.

Some of the islands have been home to Native Americans, Boston Colonials, and even prisoners of the Civil War. Campers will find a favorite with the 48-acre Lovells Island, whose trails, picnic areas, and swimming beach make for a great weekend outdoors.

To most islands, a round-trip ferry costs $10 for adults ($12 Thurs-Sun) and leaves from Boston at Long Wharf (T (Blue):

Aquarium). Water shuttles between the islands are FREE. For ferry times, call 617-223-8666, visit the Harbor Express office at Long Wharf, or see the schedule online:
http://www.nps.gov/boha/parkdocs/boatschedule.pdf.

WALDEN POND, MA

Take a tip from Henry David Thoreau and shake off the busy city life. The famed Walden Pond, where the naturalist, writer, and philosopher lived from 1845 to 1847, is now one of the areas most convenient beaches and camp sites—about a 30 minutes drive.

The water stays cold until mid-summer, but the shore is perfect for sunning or picnicking. Campers and hikers can enjoy the natural surroundings, which are particularly striking in late October as the leaves change color. Take I-90 W to 128 N to exit 29B onto Rt 2W. At the 3rd set of lights, take a L onto Rt 126S. Park ¼ mile down on left.

PROVINCETOWN, MA

P-Town, situated 120 miles from Boston by land and 50 by sea, is one of Cape Cod's most bustling and accessible towns. Stunning beaches, unique retailers, scenic bike riding, and a happening night life make it near impossible not to have a good time here. Religious right be warned: It is also home to one of the country's largest and proudest gay communities.

Boston Harbor Cruises leave Boston's Long Wharf Ferry Terminal at 9am, and arrive at MacMillan Wharf around 10:30am. (Schedules and the number of departures vary by season.) Trips cost $25 one-way, $45 round-trip; call 617-227-4321. Return on the ferry at 4pm, or splurge on one of the areas gorgeous bed and breakfasts. Off-season trips will make for a discounted romantic weekend.

NEWPORT, RHODE ISLAND

For a relaxing getaway, try Newport, RI. The 90 minute drive will land you in a turn-of-the-century landscape, complete with elaborate, beach-front mansions of the rich and famous. This quintessential New England town is a people-watchers' and architecture-lovers' paradise. Go on a warm day for sunning or fishing on the beach. For cheap dining, make a meal of the town's renowned clam chowder. Big bowls are on the menu at most pubs and waterfront restaurants, and they'll fill you up for $5-10.

Take I-93 S out of Boston to Rt 24 S to Rt 114 S (West Main Road). Continue through Portsmouth and Middletown until you reach Newport (the road becomes Broadway).

FREEPORT, MAINE

Thrifty Shopaholics can bask in the bastion of deals found in Freeport's village of 170 outlet stores, including well-knowns like LL Bean, Burberry, and Banana Republic. Household and specialty outlets will furnish that new apartment or dorm on the cheap. For coupons, check out *www.freeportusa.com.*

Take I-95N to the Maine Turnpike (Exit 52). Follow signs to I-295N and take Exit 17 for Freeport, which leads directly to US Route 1 (Main Street).

CONNECTICUT CASINOS

Sick of feeling broke in Boston? If you're ready for an upgrade, take your chances at one of the country's biggest casinos (believe or not), Foxwoods (1-800-FOXWOODS), and its regional, cooler competitor Mohegan Sun (1-888-226-7711). Both are an-hour-and-half drive or bus ride away. For the puritan in the group, each offers gambling alternatives like shopping, spas, dining, and entertainment.

Check out *www.peterpanbus.com* to reserve $20 fares and find the occasional promo package to Foxwoods. A visit to *www.gotobus.com* gets $10 fares to Mohegan Sun.

NEW YORK CITY

On the off chance you've exhausted things to do in Boston, New York is just a short, $15 ride away. Various competing bus lines—infamously called the Chinatown buses—make the four-and-a-half hour trek between the cities almost hourly.

Most Boston departures leave from South Station (Red Line T), but each bus line drops off at a different location in New York. Pick a vendor based on its drop-off point so that it's convenient to your Big Apple destination. Make reservations online to ensure a seat; Good choices are *www.fungwahbus.com* and *www.gotobus.com.*

Cheap Eats

** Signifies the Editor's Choice

Allston/Brighton

The Breakfast Club *(T (not available): 270 Western Ave, 617-783-1212)* American: This down-home diner serves up hearty portions of their aptly named breakfast and lunch (no dinner) combinations to a mostly college crowd daily.

**Eagle's Deli *(T (Green C): Cleveland Circle 1918 Beacon St, 617-731-3232   Dir: exit T E on Beacon St)*
American: This popular Boston College brunch spot and burger joint was rated one of the top ten places "to pig out" in the US by the Travel Channel. Finish their one-pound Godzilla Burger (or any burger larger, such as the five-pound "Chillerama") and you'll get yourself enshrined on the Burger Wall of Fame. For the less adventurous, try the (not so) Kiddie Burger, served with a heaping portion of homemade fries. Tip: be nice to the grill master and you'll get your order faster.

First Bite Café *(T (Green B): Packard's Corner   76 Brighton Ave, 617-782-2228   Dir: walk W on Brighton Ave)*
American: This tiny noshing spot is the quintessential university-feeding trough and has been known to name its creative sandwiches after local fraternities. The ZBT piles chicken fingers, mozzarella sticks, and french fries between two slices of bread. Salads, pizzas, wraps—you name it they got it, and for cheap. Bring an appetite.

Spike's Junkyard Dogs *(T (Green B): Harvard Ave   108 Brighton Ave, 617- 254-7700   Dir: exit T, head N on Harvard, R on Brighton)*
American: With their creative variations on the classic hot dog and other fast foods like chicken fingers and fries, Spike's provides the stomach padding necessary for a night of heavy drinking. Veggie dogs are also available.

Wing It Café *(T (Green B): Harvard Ave   1153 Commonwealth Ave, 617- 783-2473   Dir: exit T, walk S on Comm Ave)*
<u>American</u>: With over 30 varieties of wings—from Pterodactyl hot to boneless—this popular university eatery creates the ultimate game-time snacks. Try the honey barbeque: the perfect combination of sweet, spicy, and tangy.

**Super 88 Market Place *(T (Green B): Packard's Corner   1095 Commonwealth Ave, 617-787-2288   Dir: market on corner Hours: 10:30am-midnight for market, 11am-10:30 pm for stands)*
<u>Asian</u>: With eight predominately Asian fast-food restaurant stands—all of which offer very cheap food—connected to a large Asian market, you'd be wise to make this your first stop if hungry. Thai, Vietnamese, Chinese, Indian, Japanese, and Korean specialties are all represented with few items exceeding $8. So tear into some pho soup, pad Thai, satay chicken, lamb saag, or whatever else tempts your palate. Alternatively, pick up some frozen Asian dishes or a bag of live crabs and create your own masterpiece.

Harvard Chinese Restaurant *(T (Green B): Harvard Ave   145 Harvard Ave, 617-783-0270   Dir: exit T N on Harvard Ave)*
<u>Chinese</u>: The easy-to-miss storefront may look like all the other Chinese restaurants on Harvard Ave, but don't be fooled, Harvard rises above their competitors, offering free hot tea while you watch your food being made right in front of you. The multiple flavors of lo mein come in generous portions.

The Kinvara *(T (Green B): Harvard Ave   34 Harvard Ave, 617-783-9400 Dir: exit T N on Harvard Ave)*
<u>Irish Pub</u>: This low-key Irish pub is worth going to for its food alone; just make sure you get there before the bar-hoppers take all the seats. The native Irish staff serves up classic bar foods (sandwiches, fries, wings, etc.) along with time-honored Irish dishes like shepherds' pie and Irish sausage.

Cookin' Café & Grill *(T (Green B): Packard's Corner   1096 Commonwealth Ave, 617-566-4144   Dir: exit T onto Commonwealth Ave)* <u>Italian</u>: This laid-back neighborhood stop serves up six different daily breakfast and dinner specials that are perfect for large groups. Try two large pizzas or two roll-ups and a large fries for $13. Carb counters and carnivores will find plenty of salad, sandwich, and dinner options for under $8.

Porter Belly's Pub *(T (Green B): Washington St   338 Washington St, 617-254-3300 Dir: exit T N on Washington, L at base of the hill)*
<u>Irish</u>: The laid-back coziness and affordable prices at this Brighton Center pub keep the locals coming back. Indulge in the fish and chips ($10) or keep it healthy with the piquant chicken curry and rice ($9).

**Sunset Grill and Tap *(T (Green B): Harvard Ave   130 Brighton Ave, 617-254-1331   Dir: exit T N on Harvard, R on Brighton)*
<u>Tex-Mex</u>: The fast and friendly service makes this popular Tex-Mex spot ideal for grabbing a quick drink and dinner, but the cool atmosphere and blaring classic rock will make you want to stay all night. The beer selection is exceptional (112 on tap, 380 microbrews and exotic imports) and the appetizers are the perfect complement to whatever game is playing on the TVs around the bar.   Go Tuesday's for two-for-one dinner specials.

Back Bay

Café Jaffa *(T (Green B/C/D): Hynes 48 Gloucester St, 617-536-0230 Dir: exit T to Mass Ave, L on Mass, L on Boylston, L on Gloucester)*
<u>American/Middle Eastern</u>: Two worlds converge here, so bring your sense of adventure. Serving a variety of dishes from steak tips to hummus and chicken kebabs, this larger-than-average café's food and décor is simple but enjoyable.

Trident Booksellers *(T (Green): Hynes   338 Newbury St, 617-267-8688, Dir: exit T to Newbury, R on Newbury)*
<u>American</u>: This café/bookstore serves light fare and breakfast all day. Studious patrons can enjoy the quiet and FREE internet access. Bring a laptop and your work, or savor a coffee while dreaming up your first novel.

The Wrap *(T (Green B/C/D): Hynes   137 Massachusetts Ave, 617-369-9087   Dir: exit T to Mass Ave, L on Mass Ave)*
<u>Deli</u>: Not surprisingly, The Wrap specializes in well, wraps, with a wide selection to suit even the pickiest of eaters.

**Prudential Center Food Court *(T (Green B/C/D): Hynes   800 Boylston St, 617-236-3100   Dir: exit T to Mass Ave, L on Mass Ave, L on Boylston)*

Food Court: If you are pressed for time and want everything in one place, the Prudential Center has it. The food court will fulfill your ethnic quota—Gourmet India, Qdoba Mexican Grill, Sakkio Japan—as well as your sweet tooth with Ben and Jerry's and Paradise Bakery and Café. Hours: M-Sa 7am-10pm; Su 9am-8pm.

Steve's *(T (Green B/C/D): Hynes   316 Newbury St, 617-267-1817 Dir: exit T to Newbury St, R (E) on Newbury)*
Greek: With the exception of Steve's, there are few places in Back Bay to get cheap food and hardly any on Newbury Street. Steve's serves up traditional Greek dishes and breakfast (until 11:45 Sa, 12:45 Su) cheap. Get a window spot and watch the Newbury hustle and bustle.

Other Side Café *(T (Green B/C/D): Hynes   407 Newbury St, 617-536-8437 Dir: exit T to Newbury St, L on Newbury)*
Health Food: An affordable health food repast. The tables are packed together, so forget about spilling your deepest, darkest secrets to a friend, unless you want neighbors to overhear. Despite the lack of privacy, this café packs in just as much fun as it does people. The atmosphere is energetic thanks to the young, eclectic crowd.

Gourmet India *(T (Green B/C/D): Hynes   800 Boylston St, 617-247-9500   Dir: exit T to Mass Ave, L on Mass Ave, L on Boylston)*
Indian: Authentic Southern Indian dishes all less than $8 served in the food court at Prudential Center. Various weekend specials run less than $6. Even if you can't pronounce the names, you will enjoy the food—just remember to breathe betweens bites because most dishes run spicy.

Shino Express Sushi *(T (Green): Copley   144 Newbury St, 617-262-4530   Dir: exit T E (R) on Boylston St, L on Dartmouth St, L on Newbury)*
Japanese: Shino doesn't have a lot of room to house diners but that doesn't seem to deter its loyal customers who come back for $6 house specialties like the crispy eel roll, the scorpion roll (shrimp, eel, avocado, cucumber, tobikko and eel sauce), and Chirashi Don—fish over sushi rice ($9.50).

Whole Foods Market *(T (Green E): Symphony   15 Westland Ave, 617-375-1010   Dir: exit T on Huntington Ave, L (N) on Mass Ave, walk 1 block, L on Westland)*
Market: This market doesn't cut any corners, mainly because it is located in a modern, round building and doesn't have any. With its

wide selection of prepared foods, ranging from sushi to egg salad, you are bound to find something agreeable.

**Bukowski's (T (Green B/C/D): Hynes   50 Dalton St, 617-437-9999   Dir: exit T to Mass Ave, L on Mass Ave, L on Boylston St, R on Dalton) Pub Grub: You might not expect much from its looks, and even though it can get a bit cramped, this dive bar rocks. Once you squeeze through the narrow hallway that is the entrance, you will be greeted with a great selection of microbrews and foods like roasted red pepper and goat cheese quesadillas, four-cheese Mac and Cheese with broccoli, and the Dollar Dog. Highlights: $1.69 burgers M-F 11:30am-8pm.

**The Pour House (T (Green): Copley   907 Boylston St, 617-236-1767   Dir: exit T W (L) onto Boylston)
Pub Grub: Great service, fantastic music, eccentric décor, and a long bar make the Pour House a hotspot for the young and hungry. Dine on typical pub food and daily specials such as $2.50 chicken sandwiches Wednesday nights; half-price Mexican food Th 6-10pm; and half-price burgers Sa 6-10pm.

Beacon Hill

21st Amendment (T (Green/Red): Park St   150 Bowdoin St,   617-227-7100   Dir: exit T, L on Park St, R on Beacon, L on Bowdoin)
American: Everyone's favorite amendment is happily abused at this state house pub serving tasty salads, sandwiches, soups, burritos, and loads of beer. Entrées run $7-9.

**Hill Tavern (T (Red): Charles/MGH   228 Cambridge St, 617-742-6192   Dir: exit T onto Cambridge St and walk east)
American: This classy, laid-back pub—with its exposed brick walls and shiny wood paneling—is the perfect spot for an after-work drink, a quiet dinner, or simply to satisfy a craving for a juicy burger. Prices run $8-10 but half-price appetizers are available weekdays 4-6pm.

**Paramount Deli (T (Red): Charles/MGH   44 Charles St, 617-720-1152) American: Upbeat and lively by day, cozy and relaxed by night, this Charles St nook is perfect for any occasion with its simple, pleasant décor and flavorful food. Paramount's diverse menu—everything from elaborate omelets and salads to Korean-style baby back ribs—and affordable prices (most daytime offerings are less than $7 with dinner ranging from $5-15), draws a mix of students, young professionals, and locals.

Osaka Sushi Express *(T (Red): Charles/MGH   106 Cambridge St, 617-624-3939   Dir: exit T onto Cambridge St and walk east)* <u>Asian</u>: Cambridge St is always bustling, so it's no surprise that long lines form at lunch for the cheap, fresh sushi and Asian dishes perfect for those on the go.

Café Bella Vita *(T (Red): Charles/MGH   30 Charles St, 617- 720-4505)* <u>Café</u>: This laid-back coffee and sandwich spot offers quite an assortment of beverages, bagels, linguine dishes, and gelati. A number of outdoor tables give a prime view of Charles St without the hassle of a sit-down meal, or the high price (most dishes are $7-10).

The Capitol Coffee House *(T (Green/Red): Park St   122 Bowdoin St, 617-227-4865   Dir: walk away from station exit, L on Park St, R on Beacon St, L on Bowdoin)* <u>Café</u>: In view of the state house, this cute takeout spot offers an eat-on counter, a few tables, and a selection of bagels, sandwiches, salads, and pancakes and french toast at breakfast. Hours: 6am-6pm.

Shangri-La Chinese Restaurant *(T (Red): Charles/MGH   138 Cambridge St, 617-523-0557   Dir: exit onto Cambridge St and walk E)* <u>Chinese</u>: While Shangri-La's dark windows make it appear a bit shady from the outside, inside the loyal locals munch happily away on traditional Chinese dishes without real concern for the generic décor. Most plates run $7-10.

**Café Podima *(T (Red): Charles/MGH   168 Cambridge St, 617-227-4959   Dir: exit T onto Cambridge St and walk E)* <u>Deli</u>: This takeout spot (there are only three tables inside) serves up out-of-this-world hot and cold sandwiches—all very filling—for just $5-6.50, along with pizza, salads, ice cream, and protein shakes. FREE delivery for orders over $7.

City Covenience *(T (Green/Red): Park St   23 Beacon St, 617-227-7989   Dir: walk away from station exit, L on Park St, R on Beacon)* Above-average convenience store (like a small supermarket) carrying sandwiches ($3-5), frozen foods, and produce. Open until 11pm M-Sa, Su until 8pm.

Fill-a-buster *(T (Green): Park St   142 Bowdoin St, 617-523-8164*
Dir: exit T, L on Park St, R on Beacon, L on Bowdoin)
Fast Food: This greasy spoon is a state house favorite despite its less
than pristine décor, offering a mix of Mediterranean staples such as
spinach pies and falafel as well as American favorites like sandwiches
and burgers. Open only until 4pm M-F.

Nino's Pizza *(T (Red): Charles/MGH   79 Charles St, 617- 523-3974)*
Italian: This homey, hole-in-the-wall pizza and sub shop may seem a
bit out of place among its fancy Charles St neighbors, but it's a gem—
with delicious homemade sauce, dough, and subs in the $4-6 range.

Venice Ristorante *(T (Red): Charles/MGH   204 Cambridge St, 617-*
227-2094   Dir: exit T onto Cambridge St and walk E)
Italian: Venice Ristorante may not look like much from the outside, but
it's all that you could ask for in a pizza and sub shop: warm, friendly,
cheap, and open late (until 12:30am weeknights, 2am weekends).

Red Hat Café *(T (Red): Charles/MGH   9 Bowdoin St, 617-523-2175*
Dir: exit T onto Cambridge St, walk E, R on Bowdoin) Pub Grub: This
cozy, dark, hole-in-the wall is a local secret with cheap drinks and
sandwich/burger/fried fish plates in the $5-10 range.

Sevens Ale House *(T (Red): Charles/MGH   77 Charles St, 617-523-*
9074) Pub Grub: This dimly-lit bar serves up standard pub fare to a
loyal, local crowd for $6-7 per entrée.

King and I *(T (Red): Charles/MGH   145 Charles St, 617- 227-3320)*
Thai: With everything on the extensive menu around $7, and a large
vegetarian selection, it's hard to be unhappy at the end of a meal—
especially when the food is actually good. Although casual and
unassuming, the artwork and wood paneling provide ample
decorations to make this place inviting.

Brookline

The Java Stop *(T (Green D): Brookline Village   4 Brookline Pl, 617-*
566-4884   Dir: exit T, R on Station St, L on Harvard St, L on Boylston,
L into Brookline Place)
American: With a café feel, the Java Stop is a convenient and quiet
place to grab coffee and a sandwich for under $7. Only a couple tables

litter the dining area, so plan on alternate places to sit just in case they are full.

New England Soup Factory *(T (Green D): Brookline Village   2 Brookline Pl, 617-739-1899   Dir: exit T, R on Station St, L on Harvard St, L on Boylston, L into Brookline Place)*
<u>American</u>: A small, comfortable place to have lunch, this franchise takes soup to a whole new level. The menu's imaginative creations include Curried Crab and Coconut, African Chicken and Peanut, and Tomato Crab Bisque. There are also a variety of iced soups like White Peach and Raspberry and Blueberry Sour Cream with Cinnamon Stick. Highlights: clam chowder.

Sichuan Garden *(T (Green D): Brookline Village   295 Washington St, 617-734-1870   Dir: exit T, R on Station St, R on Washington St)*
<u>Chinese</u>: If you are looking to add a little spice to your life, Sichuan Garden is the place to go (as evidenced by the largely Asian clientele). They serve non-traditional Chinese dishes like shredded tripe with roasted chili vinaigrette ($7.50) and pan seared pork dumplings ($5). Small, spicy servings of meats and vegetables will have you ordering dish after dish. Don't bother saving room for dessert; there isn't any.

Brookline Spa *(T (Green D): Brookline Village   75 Harvard St, 617-566-9446   Dir: exit T, R on Station St, L on Kent St, R on Harvard St)*
<u>Deli and Subs</u>: This Brookline Village staple is a favorite among locals for pizza and subs. Sparsely decorated but infused with the smell of baking bread. Highlights: Subs $6-8.

Zathmary's *(T (Green C): Coolidge Corner   299 Harvard St, 617-731-8900   Dir: exit T and head N on Harvard St)*
<u>Deli/Market</u>: This market provides a great selection of prepared foods (think Whole Foods but better) like grilled salmon, London broil, and chicken parmesan as well as an array of cooked veggies and subs. Most meals fall between $7-12. Highlights: 20 percent off sushi on Saturdays.

Paris Creperie *(T (Green C): Coolidge Corner   278 Harvard St, 617-232-1770   Dir: exit T, head N on Harvard St)*
<u>French</u>: If you're looking for authentic Parisian crepes, this tiny place is your answer—just be ready to take your Nutella hot chocolate or western omelet crepe on the go, as seating is limited. Smoothies are also available.

Bottega Fiorentina *(T (Green D): Brookline Village   41 Harvard St, 617-232-2661   Dir: exit T, R on Station St, L on Kent St, R on Harvard St)*
<u>Italian</u>: Bottega Fiorentina gives diners a taste of la dolce vita with a menu boasting inventive dishes infused with the freshest ingredients— think porcini mushrooms, clams, Gorgonzola cheese, and prosciutto. Open M-Sa, there are daily specials including the popular lasagna alla Bolognese ($6) every Tuesday. Prices are reasonable—dishes are under $10.

**Anna's Taqueria *(T (Green C): Summit Ave   1412 Beacon St, 617-739-7300)*
<u>Mexican</u>: Fast, cheap, and fresh, Anna's provides a full meal in the Super Burrito. It's an area favorite, so be prepared for long lines, but don't be discouraged; the staff works quickly. Highlights: $4 burritos.

Boca Grande *(T (Green C): St. Paul   1249 Beacon St, 617-739-3900   Dir: exit T, walk W down Beacon St)*
<u>Mexican</u>: Low prices, great food, and fast service make Boca Grande fantástico. Dine-in at a limited number of tables or carry the food home, either way you get your money's worth: $3-4 burritos and quesadillas, $2-3 sides of guacamole and corn chips.

Village Fare Pizza *(T (Green D): Brookline Village   387 Washington St, 617-739-2774   Dir: exit T, R on Station St, R on Washington)*
<u>Pizzeria</u>: Take out or sit to enjoy some pizza or great subs. Village Fare keeps the ingredients fresh and has more choices than the local chain sub shop. Village Fare Pizza is one of the only places where you can get a 20-inch pizza for less than it would cost to send you to college.

Coolidge Corner Clubhouse *(T (Green C): Coolidge Corner   307 Harvard St, 617-566-4948   Dir: exit T and walk N on Harvard St)*
<u>Sports Bar</u>: Don't expect to pay much attention to other people in your party, as this sports bar is packed with TVs broadcasting games from across the country. Highlights: Cam Neely Burger or Larry Bird Sandwich ($7-9) and a decent brunch.

Baja Betty's Burritos *(T (Green D): Brookline Village   3 Harvard Sq, 617-277-8900   Dir: exit T, R on Station St, L on Kent St, R on Harvard St)*

Tex-Mex: The casual yet colorful atmosphere will add some spice as you chow down on cheap chalupas, tacos, and burritos.

Dok Bua *(T (Green C): Harvard St   411 Harvard St, 617-277-7087 Dir: exit T, head N down Harvard St)*
Thai: Disguised as a market, this Thai restaurant keeps the décor simple with cans, boxes, and other products surrounding diners. Restaurant-goers can sample appetizers of vegetarian spring rolls for less than $4 and entrées—ranging from chicken to squid—are only $6-9.

Rod Dee Thai *(T (Green C): Summit Ave   1430 Beacon St, 617-738-4977   Dir: exit T, head W on Beacon St)*
Thai: Rub elbows with Brookline locals, literally, as Rod Dee's is a tiny closet of a restaurant that serves up full Thai meals for less than $10, proving that size does not matter.

Cambridge

**Cambridge Common *(T (Red): Harvard or Porter 1667 Mass Ave, 617-547-1228   Dir: exit T onto Mass Ave, walk 3/4 mile)*
American: Serving upscale bar food, Cambridge Common's decent prices and hearty eats attract a lot of Harvard Law School students and other Mass Ave traffic. With cozy booths, colorful paintings from local artists, and a number of large-screen TVs, it's the perfect place to relax with friends over dinner or drinks and catch the big game. Highlight: sweet potato fries, $5 a basket.

**Charlie's Kitchen *(T (Red): Harvard   10 Eliot St, 617-492-9646 Dir: exit T onto JFK St, R on Mt Auburn, L on Eliot)*
American: This diner-meets-dive-bar is the Square's most classic burger joint. Sit downstairs in one of the cozy booths for dinner—the double cheeseburger special is just $5—or brave the noise of the bar upstairs. Charlie's has Trivia Night Sundays, Live Band Mondays, and a rowdy Karaoke Tuesdays at 10pm. Drink special: 23 oz Sam Adams for $4.75.

**Mr. Bartley's Burger Cottage *(T (Red): Harvard   1246 Mass Ave, 617-354-6559   Dir: exit T onto Mass Ave, walk 4 blocks S)*
American (classic): You can't leave Harvard Square without paying a visit to Mr. Bartley's, a Cambridge landmark for over 40 years. At this

vintage hole-in-the-wall, burgers are thick, round, cooked perfectly, and given clever names for elaborate flavor combinations like the Hillary Clinton Burger.

Au Bon Pain *(T (Red): Harvard   1360 Mass Ave, 617-661-1513   Dir: exit T onto Mass Ave)*
<u>Deli</u>: Au Bon Pain is a national chain, but this particular location is a Harvard Square fixture. With a seemingly endless set of outdoor tables stretching all the way to Mass Ave and a row of chess boards to boot, Au Bon Pain is the Paris of the Square, the perfect spot to lounge on a nice day, run into friends, and people watch. You may recognize the outdoor tables from a scene that was filmed there in *Good Will Hunting*.

Darwin's *(T (Red): Harvard   148 Mt Auburn St, 617-354-5233   Dir: exit T onto JFK, R on Mt. Auburn, walk 3/4mi)*
<u>Deli</u>: Go to Darwin's for crazy-but-delicious combinations like egg salad and avocado. The sandwiches (around $7) are like two meals in one, so save room or half for later. If the weather is nice, grab one of the few tables outdoors.

Pressed Sandwiches *(T (Red): Central   736 Mass Ave, 617-864-9600   Dir: exit T NW on Mass Ave)*
<u>Deli</u>: Hot-pressed, delicious, gourmet sandwich combinations and salads for under $10; need we say more? Closes at 8pm.

The Wrap and Smoothie Bar *(T (Red): Harvard   71 Mt Auburn St, 617-354-5838   Dir: exit T onto Mass Ave, R on Dunster St, L on Mt. Auburn)* <u>Deli</u>: A favorite among Harvard students, The Wrap will wrap up just about anything—from veggies and caramelized onions to turkey with stuffing and cranberry sauce—in a hurry. It's also a great place for smoothies.

S&S *(T (Red): Harvard   1334 Cambridge St, 617-354-0777 Dir: from Harvard Station, take the #69 bus to Inman Sq or walk ten minutes E on Cambridge St)*
<u>Deli</u>: A traditional deli and Cambridge landmark since 1919, this clean, cheery space gets packed on Sundays for their legendary brunch.

Greenhouse Coffee Shop Inc. *(T (Red): Harvard   3 Brattle St, 617-354-3184   Dir: exit T S onto JFK St, R on Brattle)*

Diner: Greenhouse's eats and service can be hit-or-miss, but the quaint one-room diner is always on point in terms of portion size. Go for all-day breakfast, stay and people watch, as tables by the window offer a great view of Harvard Square traffic.

Punjabi Dhaba Restaurant *(T (Red): Harvard   225 Hampshire St, 617-547-8272   Dir: from Harvard Station take the #69 bus to Inman Sq or walk 10 min E on Cambridge St)*
Indian: Even in the midst of restaurant-filled Inman Square, Punjabi Dhaba is a rare find—a fast-food Indian spot serving authentic fare at reasonable prices. Sit in a booth downstairs for faster service or in the dining space upstairs for a relaxed dinner out. The chicken tikka masala is a good, safe bet.

**Pinocchio's Pizza & Subs *(T (Red): Harvard   74 Winthrop St, 617-876-4897   Dir: exit T onto JFK St, L on Winthrop)*
Italian: *The Harvard Crimson* once ran a story about an employee who had eaten "Noch's" for lunch and dinner every day for 20 years...after one trip there you'll understand why. The tiny, cramped seating area with its mural of mermaids and other mythical beings may not seem like the stuff of legends, but the pizza is. The freshly-made, deep-dish Sicilian slices and sub bread are always perfect.

Moody's Falafel Palace *(T (Red): Central   25 Central Square, 617-864-0827   Dir: exit T and follow Magazine St to Western Ave)*
Mediterranean: Very cheap falafel sandwiches ($4) and platters ($6) as well as kebabs served quickly without frills.

**Felipe's Taqueria *(T (Red): Harvard   83 Mt Auburn St, 617-354-9944   Dir: exit T onto JFK, L on Mt. Auburn)*
Mexican: Popular at all hours of the day, Felipe's transformed Harvard student life when it opened this past year, fast becoming the main campus staple. The high-speed assembly line pumps out delicious burritos, tacos, and quesadillas. Felipe's is open until 1am during the week and sometimes as late as 2am on weekends, depending on the crowd.

Campo Di Fiori *(T (Red): Harvard   1350 Mass Ave, 617-354-3805 Dir: exit T onto Mass Ave, R into Holyoke Center (a glassed-in corridor to the left of Au Bon Pain)*
Pizzeria: Named after a vibrant section of Rome, what Campo Di Fiori lacks in Italian ambiance it makes up for in Italian flavor. This takeout

spot serves up traditional Roman pizza with a thinner crust and less cheese than the average slice. Sample the strange but delicious topping combinations like gorgonzola, pine nuts, and raisins.

Christopher's Restaurant and Bar *(T (Red): Porter   1920 Mass Ave, 617-876-9180   Dir: exit T and walk N on Mass Ave)*
American: Considering the warm décor provided by the exposed brick walls and fireplace, the food—primarily sandwiches and burgers—is extraordinarily cheap (under $8). Pizzas, nachos, and soups are also available to pad your stomach for the wide variety of beers on tap.

Chinatown/Theater District

China Pearl *(T (Orange): NE Med Center   9 Tyler St, 617-426-4338 Dir: exit T N on Washington St, R on Kneeland, L on Tyler)*
Chinese: Famous for its reasonable $2-$6 Dim Sum (meat wrapped in dough) and voted "Boston's Best" by Boston Magazine, China Pearl is bedecked with an ornate Chinese décor and red accents that nicely complement their authentic cuisine. Bonus: A recently updated menu includes additional vegetarian options.

New Shanghai Restaurant *(T (Orange) NE Med Center   21 Hudson St, 617-338-6688   Dir: exit T N on Washington St, R on Kneeland, L on Hudson)*
Chinese: Slightly more elegant than your average inexpensive Chinatown dining, but still cheap (entrées are $5-$11). The Peking Duck or General Gao's Chicken are both very good and carryout is available.

New York Pizza *(T (Green): Boylston   224 Tremont St, 617-482-3459 Dir: exit T S on Tremont St)*
Greek: A decidedly non-Asian find in the Chinatown area, this pizza shop sells large $2 slices and makes great grinders on fresh bread: Try the Italian sausage or hot pastrami (sm: $5, lg: $6). The restaurant is really small so plan on doing takeout.

**Penang *(T (Orange): Chinatown 685 Washington St, 617-451-6373 Dir: exit T S on Washington)*
Malaysian: An inventively and tropically decorated casual spot that serves Pacific favorites like fried noodles ($6), ginger chicken ($12.55)

and beef or chicken satay ($7). Bear in mind that certain Malaysian dishes are prone to non-Western ingredients (like chicken feet), so consult your server first. Try the Mee Siam—it is perfection in a bowl—and finish up with their amazing fried ice cream with bananas drizzled with honey.

Montien Thai Restaurant & Lounge *(T (Orange): NE Med Center 63 Stuart St, 617-338-5600   Dir: exit T N on Washington St, L on Stuart St)*
Thai: The entrées are a little pricey ($10-20) but the cheap and flavorful appetizers make this stop a no-brainer. The Thai wings ($6) or calamari ($7) each serve as great pre-game fare.

Hu Tieu Nam Vang *(T (Green): Boylston   7 Beach St, 617-422-0501 Dir: exit T S on Tremont St, L on Lagrange St – turns into Beach St)*
Vietnamese: This tiny place serves up incredibly cheap and tasty soups, noodle dishes, and exotic house specialties like jellyfish and shrimp salad. So if you're feeling adventurous or just want to keep it cheap—most entrées are under $6—this place will not let you down.

Pho Vietnam *(T (Green): Boylston   1 Stuart St, 617-292-0220   Dir: exit T E on Boylston, R on Tremont St, R on Stuart)*
Vietnamese: With nearly everything on the menu under $6, it's hard to go wrong but your best bet here is to order the Pho, a traditional, thin broth chock full of chicken, beef, or anything else you want in it. The only catch here is that they don't serve alcohol.

Downtown

**Quincy Market *(T (Green): Gov't Center   Dir: exit T and walk straight across City Hall plaza, down the back steps, and across Congress St)* Quincy Market is the most visited spot in all of Boston. The 535 foot-long building built in 1822 is part of the larger Faneuil Hall Marketplace surrounding it.   Historically, the building was used as a large grocery market. Nowadays, it houses dozens of vendors peddling delicious cheap eats, snacks, and deserts.

Emerson's Café and Catering *(T (Green): Boylston St   80 Boylston St, 617-824-8070)*
Café: This bright little café serves up coffee, drinks, sandwiches, and salads to Emerson students, area workers, and passersby.

60   Cheap Eats

Finagle-A-Bagel *(T (Green/Red): Park St   129 Tremont St, 617-426-3300   Dir: exit T onto adjacent Tremont St)*
<u>Deli</u>: Getting a freshly baked bagel doesn't take much finagling at this local chain, just a couple of bucks. Bagel flavors range from triple chocolate chip to jalapeño cheddar cheese. Finagle also serves up tasty sandwiches, pizzas, and salads.

**Beantown Pub *(T (Red): Park St   100 Tremont St, 617-426-0111   Dir: exit T, L on adjacent Tremont)*
<u>Pub Grub</u>: A narrow but deceivingly large wood-adorned tavern that serves great food and houses an unpretentious meet-and-mingle scene at night. Complete with pool tables, TVs, and draft beers under $5, Beantown attracts a young-professional crowd and many lawyers-to-be from the adjacent Suffolk Law School. After 6pm the bar starts carding.

Bell In Hand Tavern *(T (Orange/Green): Haymarket   45 Union St, 617-227-2098   Dir: exit T, walk away from I-93 overpass (W) on New Sudbury, L on Congress, L on Hanover, R on Union)*
<u>Pub Grub:</u> Sit down for a cheap (and extra large) draft at the nation's oldest tavern. Open since 1795, this simplistic, laid-back watering hole is packed with 20-somethings on the weekends but thins out during the week. Go and get a taste of the building's well-preserved history and character.

Emmet's Pub and Restaurant *(T (Red): Park St   6 Beacon St, 617-742-8565   Dir: exit T, walk straight, L on Park St, R on Beacon)*
<u>Pub Grub</u>: A quiet, casual Irish Pub with traditional bar food, beer, and wine.

Purple Shamrock *(T (Green): Gov't Center   1 Union St, 617-227-2060   Dir: exit T and walk across City Hall Plaza and down steps towards Faneuil Hall)*
<u>Pub Grub</u>: There's a nice selection of burgers, sandwiches, pastas, and seafood at this laid-back Irish pub. In the spring and summer, get a spot by the enormous open windows and watch the craziness fall with night upon the area to the beat of live music. It's Boston at its very best.   Trivia night (Mondays) will give you a chance to win free stuff.

Downtown Crossing/South Station Area

Sam La Grassa's *(T (Green): Park St   44 Province St, 617-357-6861 Dir: exit T N on Tremont St, R on Bromfield St, L on Province)*
<u>American/Deli</u>: Stop by for a sandwich at this glorified deli where students at nearby Suffolk Law School frequently dine between classes. Try one of their grilled sandwiches ($9) or create your own overstuffed sandwich from a variety of fillers and freshly baked breads ($7).

Sandwich Express *(T (Orange): Downtown Crossing   99 Summer St, 617-345-0923   Dir: exit T N on Washington St, R on Summer St)*
<u>American</u>: Ideal for people on the go, this inviting sandwich shop offers fresh soups and affordable sandwiches (small: $4, large: $5). Try the Midnight Special, an Italian-style hard salami blended with roasted red peppers and Monterey Jack cheese.

**South Street Diner *(T (Orange): NE Med Center   178 Kneeland St, 617-350-0028   Dir: exit T N on Washington St, R on Kneeland)*
<u>American</u>: Quite possibly the *only* 24-hour diner in the Metro-Boston area, South St is a haven for drunken students after bars close, but the food is good enough to eat sober. Try the stack of chocolate-chip pancakes for $5.50. Not a morning person? Burgers and most sandwiches don't exceed $6.

Finagle-A-Bagel *(T (Orange): Downtown Crossing   70 Franklin St, 617-261-1900   Dir: exit T N on Washington St, R on Franklin)*
<u>Breakfast/Sandwiches:</u> The fare at this NE chain is hearty, healthy, and light. Choose from breakfast or lunch sandwiches, soups, and salads. Bagels with one topping are under $2, and lunch is also a good deal (most sandwiches are under $7): Try the Santa Fe Smoked Turkey Melt.

**El Chacarero *(T (Orange): Downtown Crossing   426 Washington St, 617-542-0392   Dir: exit E on Washington St towards Gov't Center)*
<u>Chilean</u>: Get your lunchtime fill during a work or shopping break at this delicious and fast South American-style takeout joint. Your sandwich comes stocked with your choice of meat, guacamole, cheese, green beans, and whatever else you ask them to throw on. Try the "extra spicy" if you dare. Vegetarian options available.

Souper Salad *(T (Orange): Downtown Crossing   82 Summer St, 617-292-4870   Dir: exit T N on Washington St, R on Summer St)*
Deli Food: Another favorite of the Downtown Crossing working crowd, this small lunch stop's name nearly covers everything. Besides their five+ daily soup offerings ($3-$5) and stocked salad bar, Souper Salad also specializes in fresh sandwiches (try the roasted turkey, $5) and hot wraps (try the spicy buffalo, $6).

Corner Mall Food Court *(T (Orange): Downtown Crossing   Corner of Washington and Summer St   Dir: exit T N on Summer St)* Fast Food/Variety: This conveniently located subterranean food court is perfect for a quick mid-shopping refueling and offers a wide variety of fast classics like McDonald's, Dunkin' Donuts, Sakkio Japan and India Express.

Qdoba *(T (Orange): Downtown Crossing   62 Summer St, 617-357-0791 Dir: exit T N on Summer St)*
Fast Food/Mexican: Fairly new to Boston, this Mexican grill offers fresh (but fast) Southwestern classics like burritos, tacos, salads, and quesadillas. Choose your toppings and fillings while they grill and stuff your food right in front of you. The best deal is the tortilla soup combo, which includes a bowl of their spicy vegetarian tortilla soup (add chicken for no additional charge!), a taco, and a drink for just $7.

Fajitas and 'Ritas *(T (Green): Park St   25 W St, 617-426-1222   Dir: exit T and walk with traffic (S) on Tremont St, L on W St)*
Mexican/Southwestern: This funky Tex-Mex bar and restaurant serves up its namesake specialties for low prices but doesn't skimp on freshness or flavor. Go for lunch and grab some chicken, vegetable, or pork fajitas for under $7 and be sure to try the house margarita for a mere $4.

Herrera's Mexican Grill *(T (Green): Park St   11 Temple Place, 617-426-2350 Dir: exit T S on Tremont and turn L on Temple Pl)*
Mexican: Given its super-fresh ingredients, authentic techniques and recipes, and friendly service, Herrera's is not the average Mexican fast-food stop. In fact, it's simply an added bonus that the food happens to be fast. This stop is right on par with Brookline's Anna's Taqueria in terms of bang-for-your-buck goodness. Try their enchiladas ($6) with a side of Spanish rice.

Hub Pub *(T (Green): Park   18 Province St, 617-523-6168   Dir: exit T and walk against traffic (N) on Tremont St, R on Bromfield St, L on Province)* <u>Pub Grub</u>: This bar clearly spent all of its decorating money on TVs and projectors so you can watch sports from any vantage point inside. Although the décor isn't easy on the eyes, the prices of the standard bar food and drinks are easy on the wallet and there's plenty of room for big groups.

Fenway

Audubon Circle Restaurant *(T (Green): Kenmore   838 Beacon St, 617-421-1910   Dir: exit T N on Beacon St)*
<u>American</u>: A cheap, chic spot with one of the city's best hamburgers, good vegetarian options, and very reasonable prices ($7-13). Those seeking solace from the often-hectic Kenmore scene will find comfort here amongst the wooden walls and sleek, modern décor. Not in the mood for a burger? Eat a quesadilla.

India Quality *(T (Green): Kenmore   484 Commonwealth Ave, 617-267-4499 Dir: exit T and head downtown (E) on Commonwealth Ave)*
<u>Indian</u>: One of the few Indian restaurants in the area, this sit-down restaurant serves Northern Indian cuisine to an eclectic crowd. Entrées, such as the delicious Chicken Tikka, start at $8. So don't be put off by the name—it really is high quality—and when you're feeling lazy, don't forget that they deliver.

El Pelon Taqueria *(T (Green D): Fenway   92 Peterborough St, 617-262-9090   Dir: exit S on Park Dr, L on Peterborough)*
<u>Mexican</u>: This authentic Mexican burrito and taco shop ranks with the likes of Anna's as one of the best taquerias in Boston. The tiny but cheerful Pelon is ideal for a quick and filling lunch. All burritos are under $6, but the menu offers so much more.

**Boston Beer Works *(T (Green): Kenmore   61 Brookline Ave, 617-536-2337   Dir: exit T, walk away from city (W) on Brookline)*
<u>Pub Grub</u>: If we said this giant bar has 16 changing brews on tap and large portions of cheap bar foods ($5-13) ranging from buffalo wings to fresh salads and grilled fish, would you be interested? What if we also said all the beer is brewed on-site and the place was littered with TVs? Not a beer drinker? Become one by trying the blueberry ale; it's

undoubtedly like at least one of your friends: fruity yet oddly appealing.

Cask 'n' Flagon *(T (Green): Kenmore   62 Brookline Ave, 617-536-4840   Dir: exit T and walk away from city (W) on Brookline)*
Pub Grub: This Fenway landmark may be located in the shadows of the Green Monster, but the food and drinks are decidedly cheaper than Fenway fare. The menu is stocked with traditional bar provisions and nearly all items are under $10. Grab a beer and a burger and be prepared to talk baseball. No tickets? Don't worry—there are plenty of TVs around.

**Tiki Room *(T (Green D): Kenmore   1 Lansdowne St, 617-351-2580   Dir: exit T, walk away from city (W) on Brookline Ave, L on Lansdowne)*
Tahitian: A slightly hokey palm and bamboo-adorned oasis amidst the beer and baseball land in the vicinity of Fenway Park. Tiki Room is a jovial and tropical drink/dinner spot. The Polynesian-infused menu includes fancy sandwiches and the popular "Build Your Own Pu Pu Platter" (guests choose six items).

Jamaica Plain

El Embajador *(T (Orange): Green Street   3371 Washington St, 617-524-6812   Dir: exit T, walk N on Green St, R on Washington)*
Caribbean: El Embajador will definitely provide a unique dining experience in a cozy, intimate setting suitable for smaller groups and couples. If you've never had fried plantains, try them here. Order stews, soups, paellas, or the steak and onion Cuban sandwich for under $8.

El Oriental de Cuba *(T (Orange): Jackson Square   416 Centre St, 617-524-6464   Dir: exit T, R on Centre St and walk .4 mi or avoid the T and take the #39 bus)*
Cuban: If you are unfamiliar with Cuban food, El Oriental is a good place to be introduced to it. Sides of spicy tamales, rice, and peppers complement roasted pork and steak sandwiches. Note: During production, this restaurant burned down. Plans are under way to rebuild.

Miami Restaurant *(T (Orange): Jackson Square   381 Centre St, 617-522-4644   Dir: exit T, R on Centre St and walk .3 mi or avoid the T and take #39 bus)*
<u>Cuban</u>: The hefty Cuban sandwiches and spiced soups are a lot to handle, but the prices won't kill the joy—so eat up.

**Sorella's *(T (Orange): Stony Brook   388 Centre St, 617-524-2016 Dir: exit T, head W on Boylston St .3 mi, R on Centre St, or avoid the T and take the #39 bus)*
<u>Diner</u>: The best breakfast place around, but be careful not to sleep through their hours (6:30am-2pm) and expect about a 20-30 minute wait on weekends. Oversized omelets and creative pancake options will make your mouth water as the plates go by.

Alex's Chimis *(T (Orange): Jackson Square   358 Centre St, 617-522-4644   Dir: exit T, R on Centre St and walk .3 mi or avoid the T and take #39 bus)*
<u>Dominican</u>: Come here for fantastic and cheap Dominican derivations of chicken sandwiches and hamburgers.

Pizza Oggi *(T (Green E): Health Street   8 Perkins Street, 617-345-0022   Dir: exit T, walk S on S. Huntington .4 mi or take #39 bus to Centre St, L on Centre St, R on Perkins St)*
<u>Italian</u>: It's no exaggeration to say this is some of the best and most interesting thin-crust pizza in Boston. Salads, sandwiches, and pastas are also available for takeout only.

Taco's El Charro *(T (Orange): Jackson Square   349 Centre St, 617-522-2578   Dir: exit T, R on Centre St and walk .3 mi or avoid the T and take #39 bus)*
<u>Mexican</u>: Authentic, spicy cuisine that will leave your wallet and belly full: Try the soft or crispy tacos with any variety of fixings like pineapple-flavored pork or beef (under $9).

Costello's Tavern *(T (Orange): Green Street   723 Centre St, 617-522-9263   Dir: exit T, walk (N) up Green .4 mi, L on Centre St, or avoid the T and take #39 bus)*
<u>Pub Grub</u>: Costello's is a low-lit bar with a blaring jukebox, live music on the weekends, TVs, and dart boards where you can grab cheap burgers, fries, and sandwiches.

The Purple Cactus Burrito and Wrap *(T (Orange): Green Street 674 Centre St, 617-522-7422   Dir: exit T and walk (N) up Green (.4 mi), L on Centre St or avoid the T and take the #39 bus)*
<u>Tex-Mex</u>: The burritos are packed with fresh chicken or steak, rice, and beans and will leave you wanting nothing more than a cold beer. The menu has something for meat lovers and vegetarians alike—all for under $5.

North End

**Bova's Bakery *(T (Green/Orange): Haymarket   134 Salem St, 617-523-5601   Dir: exit T, follow walkway to North End, R on Cross St, L on Salem)*
<u>Bakery</u>: This place is truly a hidden treasure of bliss. Allow yourself to be lured in by the smell of freshly baked breads and pastries and you'll soon be starving—good thing a hard working family keeps it open 24-hours-a-day and sells a myriad of super cheap sandwiches and baked delights.

**Cafe Paradiso *(T (Green/Orange): Haymarket   255 Hanover Street, 617-742-1768   Dir: exit T, follow walkway to North End, R on Cross St, L on Hanover)*
<u>Café</u>: Everything you could ask for in a local neighborhood café: coffee, cocktails, and cheap, traditional food packed into a quaint, eclectically decorated space (there is a bicycle hanging from the ceiling). Try the unique Torta Rustica (eggplant parmigiana-style pouch filled with vegetables and cheese) for a mere $6 or one of their signature salads or sandwiches. Open daily until 2am.

Caffe Dello Sport *(T (Green/Orange): Haymarket   308 Hanover St, 617-523-5063   Dir: exit T, follow walkway to North End, R on Cross St, L on Hanover)*
<u>Café</u>: A festive, larger-than-average café open from 6am to midnight every night, featuring live soccer televised weekly. Must-try menu selections include the various Panini sandwiches (all under $6), pastries, and gourmet coffee.

Dino's *(T (Green/Orange): Haymarket   141 Salem St, 617-227-1991   Dir: exit T, follow walkway to North End, R on Cross St, L on Salem)*
<u>Italian</u>: Don't let the fast-food ambience—or its tiny size—fool you, the food here is excellent. Dino's serves up a good variety of hot and cold sandwiches and salads, most of which fall under $7. Chip in a couple

extra bucks for a plate of pasta with homemade sauce and sit down at one of the dozen tables.

Pizzeria Regina *(T (Green/Orange): North Station   11½ Thatcher Street, 617-227-0765   Dir: exit T NE on Causeway St, R(S) on Joe Tecce Way/N Washington St, L on Thatcher)*
Italian: Sure, the North End is home to a plethora of pizzerias, but get a real (and cheap) taste of history at "Boston's Original Pizzeria" which boasts great service, a time-perfected recipe (open since 1926), and most importantly, huge slices of brick-oven pizza. Stick to the basics with the Margherita ($10), or spice things up with one of 15 other variations on the classic Italian pie.

Pushcart Café & Pizzeria *(T (Green/Orange): Haymarket   115 Salem St, 617-523-8123   Dir: exit T, follow walkway to North End, R on Cross St, L on Salem)*
Italian: An inviting pizzeria blanketed with flat screen TVs around a bar, making it a great place for watching games. To draw the Monday night game crowds, Pushcart offers FREE slices of pizza with the purchase of an alcoholic drink. Otherwise, pies are $7 for a 16-incher.

Corner Café *(T (Green/Orange): North Station   87 Prince St, 617-523-8997   Dir: exit T NE on Causeway St, R on Prince)*
Pub Grub: This small, dark, and rowdy neighborhood pit stop offers a variety of cheap eats ranking from franks and beans to chicken parmigiana (all for under $8). Order a $10 pitcher or $3 bottle of Red Hook with your sausages—highly recommended by the local clientele—and enjoy views of passing foot traffic until 2am.

Tutto Italiano *(T (Green/Orange): Haymarket   20 Fleet St, 617-557-4002   Dir: exit T, follow walkway to North End, R on Cross St, L on Hanover St, R on Fleet)*
Specialty Grocer: A great place to come for special Italian ingredients like fresh mozzarella or gorgonzola cheese, olives, prosciutto, or tasty jams. You can also find pretty mean subs and pastries. Hours vary according to the owner's whims, but seem to run on average as follows: 10am-7pm T-Th, 10am-6pm F, 10am-3pm Sa, 9am-3pm Su; closed M.

O'Natural's Café *(T (Red): Davis   187 Elm St, 617-666-2233   Dir: exit T to Holland St, R on Holland, cross Davis Sq to Elm)* <u>American, Health Food</u>: O'Natural's makes health food accessible, dubbing its menu of flatbread sandwiches, salads, soups, and Asian noodles "Fast food, naturally." Popular among young professionals at lunchtime. Don't miss the flatbread pizza, which is served after 4pm. Open until 8 pm.

Renee's Café *(T (Red): Davis   198 Holland St, 617-623-2727   Dir: exit T to Holland St, L on Holland)*
<u>American</u>: A sweet local diner with slow service and hearty breakfast and lunch eats (closes at 1:30pm).

**Soleil Café and Catering *(T (Red): Davis   1153 Broadway St, 617-625-0082   Dir: exit T to Holland St, L on Holland to where it intersects Broadway)*
<u>American</u>: Colorful photos by local artists decorate the walls of this breakfast and lunch stop (open 9am- 4pm). Local professionals, yuppies and funkier types alike enjoy fresh sandwiches and salads. Interesting flavor combos include the Napa—herb-grilled chicken with brie, avocado, bacon, and aioli on garlic focaccia—or the Woodstock—tofu, Thai peanut sauce, cilantro, carrot, red onion, red pepper, and cucumber in a spinach wrap. www.soleil-cafe.com

Wing Works *(T (Red): Davis   201 Elm St, 617-666-9000   Dir: exit T to Holland St, R on Holland, cross Davis Sq to Elm)*
<u>American</u>: A take-out spot with cheap, finger-licking good wings. Also caters platters perfect for Super Bowl parties.

Rosebud Diner *(T (Red): Davis   381 Summer St, 617-666-6015   Dir: exit T to Holland St, R on Holland, cross Davis Sq to Elm, L on Summer)*
<u>Diner</u>: Typical diner fare served up in an old-fashioned diner car. Go for breakfast or a late snack (8am-midnight F-Sa, 8am-11pm M-Th).

**Sound Bites *(T (Red): Davis   708 Broadway, 617-623-8338   Dir: exit T to College Ave, R on College to Powderhouse Sq, R on Broadway)*

<u>Diner</u>: This tiny breakfast stop serves some of the best pancakes and omelets around—delicious, cheap, and generous portions—but be prepared for long waits and fast turnover. Closes at 2:45pm.

**Blue Shirt Café *(T (Red): Davis   424 Highland Ave, 617-629-7641 Dir: exit T to College Ave, L on Highland)*
<u>Health food</u>: This funky health-food spot is a favorite for Davis vegetarians with its zesty sandwiches, wraps, and salads. Thirsty? Cool off with one of many juice and smoothie infusions.

Amelia's Kitchen *(T (Red): Davis   1137 Broadway St, 617-776-2800 Dir: exit T to Holland St, L on Holland to where it intersects Broadway)*
<u>Italian</u>: A neighborhood pizza and pasta place, this cozy eatery has a loyal following. Locals swear by the homemade fettuccine and focaccia bread. Limited outdoor seating is available during the summer.

Angelina's Pizza *(T (Red): Davis   230 Holland St, 617-776-1240 Dir: exit T to Holland St, L on Holland)*
<u>Italian</u>: Angelina's, popular amongst Tufts students and locals, is a classic stool and table pizza stop with cheap and delicious slices, calzones, and subs.

Mike's Restaurant *(T (Red): Davis   9 Davis Square, 617-628-2379 Dir: exit T to Holland St, R on Holland to Davis Sq)* <u>Italian</u>: This Davis staple has been serving up greasy but wonderful slices for years (regular $1.89, Sicilian $2.05), along with a standard selection of cold-cuts, calzones, pasta, and beer. Grab a chair by the window or a table outdoors and watch Davis traffic go by.

Anna's Taqueria *(T (Red): Davis   236A Elm St, 617- 666-3900   Dir: exit T to Holland St, R on Holland, cross Davis Sq to Elm)*
<u>Mexican</u>: Choose your own toppings at this assembly-line burrito joint. Burritos not your thing? Their authentic quesadillas, tacos, and Mexican plates will fill you up for less than $4.

Tip Top Thai *(T (Red): Davis   1127 Broadway St, 617-627-9333 Dir: exit T to Holland St, L on Holland to where it intersects Broadway, slight R on Broadway)*
<u>Thai</u>: A new addition to the neighborhood with classic dishes. Meals in this quaint setting are a steal: nothing on the menu is over $8. Show a student ID for 10% off.

South End

**Charlie's Sandwich Shoppe *(T (Orange): Mass Ave   492 Columbus Ave, 617-536-7669   Dir: exit T S on Mass Ave, L on Columbus)* American: An old-school joint that's been serving up huge breakfasts and their signature turkey hash since 1927. Sit at the counter and catch the chaos around the grill, or relax in a booth as you dine on heaping portions of any greasy American favorite you can dream up at Boston's famed breakfast institution (served all day).

Flour Bakery and Cafe *(T (Orange): Mass Ave   1595 Washington St, 617-267-4300   Dir: exit T S on Mass Ave, L on Washington St)* Bakery: Stop by for a muffin ($2.50) or satisfy your sweet tooth with a scone ($1.50) while soaking up the casual, feel-good ambiance. The staff is friendly and the sour cream coffee cake is better than your grandmother's.

Yum Mee Garden *(T (Green E): Prudential   665 Tremont St, 617-267-0488   Dir: exit T, walk S on W Newton, L on Tremont)* Chinese: Yum Mee is exactly that, serving any type of Chinese you can dream up from its ginormous menu of offerings, almost all of which are less than $8. Takeout and delivery only

Miami Café *(T (Green E): Prudential   68 Aguadilla St, 617-859-8105 Dir: exit T, walk S on W Newton, R on Aguadilla)* Cuban: Ever been to Cuba, the Dominican Republican, or Puerto Rico? If not, here's a chance to taste some of the finest dishes from those countries. Take a break from mainstream S End by soaking in some salsa music, a daiquiri or two, and dirt cheap appetizers before filling up on one of many exotic dishes and sandwiches ranging from $4-12. Highlights: $4 tamales and $1 empanadas. Hours: 8am-8pm; cash only.

Garden of Eden *(T (Orange): Back Bay   571 Tremont St, 617-247-8377   Dir: exit T S on Dartmouth, L on Tremont)* Deli: Although nothing about the menu or venue stands out, the huge variety of salads, heaping sandwiches, homemade soups, and weekend brunch options should be able to satisfy most customers given that everything is under $8.

Mike's City Diner *(T (Orange): Mass Ave   1714 Washington St, 617-267-9393   Dir: exit T S on Mass Ave, L on Washington)*
<u>Diner</u>: With its red countertop, checked tablecloths, bottomless coffee, and to-die-for home fries (with cheese), Mike's seems almost a parody of the quintessential diner. The portions are hearty, the service is friendly, the prices are great, but there is a catch: It's only open 6am-3pm.

Victoria's Diner *(T (Orange): Mass Ave   1024 Massachusetts Ave, 617-442-5965   Dir: exit T S on Mass Ave)*
<u>Diner</u>: This laid-back spot in Newmarket Square features great sandwiches (try the open-faced turkey) and breakfast at any hour for an eclectic crowd daily from 6am-10pm.

Delux Café *(T (Orange): Back Bay   100 Chandler St, 617- 338-5258 Dir: exit T S on Dartmouth St, L on Chandler)*
<u>Eclectic</u>: A hip, funky hole-in-the-wall restaurant/bar that is constantly packed with boisterous post-work crowds. The eclectic menu is stocked with a variety of good eats from pan-seared tuna with garlic potatoes ($9) to good old-fashioned grilled cheese ($4). Bring cash—credit cards are not accepted.

Rome Pizza *(T (Green): Arlington   416 Tremont St, 617-695-1640 Dir: exit T S on Arlington St, R on Tremont)*
<u>Italian</u>: Large cheese pizzas for $8.50, $6 wraps, pasta dishes under $7, and meat dishes under $8...need we say more?

Morse Fish Company *(T (Silver): Union Park St   1401 Washington St, 617-262-9375   Dir: exit T and take Union Park St S to Washington St)* <u>Seafood</u>: When a restaurant can boast having been around for over 100 years, you know there must be something special about the place—at Morse Fish, it's the prices. Diners here scarf down cheap, fresh seafood off paper plates with plastic forks in a bare bones environment. Warm up with a shrimp cocktail (ten shrimp, $6) and end with a haddock sandwich ($6) or one of many cheap fish dinners ($8) complete with fries and cole slaw. Note the hours: M-Th & Sa 11am-8pm, F 11am-9pm, Su 12-6pm.

State Street Area/Financial District

Al's State Street Café *(T (Blue): Aquarium   114 State St, 617-720-5555   Dir: exit T, walk away from water (W) on State St)*
American: Hot and cold subs on freshly baked bread and salads are served expeditiously at this light-lunch stop. Very large subs are $6, smaller ones $4; try the Lady Café Special (fresh mozzarella, sweet plum tomatoes, and basil, drizzled with olive oil and balsamic vinegar).

The International *(T (Blue): Aquarium   184 High St, 617-542-4747   Dir: exit T S .3 mi on Atlantic Ave, R on High St)*
American: This multi-faceted venue morphs seamlessly from after-work bar to billiard-playing hangout to dinnertime fine-dining. Be sure to sample their signature International Burger, which at $10 may seem like a splurge until you see the size of that monster and the pile of fries that accompanies it. Note the early hours: M-W 11:30am-8pm; Th-F 11:30am-9pm.

Pressed Sandwiches *(T (Orange): State St   2 Oliver St, 617-482-9700   Dir: exit T onto State St, head toward Faneuil Hall (E), R on Kilby St which becomes Oliver St)*
Italian: This panini shop specializes in perfecting flat sandwiches. Fresh ingredients like hummus, vegetables, prosciutto, and mozzarella are placed between slices of high-quality bread and then heated in the press. Bottom line: a genuinely healthy and tasty lunch for less than $8. Hours: 7am-3pm.

Andale *(T (Red): S Station   125 Summer St, 617-737-2820   Dir: exit T onto Summer St and take a L)*
Mexican: Add some spice to a business lunch at this small vegetarian-friendly Mexican spot. One of their burritos ($6.25) is sure to fill you up and it comes stuffed with ingredients you pick. If you're looking for something light, their stocked nachos are just $4.25. Seating is minimal, so get your lunch to go.

Pizza Oggi *(T (Blue): Aquarium   131 Broad St, 617-345-0022   Dir: exit T S on Atlantic Ave, walk a few blocks, R on Broad St)*
Pizza: Flavorful, creative pizzas and sandwiches make this Boston chain a necessary stop on your to-eat list. Try their Hawaiian pizza (scallions, roasted pineapple, and smoked ham); a small is $12 and worth every penny. Sandwiches ($6) are a little cheaper and just as delectable.

Cosi Sanwich Bar (Two Locations in the area) *(T (Red): S Station 133 Federal St, 617-292-2674 Dir: exit T onto Summer St and take L, R on Purchase St, L on Federal St)*
(T (Blue): State 14 Milk St, 617-426-0593 Dir: exit T and walk down Washington St, L on Milk St)
<u>Soup/Sandwich</u>: A hip and innovative chain of laid-back coffee and sandwich shops that are easy on the wallet and offer cozy ambiance. Cuisine is on the gourmet end, so expect the average sandwich to cost around $7.25.

Cheap Drinks

Allston/Brighton

**The Avenue *(T (Green B): Harvard Ave   1249 Commonwealth Ave, 617-782-9508   Dir: NW corner of Harvard and Commonwealth Ave)* This relaxed hangout—prone to a younger crowd—stakes the proud claim of pouring a decent selection of $1 pints every night of the week. The Avenue is great for meeting up early for drinks and food (those under 21 may eat until 8pm), but equally perfect as a final destination, with its sports broadcasting flat screen TVs, pinball machines, and pool table.

**The Green Briar Pub *(T (Green B): Washington St   304 Washington St, 617-789-4100   Dir: exit T N on Washington St, L at base of hill onto Washington)* This lively and friendly Irish pub will make you want to become a regular. The warm environment justifies the $3 drafts. Go on a Friday night when the bar has beer promotions with companies like Newcastle and Corona (translation: free stuff & cheap drinks).

**The Kells *(T (Green B): Harvard Ave   161 Brighton Ave, 617-782-9082   Dir: exit T N on Harvard, L on Brighton)*
A huge Irish bar with Asian-infused décor and cuisine, The Kells is one of the few bars in the area that features the coveted $1 draft and a packed dance floor. If your priorities are people and dancing, go on a Thursday (any other night, there seems to be more bouncers than drinkers). Possessors of fake IDs beware: Kells' bouncers enjoy confiscating IDs.

The Kinvara *(T (Green B): Harvard Ave   34 Harvard Ave, 617-783-9400   Dir: exit T N on Harvard Ave and walk .5 mi)*
This parody of a traditional Irish bar is a dark, wood-furnished cove festooned with the staples of Boston living: (cheap) beer, baseball,

and music. Catch a Sox game and enjoy some traditional Irish singing on a Thursday night.

Mary Ann's *(T (Green C): Cleveland Circle   1937 Beacon St)*
There is something endearing about this slightly-sketchy, stale smelling BC hole-in-the-wall and that something just may be its $1.50 Bud Light drafts and $1 bottles for the barely-legal crowd to sip on at happy hour.

The Model Café *(T (Green B): Harvard Ave   7 N Beacon St, 617-254-9365   Dir: exit T N on Harvard, L on Brighton Ave, walk .3 mi past Cambridge St)* Allston's Mecca for urban hipsters seeking reprieve from trendy downtown alternatives has served as a great local dive bar for the better part of a century. Enjoy a $3.50 pint and decent bar food (kitchen closes at 10pm when the drinking crowd pours in).

Our House *(T (Green B): Griggs   1277 Commonwealth Ave, 617-782-3228   Dir: exit T and walk E towards Harvard Ave)*
This subterranean lounge and pre-game spot becomes the game, literally—grab the Jenga set or another forgotten game from your childhood and settle into a corner on a comfy couch with a $2 Brubaker and enjoy the rarity of a cheap drink in Boston.

Silhouette Lounge *(T (Green B): Harvard Ave   200 Brighton Ave, 617-254-9306   Dir: exit T N on Harvard, L on Brighton)*
Stray from the beaten path for a night and head out to this self-proclaimed dive bar for strong drinks and free baskets of popcorn. If it's beer you seek, take advantage of $1.25 Old Milwaukee drafts until you feel bold enough to challenge the regulars to pool or darts.

Back Bay

**Bukowski's *(T (Green B/C/D): Hynes   50 Dalton St, 617-437-9999   Dir: exit T to Mass Ave, L on Mass Ave, L on Boylston St, R on Dalton)*
"99 bottles of beer on the wall" isn't just a song lyric any more, it's the number of beers on the menu at Bukowski's, all of them cheap for Boston including Schlitz, Pabst, and Genesee beer for just $2.25.

Foggy Goggle *(T (Green B/C/D): Hynes   911 Boylston St, 617-266-3399   Dir: exit T to Mass Ave, L on Mass Ave, L on Boylston St)* Once featured as Playboy's College Bar of the Month, the Foggy Goggle is a hotspot that serves up large drinks on the cheap. With three bars tended by hot-bodied females and a large open dance floor, expect the energy level high, the '80s and '90s rock deafening, and the fishbowl-sized mixed drinks fairly weak.

Our House East *(T (Green E): Symphony   52 Gainsborough St, 617-236-1890   Dir: exit T, L (SW) on Huntington, R on Gainsborough)* A pre-game favorite for college students, Our House East goes easy on the wallet with its $2 beers.

**Pour House *(T (Green B/C/D): Hynes   909 Boylston St, 617-236-1767   Dir: exit T to Mass Ave, L on Mass Ave, L on Boylston)* College students and young professionals flock to the Pour House for its friendly pub/sports bar atmosphere and cheap selection of mixed drinks and beers like 22oz Pabsts for under $4.

TC's Lounge *(T (Green B/C/D): Hynes   1 Haviland St, 617-247-8109   Dir: exit T to Mass Ave, L on Mass Ave, R on Haviland)* The Berklee College of Music claims TC's as its own, but that doesn't deter other students and locals from drinking and hanging out at this bargain bar. There is limited seating and no food at this dimly-lit pub but the casual atmosphere makes this bar a popular hang out for its often boisterous clientele.

Beacon Hill

**Beacon Hill Pub *(T (Red): Charles/MGH   149 Charles St)* This noisy dive bar draws a youthful, energetic crowd and stands in stark contrast to its fancy neighbors as the only true college bar in the area. Throw some darts, shoot some hoops, and grab a Bud ($1.55, $3 for the stay-cold cans).

Hill Tavern *(T (Red): Charles/MGH   228 Cambridge St, 617-742-6192   Dir: exit T onto Cambridge St and walk E)* By night, the Hill Tavern draws a laid-back but lively crowd of Beacon Hill locals ranging in age. This classy, laid-back pub with its exposed brick walls and shiny wood paneling is the perfect spot for an after-work drink.

Red Hat Café *(T (Red): Charles/MGH   9 Bowdoin St, 617-523-2175   Dir: exit T onto Cambridge St, walk E, R on Bowdoin)* This cozy, dark, hole-in-the wall is a local secret with cheap drinks and sandwich/burger/fried fish plates in the $5-10 range.

Sevens Ale House *(T (Red): Charles/MGH   77 Charles St, 617-523-9074)* Dark and laid-back, this local favorite is about as divey as Charles St gets, though Polo shirts still abound. Grab a beer and play some darts but watch where you throw—the small space fills quickly. Beer and wine only: pints $4.25.

Brookline

Best Cellars *(T (Green C): Coolidge Corner   1327 Beacon St, 617-232-4100   Dir: exit T onto Beacon St)* Wine shopping's made easy, as Best Cellars stocks their reasonably-priced bottles by taste: juicy, fizzy, sweet, smooth, etc. Just bring your taste buds and you'll be a connoisseur in no time. Most Saturdays between 2-4pm, Best Cellars offers free food—cooked by a professional chef—and wine to its customers. They also have daily wine tastings (5-8pm weekdays, 2pm weekends) so if you are not yet a wino, maybe it's time to become one.

**The Publick House *(T (Green): Washington Square   1648 Beacon St, 617-277-2880   Dir: exit T onto Beacon St)* Patrons come here for exotic beer (24 on tap) by candle and firelight. Savory suds are reasonably priced for microbrews: Smuttynose IPA $4.50, North Coast Scrimshaw Pils $4.50, Six Point Righteous Ale $4.

T's Pub *(T (Green B): Babcock Street   973 Commonwealth Ave, 617-254-0807   Dir: exit T and take R on Commonwealth Ave)* Whether you came for a drink or a game, T's Pub has great service and an energetic college crowd. Highlights: $2.25 16oz drafts.

Trader Joe's *(T (Green C): Coolidge Corner   1309 Beacon St, 617-278-9997   Dir: exit T onto Beacon)* An affordable place to buy groceries for the week or the evening's dinner fixings. It also carries a large selection of wines, beers, liquors, and gourmet foods—Trader Joe's is a fun one-stop-shop.

Unfortunately, we were unable to locate bars in Harvard Square selling cheap drinks. However, we didn't want to leave you empty-handed after a stressful day, so we've prepared a list of unpretentious local favorites in Harvard Square where you won't be broken by your tab but will be paying average prices for drinks. If you have any suggestions where one might find cheap drinks around Harvard Square, please let us know via our website (www.brokeinboston.com).

Brother Jimmy's *(Closed at present time; plans to re-open on Eliot St Dir: exit T onto JFK, walk 3 blocks, R on Eliot)* After a two-year stay in the old location of the House of Blues, this southern beer and BBQ spot has plans to reopen around the corner from Redline on Eliot St. Before its relocation, Brother J's was the spot for heavy boozing and country tunes, with cheap beers, liquor-laden Swamp Bowls, and a laid-back vibe.

**Border Café *(T (Red): Harvard   32 Church St, 617-864-6100 Dir: exit T onto Mass Ave, walk towards Porter Sq, L on Church)* Border gets packed every night of the week with students and twentysomethings looking to take the edge off their day with a margarita or a glass of sangria.

The Cantab Lounge *(T (Red): Central   738 Mass Ave, 617-354-2685 Dir: exit T NW onto Mass Ave towards Harvard Sq)* Crowds gather at this dive bar mostly for the live music every night. Open mic M-W & Su for folk, bluegrass, and blues; F and Sa Little Joe Cook, a long-time Cambridge performer, plays with his group the Thrillers. Cover prices range from $3-8; drafts of Busch $1.75 every night, bottled beer $3, mixed drinks $3.25.

The Cellar *(T (Red): Harvard   991 Mass Ave, 617-876-2580 Dir: exit T onto Mass Ave, walk 3/4 mi towards Central Sq)* Known mostly among Harvard students as an upscale liquor mart, the Cellar also has an attractive, relaxed space downstairs where the mostly older, local crowd sips good beer for decent prices (Guinness, Newcastle, Sierra Nevada $4).

Flat Top Johnny's *(T (Red): Kendall   1 Kendall Sq, 617-494-9565)* Primarily a pool hall, Flat Top Johnny's is a hip spot to sip a beer or hang out. FREE pool after 11pm on Wednesday nights always draws a crowd.

**The Hong Kong *(T (Red): Harvard   1236 Mass Ave, 617-864-5311   Dir: exit T onto Mass Ave, walk towards Central Sq)* The Kong's got it all for a night of messy fun: a restaurant on the first floor, a bar on the second, a dance floor on the third, and a fun, strange, drunken mix of people ranging from Harvard undergrads to townies. Buy a couple liquor-laden Scorpion bowls with friends ($14 each), grab the footlong straws, and race to see who can get the most ridiculous the fastest. On weekends, long lines often form after midnight.

People's Republik *(T (Red): Harvard or Central   876 Mass Ave, 617-491-6969   Dir: exit T onto Mass Ave)* Standing in no-man's land between Harvard and Central Square, the People's Republik is like a sanctuary amidst Siberia, with a dark, warm, and inviting atmosphere of casual locals. With bottles of buds for $2.50, you'll be glad you made the trek.

Phoenix Landing *(T (Red): Central   512 Mass Ave, 617-576-6260   Dir: exit T SE onto Mass Ave towards MIT)* Phoenix Landing is the most college-y bar in Central Sq. In this packed, noisy space buzzing patrons mingle and dance to Top 40 beats and house music as the night progresses. Get there before 10pm to avoid the nominal cover charge. Half-priced appetizers 4-6pm weekdays.

The Plough and Stars *(T (Red): Harvard or Central   912 Mass Ave, 617-576-0032   Dir: exit T onto Mass Ave)* A boisterous Irish bar filled with locals and grad students downing pints. Live music comes on at 9pm every night (blues, folk, R&B, swing, jazz, country, bluegrass, Irish) with a cover charge Th-Sa from $0 to $6 once the music begins. Pints of Bud $2.75, 20oz "Imperial Pint" of Guinness $4.

Redline *(T (Red): Harvard   59 JFK St, 617-491-9851   Dir: exit T onto JFK; walk 3 blocks)* Be prepared to wait in line, as this small, trendy space gets packed quickly on weekends with undergrads, grad students, and young professionals looking to meet and mingle. W-Su DJs spin a mix of beats, mostly hip-hop, with no cover charge.

**Shay's *(T (Red): Harvard   58 JFK St, 617-864-9161   Dir: exit T onto JFK, walk 3 blocks)* Shay's is the closest you'll get to Cheers in the Square: A gathering of boisterous locals who pack the pub's outdoor seating at all hours of the afternoon, evening, and night.

Whitney's *(T (Red): Harvard   37 JFK St, 617-354-8172   Dir: exit T onto JFK, walk one block)* Don't expect service with a smile (or many smiles at all) at the Square's only real dive bar. What you can expect is a prime view of the Square (windows face JFK Street) and $3 bottles of Bud.

Chinatown/Theater District

Felt *(T (Orange): Chinatown   533 Washington St, 617-350-5555 Dir: exit station N on Washington)* This sleek urban lounge features music, billiards, and while it is not known for being cheap, Felt regularly hosts liquor promotions (*then* things become reasonable). Stay abreast of upcoming events at *www.feltclubboston.com*.

Jacob Wirth's Restaurant *(T (Orange): NE Med Center   31 Stuart St, 617-338-8586   Dir: exit station N on Washington and turn L on Stuart)* This self-proclaimed "Boston tradition" has a good selection of domestic and imported beers, but more importantly, offers $1.50 pints and $6 pitchers of Pabst Blue Ribbon. (It may not be the fanciest beer in the place, but it certainly is the best deal.)

The Tam *(T (Green): Boylston   222 Tremont St   Dir: exit T S on Tremont)* This small Irish pub defines the term "hole-in-the-wall" (it doesn't even have a phone) and is prone to interesting homeless visitors, but pints are $2 and most mixed drinks are under $5. Bring quarters for the stocked jukebox.

Downtown

Rattlesnake Bar *(T (Green): Arlington   384 Boylston St, 617-859-8555 (on corner of Boylston and Arlington)* A decent place to grab a burger and sandwich, but a better place to grab a drink, especially on the rooftop deck.

Sweetwater Café *(T (Green): Boylston   5 Boylston Pl, 617- 351-2515)* A laid-back bar in the midst of the general Alley debauchery,

serving upscale bar food and drawing a sizable after-work crowd. In
summer, tables are set up outside in the cobblestone Alley and give
the place a very European feel.

Downtown Crossing/South Station Area

Fajitas and 'Ritas *(T (Green): Park St   25 W St, 617-426-1222 Dir:
exit T S on Tremont St, L on W St)* This funky Tex-Mex bar and
restaurant serves up its namesake specialties for low prices but
doesn't skimp on freshness or flavor. Strawberry, raspberry, or
regular margaritas are available by the glass ($4) or pitcher $(11.50).

The Good Life *(T (Orange): Downtown Crossing   28 Kingston St,
617-451-2622   Dir: exit T S on Summer St, R on Kingston)* Add this
1950s-style bar and lounge—with its reasonably-priced martinis and
Mai Tais—to your bar-hopping list immediately. Check out their live
jazz and swing on the weekends.

Jose McIntyre's *(T (Blue): Aquarium   160 Milk St, 617-451-9460
Dir: exit T S on Atlantic Ave, R on Milk St)* The cultural collision of
Mexico and Ireland is a bit random, but it somehow works for this
unique and friendly pub/cantina. The 3.5 bars specialize in the 60oz
margaritas—they're cheap already and even cheaper when you split
one...which you'll have to do. Also enjoy half-priced appetizers (try the
nachos!) every weekday from 4-7pm.

Sidebar *(T (Green): Park St   14 Bromfield St, 617-357-1899   Dir:
exit T, walk straight (N) on Tremont, R on Bromfield St)* This bar
boasts informal dining with excellent burgers, $1 drafts and $6
pitchers, nice waitresses, and a large following of regulars who pack
into the narrow space to watch whatever game is being broadcasted
on the bar's various TVs. All in all, it's everything you'd want from a
Boston bar.

Silvertone *(T (Green): Park St   69 Bromfield St, 617-338-7887   Dir:
exit T, walk straight (N) on Tremont, R on Bromfield St)* You'll feel like
you're at a friend's house in this underground hideaway, as cocktails
(like their signature raspberry vodka martini) are all in the $5 range
and can be enjoyed from the comfort of a couch.

Fenway

Copperfield's *(T (Green): Kenmore   98 Brookline Ave, 617-247-8605 Dir:exit T, walk away from city (W) on Brookline)* A college drinking and dancing hotspot aptly called "Slopperfields" by its faithful patrons, Copperfield's earns its moniker with strong, cheap drinks. The bar has either a live band or a DJ every night of the week, and openly advertises both of its rooms (each with fully stocked bars and DJ booths) for use as party venues FREE of charge.

P.J. Kilroy's *(T (Green): Kenmore   822 Beacon St, 617-266-3986 Dir: exit T, walk away from downtown (W) on Beacon)* A neighborhood dive bar with a laid-back atmosphere that's quieter (and cheaper) than the nearby An Tua Nua. Pitchers of Pabst Blue Ribbon and Bud are $6 and $8 respectively—a steal by Boston standards.

Who's On First? *(T (Green): Kenmore   19 Yawkey Way, 617-247-3353   Dir: exit T, walk away from city (W), L on Yawkey)* A popular sports bar and dance club, Who's on First? is a haven to a diverse crowd—families and game-goers by day, students and young professionals by night. Packed on game days, the bar compensates for its minimal elbow room and blasting music with $1 test-tube shots and $2 drafts.

Jamaica Plain

Brendan Behan Pub *(T(Orange): Jackson Square   378 Centre St, 617-522-5386   Dir: exit T, walk S on Alpert, R on Centre, or avoid the T and take the #39 bus)* Devoid of TVs, the attention falls on the drinks and conversation at this local watering hole voted best Irish pub in Beantown on four occasions. Relax in the dimly lit, spartan atmosphere with a pint of the black stuff and listen to live music or the occasional poetry reading. While neither truly cheap nor expensive, we think you'll enjoy it as an escape.

Costello's Tavern *(T (Orange): Green Street   723 Centre St, 617-522-9263   Dir: exit T, walk (N) up Green .4 mi, L on Centre St, or avoid the T and take #39 bus)* Costello's is a low-lit bar with a blaring jukebox, live music on the weekends, TVs, and dart boards where you can grab cheap burgers, fries, and sandwiches.

**Doyle's Café *(T (Orange): Green Street 3484 Washington St, 617-524-2345 Dir: exit T, walk E on Green St, R (S) on Washington for 3 blocks)* Since the late 1880s, Doyle's has been pouring pints for everyone from politicians to recent graduates. This pub will feel like home with its large, comfortable, friendly, laid-back atmosphere. Loud laughter is heard 'round the clock over bottles and drafts of beer ranging in price from $1.75 Miller High Life to $13 bottles of Chimay Grande Reserve (yes, it's a beer).

Galway House *(T (Orange): Green Street 710 Centre St, 617-524-9677 Dir: exit T, walk W on Green St .3 mi, L on Centre St, or avoid the T and take #39 bus)* A local favorite for an early evening pint among an older local crowd, this unassuming pub has cheap, simple bar food (hamburgers, fries, chowder) and drinks under $3.

Midway Cafe *(T (Orange): Green Street 3496 Washington St, 617-524-9038 Dir: exit T, walk E on Green St, R (S) on Washington for 3 blocks)* With acts six nights a week ranging from rock to hip hop to comedy, the Midway attracts a diverse clientele including a large lesbian crowd. So although this isn't your cheapest bet for drinks (think $4-5 bottles), and the place is a real dive, it can be worth it for the show.

Somerville

**The Burren *(T (Red): Davis 247 Elm St, 617-776-6896 Dir: exit T to Holland St, R on Holland, cross Davis Sq to Elm)* A local favorite known for its lively nightlife and traditional Irish food and drink. The outer room—abuzz with friends and families at dinner—has cozy booths and on most nights, live Irish tunes. The back room hosts popular cover bands and a dance floor full of Tufts students and twenty-somethings.

**The Independent Restaurant and Bar *(T (Red): Harvard 75 Union Sq, 617-440-6021 Dir: exit T, take 86 bus to Union Sq, E on Somerville Ave past Stone Ave)* Amid the ethnic offerings of Union Square, the Independent offers straightforward American fare. A lively spot with a quasi-intellectual vibe, the Independent keeps it light with Texas Hold'em tournaments on Mondays, Movie Nights on Tuesdays (if the Sox aren't playing!), and cheese tastings on the first Wednesday of the month. For Sox games, get FREE hotdogs during the first inning (and wash them down with $2.50 pints of PBR available all night). www.theindo.com.

The Joshua Tree *(T (Red): Davis   256 Elm St, 617-623-9910 Dir: exit T to Holland St, R on Holland, cross Davis Sq to Elm)* Popular among the college and 20s crowd, this upscale watering-hole boasts a huge central bar, flat-screen TVs showing every Sox game, and Top 40-style music. The menu offers 65 dishes, mostly bar food but with some Southwestern touches (burritos, quesadillas, etc.) Entrees range $9-13.

The Kirkland *(T (Red): Harvard   425 Washington St, 617-491-9640 Dir (10 min walk): exit T, R on Massachusetts Ave, becomes Harvard St, L on Quincy St, R on Kirkland St, becomes Washington)* A cozy spot complete with fireplace and wood floors that specializes in serving beer, burgers, and other upscale comfort food to the beat of live tunes. Bands play on Th, F, and Sa nights at 9pm; cover price $5. On Wednesdays, enjoy $2 burgers and half-price apps.

PJ Ryan's *(T (Red): Davis   239 Holland St, 617-625-8200 Dir: exit T to Holland St, L on Holland)* Though questionably authentic—neither of the bar's owners are named PJ or Ryan—the beer selection is sufficiently Irish and the full menu of upscale bar food makes it a pleasant hangout day or night.

Thirsty Scholar *(T (Red): Harvard   70 Beacon St, 617-497-2294 Dir (10 min walk): exit T, R on Massachusetts Ave, becomes Harvard St, L on Quincy St, R on Cambridge St, L on Camelia Ave, cross Line St R onto Cooney St, L on Beacon)* A classy Irish bar with delicious upscale bar food, friendly service, and a fun, upbeat atmosphere; the thirsty scholar is the perfect place to put down your studies and engage your taste buds instead. 24 beers on tap and 16 in bottles; Sunday night trivia.

**Tir na nOg *(T (Red): Harvard   366A Somerville Ave, 617-628-4300   Dir: exit T, take 86 bus to Union Sq, W on Somerville)* This local favorite is known throughout Boston by a following so loyal they created a newspaper—Tir na nEws—to keep everyone updated and connected. Friendly and relaxed, the bar really gets going at 10pm each night when live music comes on with NO COVER CHARGE. Check band listings at www.thenog.com.

South End

Wally's Jazz Café *(T (Orange): Mass Ave   427 Mass Ave, 617-424-1408   Dir: exit T S on Mass Ave)* This historic live jazz venue also features cheap beers. A word to the wise: Bring cash, because they don't take cards. Don't bother dressing up, the cramped little venue is the antithesis of pretentious.

State Street Area/Financial District

Bell In Hand Tavern *(T (Orange/Green): Haymarket   45 Union St, 617-227-2098   Dir: exit T S on Congress St, L on Hanover, R on Union)* Sit down for a cheap (and extra large) draft at the nation's oldest tavern. Open since 1795, this roomy, laid-back, wood-adorned bar is packed with twentysomethings on the weekends, but thins out during the week. Go then, and get a true taste of the building's well-preserved history and character. The standard bar food is decent and fairly cheap (most entrées ~$8).

Black Rhino *(T (Blue): State   21 Broad St, 617-263-0101 Dir: exit T E (towards Devonshire St) on State St, R on Broad St)* Two words: roof deck. Chill out and take in the Boston skyline on one of the city's only rooftop decks. As if that weren't enough, they have great appetizers, weekly music events, three levels, and cheap Harpoon drafts. It will quickly become your new favorite urban hangout.

Dockside Restaurant & Bar *(T (Blue): Aquarium   183 State St, 617-723-7050   Dir: exit T W on State St)* An engaging sports bar with good people, cheap beer, and classic bar cuisine. Hit up their 10¢wings, M-F from 5-10pm, and wash it all down with a $2 Molson. Being thrifty never tasted so good.

Hong Kong *(T (Blue): Aquarium   65 Chatham St, 617-227-2226 Dir: exit T S on State St, R on Chatham)* With 90 different beers, cheap, potent scorpion bowls downstairs, and top-40 style tunes and dancing upstairs, this casual bar caters mostly to a young, diverse crowd. Cheap meat skewers help stave away hunger.

86   Cheap Drinks

Sissy K's *(T (Blue): Aquarium   6 Commercial St, 617-248-6511 Dir: exit T W on State St, R on Commercial St)* This popular double-decker college hangout, with its dance floor, stage, $1 Bud Light drafts, and karaoke Su-Th claims it's the "place to be," and they just might be right. Although it can get crowded Th and F nights, there is rarely a cover and the place serves two-for-one appetizers every night from 10pm-1am.

Trinity *(T (Blue): Aquarium   61 Chatham St, 617-367-6172 Dir: exit T W on State St, R on Chatham)* This hidden gem ought not to be overlooked by the college kid on a budget: It has cheap beer, live music, dancing, and friendly bartenders. Claustrophobics beware; the low ceilings and dense crowds can be a bit overwhelming, but manageable after a couple drinks.

Cool Cheap Date Places

Allston/Brighton

Big City *(T (Green B): Harvard Ave 138 Brighton Ave, 617-782-2020 Dir: exit T N on Harvard Ave, R on Brighton)* American: Perfect for the casual date. Get dinner in the dimly-lit urban-style café on the first floor—make sure you take advantage of the crayons and paper tablecloths—and then head upstairs for drinks and pool.

Herrell's Renaissance Café *(T (Green B): Harvard Ave 155 Brighton Ave, 617-782-9599 Dir: exit T N on Harvard, R onto Brighton)* American: With its eclectic crowd and up-and-coming music, Herrell's is the accidental date place. Grab an espresso and some homemade ice cream and combine your artistic endeavors on the magnetic poetry wall. Alternatively, you can get to know last night's partner better over a breakfast of huge pancakes ($6).

**Wonder Bar *(T (Green B): Harvard Ave 186 Harvard Ave, 617-351-2665 Dir: exit T S on Harvard Ave)* American: High ceilings, brick walls, a spacious interior, and a dimly-lit modern, urban décor give Wonder Bar the feel of a trendy Manhattan bistro without the price gouging or bar noise. You'll actually hear your date talking! Enjoy live jazz on Sunday and Monday evenings, cheap appetizers and entrées daily. Check out the second bar and lounge downstairs, which serves as a refuge when the place gets packed.

**Carlo's Cucina Italiana *(T (Green B): Harvard Ave 131 Brighton Ave, 617-254-9759 Dir: exit T N on Harvard, R on Brighton Ave)* Italian: Known for its piles of pasta and fresh bread, Carlo's has evolved from a pizza shop into one of Allston's few off-the-boat Italian restaurants. The environment—with its close tables and painted murals—is intimate and Tuscan. Order a bottle of wine and the penne with creamy marinara and enjoy romance Italian style.

**Tasca Restaurant *(T (Green B): Washington St   1612 Commonwealth Ave, 617-730-8002   Dir: situated on SW corner of Commonwealth and Washington)*
Spanish: Get a rare, accurate taste of Spain in this dimly-lit tapas restaurant where the sangria is divine and the atmosphere is superior. Tapas are cheap ($3-$4) though small in portion, but the Paella ($18) is to die for and great for sharing. Go on a Thursday night for live Spanish guitar.

**Brown Sugar Café *(T (Green B): Babcock St   1033 Commonwealth Ave, 617-787-4242   Dir: exit T W on Commonwealth Ave)* Thai: A beacon of light amongst the region's array of Thai restaurants. Brown Sugar is constantly packed, so call ahead for reservations on weekends. The service is great and the décor is rich with tastes of Thailand. The dishes are creative and absolutely delicious. Try the Siamese Twins (a chicken and shrimp dish served in a pineapple) or the Flaming Seafood Volcano Special. You won't be disappointed, as this is definitely one of Boston's best.

Pho Pasteur Restaurant *(T (Green B): Harvard Ave   137 Brighton Ave, 617-783-2340   Dir: exit T N on Harvard Ave, R onto Brighton Ave)* Vietnamese: This Vietnamese spot is easy to overlook, but don't let the shoddy exterior deter you. Appetizers ($3.50-$8) are cheap and generous: Try the Vietnamese crepe, the summer rolls, which are perfect for sharing, or enjoy the Pho (big soup bowls). People watching provides excellent dinner entertainment as well as something to talk about if conversation is lacking—so get a table by the window.

Tempo Dance Center *(T (Green B): Washington St   380 Washington St, 617-783-5467   Dir: exit T N on Washington St, L at base of hill)* Show off your dance skills or grab a lesson at this American and international-style dance center, which offers private lessons to couples by appointment. If your skills fall short of your date's expectations, head down the street to the Green Briar and drink away the memory of it.

Back Bay

Deville Restaurant and Lounge *(T (Green B/C/D): Hynes   10 Scotia St, 617-266-2695   Dir: exit T to Mass Ave, L on Mass Ave, L on Boylston, R on Dalton St, R on Scotia)*
American: Attached to the popular bowling alley, Kings, this restaurant keeps patrons entertained and well fed while they wait for a lane. Begin with the fried calamari ($8), move on to pizza ($10-13), and end with Boston Cream Pie or chocolate cake for dessert ($6 each). Nachos and pizza served until 1am every night of the week, full menu served until 12am.

**Top of the Hub *(T (Green E): Prudential   800 Boylston St, 617-536-1775   Dir: Station located opposite Prudential Center)*
American: This is one of the most romantic places to bring a date in Boston. Impress him or her with the scenic view of the city as you look out from the 52nd floor of the Prudential Tower. Dinner is very expensive, so go to the bar for a drink, coffee, or dessert and soak up the atmosphere. There is usually a line for the elevator but it moves quickly. The entrance is inside the Prudential Mall.

**Kings *(T (Green B/C/D): Hynes   50 Dalton St, 617-266-2695   Dir: exit T to Mass Ave, L on Mass Ave, L on Boylston, R on Dalton)*
Bowling Alley: With bowling, billiards, and a lounge, no matter what your date prefers, both of you will be entertained. Home to hip music, a trendy décor, and a mostly late-20s and early-30s crowd, Kings will keep you busy throughout the Boston night. Beware: Bowling can get expensive at $5.50 per game per person (plus $5 for shoes) before 6pm, and $6.50 per game thereafter, so come Mondays when women bowl for FREE, or if you work in a restaurant or bar, you can bowl FREE Tuesdays.

Espresso Royale Caffé *(T (Green B/C/D): Hynes   288 Newbury St, 617-859-9515   Dir: exit T to Newbury, R on Newbury)*
Café: Modeled after Italian cafés, Espresso Royale's relaxed atmosphere, great coffee, and dependable espresso drinks make this a great place to meet up and get to know one another while getting your caffeine fix.

Other Side Café *(T (Green B/C/D): Hynes   407 Newbury St, 617-536-8437 Dir: exit T to Newbury St, L on Newbury)*

Health Food: The comfortable couches, spacious seating, and almost hyperactive atmosphere make this a hot date spot that will keep both you and your partner entertained. An energetic crowd and constant tunes will fill gaps in conversations, but with original, healthy food options like pear lemon ginger wheatgrass juice, there is always something to talk about. The Other Side daily 11:30am-3pm for $7.50. Café is a welcomed change from the average, quieter café.

Bombay Café *(T (Green B/C/D): Hynes   175 Massachusetts Ave, 617-247-0555   Dir: exit T to Mass Ave, L on Mass Ave)*
Indian: A great place for a date or a night out with friends. Dishes vary in spice and price ($8-12) but you can't go wrong with the $6.25 lunch buffet M-F 11:30am-5pm, Sa-Su 12-5pm.

**Cactus Club *(T (Green B/C/D): Hynes   939 Boylston St, 617-236-0200   Dir: exit to Mass Ave, L on Mass Ave, L on Boylston)*
Southwestern: Share large appetizers like the monstrous nacho platter while sipping gargantuan margaritas. A loud, fun-loving crowd of young professionals gathers at this large, popular night spot—its upbeat atmosphere is great for dates or big parties.

Tapeo *(T (Green B/C/D): Hynes   268 Newbury St, 617-267-4799 Dir: exit T to Newbury St, R on Newbury)*
Spanish: Tapeo is consistently recognized for its premium tapas and romantic setting. Each dish is small and runs about $7, so this is not the place to eat if you are super hungry and looking to dine cheaply. However, if you're looking to romance your date with drinks and a delicious, light meal, Tapeo is a great choice.

Beacon Hill

Ma Soba *(T (Red): Charles/MGH   156 Cambridge St, 866- 210-5641 Dir: exit T onto Cambridge St and walk E)*
Asian: Ma Soba's sleek, beautiful décor and quiet atmosphere make it the perfect spot for a nice dinner with friends or a date. Sample the delicious, inventive sushi and pan-Asian food (most entrées $12-17) and choose from a well-rounded selection of wines. Come at lunch during the week for combination sushi and teriyaki plates—all under $10.

**Panificio *(T (Red): Charles/MGH   144 Charles St, 617- 227-4340)*
<u>Bakery</u>: The dark wood paneling and jumbles of old photographs and
trinkets that adorn Panificio's walls will remind you of your
grandmother's sitting room. Order at the counter and then bask in the
homey atmosphere while delicious paninis, soups, and Sicilian slices
are brought to your table. At night, choose from a selection of meat
and pasta dishes. Watch out for lines on weekends as the Sunday
brunch is exceptional.

Paris Creperie *(T (Red): Charles/MGH   326 Cambridge St, 617-589-
0909   Dir: exit T onto Cambridge St and walk E)*
<u>Crepes</u>: Build your own meal or dessert crepe from Paris's many
interesting and inventive options (everything from brie with apples to
a tuna melt on a red pepper-scallion crepe). The service is friendly
and fast but it is expected that you'll linger on the tables or couches in
this clean, bright space.

Antonio's *(T (Red): Charles/MGH   286 Cambridge St, 617-367-3310
Dir: exit T onto Cambridge St and walk E)*
<u>Italian</u>: Warm, friendly, and filling; Antonio's is a little piece of the
North End right in Beacon Hill.   Dinner entrées fall under $11 and
include options like lobster ravioli and veal piccata. Eat lunch for half
the cost.

Figs *(T (Red): Charles/MGH   42 Charles St, 617-742-3447   Dir: exit
T onto Charles St)*
<u>Italian</u>: This bustling, modern spot mixes up a variety of flavorful
toppings on its gourmet thin-crust pizza ranging from asparagus to
prosciutto to (you guessed it), figs. Figs is the most affordable of
famed local chef Todd English's restaurants—all pies are $11-17 and
enough for two people.

Upper Crust *(T (Red): Charles/MGH   20 Charles St, 617- 723-9600
Dir: exit T onto Charles St)*
<u>Italian</u>: Appropriately named for its style and taste, the bright, sleek,
modern décor matches the fresh and inventive pizza at this popular
upscale eatery (pies & slices available).

**Phoenicia *(T (Red): Charles/MGH   240 Cambridge St, 617-523-
4606   Dir: exit T onto Cambridge St and walk E)*
<u>Lebanese</u>: This cozy, upscale neighborhood favorite is the perfect
place to start your Lebanese education. Begin with the taboule,

hummus, or baba ghanouj, move on to lamb or chicken kabob, or make a platter with everything that appeals to you (called a mezze). With most menu offerings in the $8-12 range, there's no excuse to go on thinking the only good thing to come out of Beirut is a drinking game.

Brookline

**The Publick House *(T (Green C): Washington Street   1648 Beacon St, 617-277-2880   Dir: exit T onto Beacon)*
Beer Bar: Exotic beer and live music by candle and firelight. Although beer is your only choice for alcohol (there are 24 on tap), your dinner choices are far from limited; try the Grilled Andouille Sausage or the Arrogant Pulled Pork ($9 each).

Martin's Coffee Shop *(T (Green C): Coolidge Corner   35 Harvard St, 617-566-0005   Dir: exit T, walk N on Harvard St)*
Café: Although the tables are packed close together, it makes for a cozy environment perfect for relaxed conversation over a light, cheap meal or coffee. Great, cheap breakfasts served daily.

JP Licks *(T (Green C): Coolidge Corner   311 Harvard St, 617-738-8252   Dir: exit T, walk down Harvard St)*
Ice Cream: This homemade ice cream parlor is the perfect place to beat the summer heat or satisfy an after-dinner craving. Tables are available but fill up fast, as all six Boston locations are constantly busy—it's just that good.

Bertucci's *(T (Green D): Brookline Village   4 Brookline Pl, 617-731-2300   Dir: Brookline Place is behind tracks)*
Italian: A classic brick-oven pizza joint that serves up pastas, sandwiches, and as many of their famous dinner rolls as you can eat. Split a large gourmet pizza for $18 and have plenty to take home, or splurge on one of their many $14 pasta dishes.

**Vinny T's *(T (Green C): Tappan Street   1700 Beacon St, 617-277-3400   Dir: exit T onto Beacon)*
Italian: An absolute Boston must! I get hungry every time I think about this place. With most single portions large enough for two, and double portions (per due) enough for 3, your money goes far here. The romantic interior, exceptional food, and friendly staff provide an ideal date or group environment. Don't miss the spicy mussels fra

diavolo ($13) or the chicken parmesan ($12). An hourly lottery gives you the chance to eat for free. Bring a big, hungry group and dine family style i.e. bottomless plates on a set menu for groups of six or more for $20/person. Tip: Do takeout to save on tip, drinks, and taxes.

The Clay Room *(T (Green C): Summit Ave   1408 Beacon St, 617-566-7575   Dir: exit T onto Beacon, place on corner)*
Heat up your date—along with that ashtray you just made—at this creative alternative to the bar scene. The Clay Room allows you to make and decorate your own clay creations, so start letting your inner artist out. Prices for use of the kiln and clay run from $5-30 depending on how big you want your masterpiece, plus $8/person for painting supplies.

Cambridge

**Green Street Grill *(T (Red): Central   280 Green St, 617 876-1655 Dir: exit T to Mass Ave, R on Magazine St, R on Green)*
Caribbean: Buried behind Mass Ave in Central Sq is Cambridge's best-kept secret boasting exotic, flavorful, Caribbean-inspired fare and great live music. Although the menu is limited, the décor is perfect for a quiet dinner with friends, a date in the elevated seating area, or sipping drinks with the after-work crowd at the bar. Don't expect to see students, as Green Street draws an older clientele. T, Th, and Sa a different live band plays for free after 10:30pm but you have to be 21+ to stay. Open for dinner only.

Baraka Café *(T (Red): Central   801/2 Pearl St, 617-868-3951   Dir: exit T SE on Mass Ave, R on Pearl)*
North African: Serves a variety of uniquely flavored dish combinations with an emphasis on lamb and veggie dishes. Reviews are consistently good and at $9-16 per entrée, you'll get your money's worth. Do note that the restaurant only accepts cash and reservations for parties of three or more.

**Daedalus *(T (Red): Harvard   45 1/2 Mt Auburn St, 617-349-0071 Dir: exit T onto Mass Ave, R on Dunster St, L on Mt Auburn)*
American (new): Trendy-chic with a European feel, Daedalus is a catch-all for undergrads, grad students, and select Cantebridgians. Sit downstairs for a quiet drink with friends or mingle upstairs in a slightly

louder atmosphere. Overlooked as a restaurant, Daedalus has a great selection of upscale bar food (lunch $7-8, dinner $10-18) Tip: The upstairs lounge can be reserved for groups of 30 or more Su-W nights.

Fire & Ice *(T (Red): Harvard   50 Church St, 617-547-9007 Dir: Exit station onto Mass Ave, walk towards Porter, left on Church)*
American (new): Billed as "inventive" dining, Fire + Ice is the place for the inspired eater. Create your own meal by selecting from vegetables, noodles, meats, and fish and their expert chefs will cook it all up for you in any sauce. With its colorful, funky décor and innovative approach to eating, Fire + Ice is a good place for groups or for dates.

La Crêperie *(T (Red): Harvard   1154 Mass Ave, 617-661-6999 Dir: exit T onto Mass Ave, walk 3/4 mi towards Central Sq)*
Creperie: La Creperie is a sweet spot that will hit your sweet-spot; a cute little eatery at the edge of The Square with delicious, classic crepe combinations like Nutella and bananas as well as a selection of mouth-watering meal crepes like the pear, blue cheese, walnuts, and arugula. Groups beware: There is limited seating, so get yours to go. Prices: $4-8.

**Cambridge, 1 *(T (Red): Harvard   27 Church St, 617-576-1111 Dir: exit T onto Mass Ave, walk towards Porter, L on Church)*
Pizzeria: Cambridge, 1 offers pizza and salad but the food is far from basic with toppings ranging from lobster and corn to chicken sausage and ricotta. A mid-20s crowd hangs out at the bar or in cozy side booths. Two big screen TVs play every Sox game, providing a nice alternative to noisy sports bars. Grab a seat at the back for a beautiful view of Harvard's most historic graveyard—it's not nearly as morbid as it sounds!

**Border Café *(T (Red): Harvard   32 Church St, 617-864-6100 Dir: exit T onto Mass Ave, walk towards Porter Sq, L on Church)*
Tex-Mex: With brightly colored wall murals and a vibrant atmosphere to match, Border Café draws a fun, young crowd for reasonably-priced Tex-Mex food and drinks every night of the week. Get a table downstairs or sip sangria by the bar. Bring a date, a friend, or an entourage.

Spice Thai Cuisine *(T (Red): Harvard   24 Holyoke St, 617-868-9560 Dir: exit T onto Mass Ave, R onto Holyoke St)*

<u>Thai</u>: Spice is the place to go for classic Thai food in a pretty but casual setting. Dimly lit and decorated in warm, rich hues, it's perfect for a relaxed date or dinner with close friends. The Pad Thai is a safe bet and the lunch menu ($6-8) is a smaller-portioned, cheaper version of the dinner menu ($7-16).

Veggie Planet *(T (Red): Harvard 47 Palmer St, 617-661-1513 Dir: exit T onto Brattle St, R on Palmer)*
<u>Vegetarian</u>: Although some complain this bohemian eatery is overpriced (most pizza and rice dishes are $10), Cambridge vegetarians (of which there are many) swear by it as a spot to get some hearty non-meat eats, with pizza toppings ranging from caramelized onions to tofu. The wait can be long but the atmosphere is pleasant, making it a great date spot—so long as your date isn't a power-lifting protein junkie.

Chinatown/Theater District

**Blu Café (At the Ritz Carlton Sports Club/LA) *(T (Orange): Chinatown 4 Avery St, 617-375-8550 Dir: exit T N on Washington St, L on Avery)*
<u>American</u>: This glass-encased gem atop the Ritz-Carlton Hotel offers lavish European-inspired dining and fantastic views of the city. Your best bet is to make it a lunch or brunch date when prices are more reasonable. The lemon-brined grilled chicken sandwich ($12) is delicious and is served with french fries or a green salad. Finish up with coffee and the daily selection of fresh pastries ($4). Who said luxury dining can't come cheap?

Finale *(T (Green): Arlington 1 Columbus Ave, 617-423-3184 Dir: exit T S on Arlington, L on Columbus)*
<u>French/American</u>: This luxurious dessert spot is very expensive, but that doesn't mean you have to pay a fortune to live well. The portions are large and decadent enough to split so order two coffees, one dessert to share, and linger while the endorphins kick in. Try the Crème Brulée ($9) or Molten Chocolate ($11).

Downtown

The Kinsale *(T (Green): Government Center   2 Center Plaza (Cambridge St), 617-742-5577   Dir: exit T, turn around and cross Cambridge St)*
Irish: This large Irish pub has fantastic and well-priced food, a good beer selection, classic Irish décor, and outdoor seating. It's a popular lunch spot and after work, the music becomes louder for the 20s and 30s crowd that converges at the bar.   Follow up the satiating steak sandwich ($9) with a chocolate chip cookie sundae ($4.50) and you'll be happy to lounge for hours.

Fenway

Heritage Café *(T (Green): Kenmore   636 Beacon St, 617-369-9400   Dir: exit T, walk towards city (E) on Beacon)*
American: A good pick for casual lunch dates, this underground sandwich shop has tons of great tasting good-for-you soups and sandwiches. Try the buffalo chicken tenders and tomato soup, and admire the local artist's black and white photography that adorns the café's bright red walls.

Umi Japanese Cuisine and Sushi Bar *(T (Green D): Fenway   90 Peterborough St, 617-536-6688   Dir: exit T S on Park Dr, L on Perterborough)*
Japanese: Umi serves up a great variety of reasonably priced authentic Japanese cuisine as well as cheap beer and wine. Escape the hustle of Kenmore and relax in ambient comfort with some sushi, sake, and tempura.

**Jake Ivory's Piano Bar *(T (Green): Kenmore   9 Lansdowne St, 617-247-1222   Dir: exit T, walk away from city on Brookline Ave (W), L on Lansdowne)*
Piano Bar: Open Th-Sa nights only, this live piano-fueled— albeit bare-boned—nightclub gets rowdy! A largely younger crowd fills the dance floor as dueling pianists play ANY song requested (they boast a knowledge of 100,000 songs). Wind down at a picnic table with after-dinner drinks, request a song, and wind up again. Jake Ivory's is best suited for drunken groups ($4 cover charges Th-Sa for 21+, $10 otherwise).

Jillian's *(T (Green): Kenmore   145 Ibswich St, 617-437-0300 Dir: exit T, walk away from city (W) on Brookline Ave, L on Lansdowne St, L on Ibswich)*
Sports Bar: This gigantic, three story sports bar and pool hall lives up to its "eat, drink, play" axiom. It houses a Vegas-style lounge with ping pong tables, large-screen TVs, pool tables, an arcade, and a bowling alley. With so many things to do, a date couldn't possibly go awry.

Jamaica Plain

Dogwood Café *(T (Orange): Forest Hills   3712 Washington St, 617-522-7997   Dir: exit T, walk E on South St, R (S) on Washington St)*
American: A favorite among locals for its selection of salads and pizza, art-adorned walls, and live music on the weekends. The constant background noise will drown out any awkward silences.

**Cha Fahn *(T (Orange): Green Street   763 Centre St, 617-983-3575   Dir: exit T, walk W on Green St .3 mi, L on Centre St, or avoid the T and take the #39 bus)*
Café: Heat up your stomach with a hot sandwich or dim sum during lunch on weekends ($7-12) or just pop in for a cup of tea or warm sake to wind down from your day in this stylish and exquisitely decorated Oriental tea room that is popular with a young crowd. Dinner entrées run on the expensive side ($16) but Wednesday nights they offer three course meals for $25.

Emack and Bolio's *(T (Orange): Green Street   763 Centre St, 617-524-5107   Dir: exit T, walk W on Green St .3 mi, L on Centre St, or avoid the T and take #39 bus)*
Ice Cream Parlor: Emack and Bolio's has something for everyone's sweet tooth including gourmet ice cream, frozen yogurt, pies, pastries, floats, coffee—the list goes on and on. This spacious establishment is a great place for an inexpensive date amid an energetic clientele on sugar highs.

**JP Licks *(T (Orange): Green Street   659 Centre St, 617-524-6740 Dir: exit T, walk W on Green St .3 mi, L on Centre St, or avoid the T and take #39 bus)*

Ice Cream Parlor: The original locale for the popular ice cream chain (hence the "JP" in the name) stands out from other parlors with its loud, colorful décor and imaginative and delicious flavors of ice cream—think Cake Batter, White Coffee, and Oatmeal Cookie. They are popular with the more health conscious for their selection of low fat options.

Bukhara *(T (Orange): Green Street   701 Centre St, 617-522-2195 Dir: exit T, head W on Green St .3 mi, L on Centre St, or avoid the T and take #39 bus)*
Indian: The quiet, elegant, ethnic atmosphere will deceive you into believing the bill will be steep. Better leave the large groups at home; seating is only good for small parties. Highlights: excellent $8 weekday buffet 11:30am-3pm.

**Bella Luna *(T (Orange): Stony Brook   405 Centre St, 617-524-6060   Dir: exit T, head W on Boylston St .3 mi, R on Centre St, or avoid the T and take the #39 bus)*
Italian: Upon arrival, your senses will be assaulted with smells, colors, art, dangling stars, and the warmth of delicious Italian cooking. This spacious, funky eatery can accommodate large parties and impress even the toughest critics with its charm, gourmet pizza, and variety of salads and sandwiches.

Wonder Spice Cafe *(T (Orange): Green Street   697 Centre St, 617-522-0200   Dir: exit T, walk W on Green St .3 mi, L on Centre St, or avoid the T and take #39 bus)*
Thai/Cambodian: Sporting a diverse menu, energetic and prompt service, Wonder Spice is a great place to impress a date with your cultural sophistication. Unobtrusive Cambodian and Thai artwork lines the walls. Come for solid dishes of Pad Thai, Pho bowls, and something called "Fruits Sizzling"—meat accompanied by a choice of seasonal fruits and vegetables all for $12 or less. Patio seating is available.

The Footlight Club *(T (Orange): Stony Brook   7A Eliot St, 617-524-6506   Dir: take the #39 bus to South St, R on Eliot from Centre St)*
Theatre: One of the oldest running community theatres in the country, The Footlight Club provides amateur comedy shows, dramas, and musicals for the blossoming Jamaica Plain neighborhoods. Admission with student ID ranges in price from $14-18, $15-20 without ID, $12-14 for kids under 12. For tickets call the Box Office at 617-524-3200.

North End

**Mike's Pastry *(T (Green/Orange): Haymarket   300 Hanover St, 617-742-3050   Dir: exit T, follow walkway to North End, R on Cross St, L on Hanover)*
Bakery: Toting one of Mike's signature string-tied boxes of sweets indicates that one has undergone a certain necessary Bostonian rite of passage. The homemade gelato, cookies, cakes, and about every other sweet concoction imaginable has quickly made this amazing bakery and dessert shop a legend and a must-go. Visit after dinner for dessert, or just turn Mike's into the entire date by grabbing one of the coveted window tables and sharing the delicious triple chocolate cake or cannoli.

Caffe Graffiti *(T (Green/Orange): Haymarket   307 Hanover St, 617-367-3016   Dir: exit T, follow walkway to North End, R on Cross St, L on Hanover)*
Coffee Shop: Leave your mark on the famous wall (it's called Caffe Graffiti for a reason) of this young hipster-oriented coffee shop with great music and menu selections. Well-known for brewing excellent cappuccino and espresso, the café's cozy ambience and nooks are highly conducive to long conversation. Open 6am–midnight daily.

**Tia's *(T (Blue): Aquarium   200 Atlantic Ave, 617-227-0828   Dir: Exit T to State St, L on State, R on Atlantic)*
Seafood: An outdoor seafood restaurant and bar right on the waterfront with a killer view of the harbor. While this place is by no means cheap but there are a few options on the menu that won't break your wallet. However, go for appetizers and drinks only—easily accomplished by setting a late night date—and get a spot on the large patio. Smoking is allowed on the patio, so if either you or your date is sensitive to it, try to sit at a table as upwind as possible to avoid choking. Make sure to try the New England clam chowder: $5/cup.

Somerville

**Johnny D's Uptown *(T (Red): Davis   17 Holland St, 617-776-2004   Dir: Exit T to Holland St, L on Holland)*
<u>American</u>: New American and vegetarian friendly fare comes with a side of live music, making this restaurant a nightly hot spot. The crowd changes depending on the show—from folk to rock to salsa—but it's always a fun, laid-back mix of people. Check out Sunday jazz brunches, open blues jam (4:30pm to 8:30pm) and evening salsa lessons. Tuesday through Friday, have an early dinner (4:30-6:30pm) with half-price entrees. Open 12:30pm-1am F-Sa.

La Contessa Pastry Shop *(T (Red): Davis   420 Highland Ave, 617-623-9193   Dir: exit T to College Ave, L on Highland)*
<u>American/Italian</u>: A Davis Landmark, serving its famous Italian and American pastries for over 30 years. The cannolis rival Mike's of the North End but are cheaper and closer.

West Side Lounge *(T (Red): Harvard   1680 Mass Ave, 617-441-5566   Dir: exit T onto Mass Ave, walk 3/4 mile North)*
<u>American (new)</u>: Nestled between Harvard and Porter Squares, West Side is a cozy spot that generally attracts an older crowd. With a warm and beautiful décor, many come for the sophisticated (but reasonably priced) food with notes of Mediterranean influence, and stay for the equally sophisticated drinks (think Candied Ginger Martinis).

Diesel Café *(T (Red): Davis   257 Elm St, 617-629-8717   Dir: exit T to Holland St, R on Holland, cross Davis Sq to Elm)*
<u>Café</u>: The young and trendy come for the coffee but stay for the sandwiches, salads, and pastries. Comfy couches and pool tables add to this hot spot's allure. Open until 12am daily.

Kebab Factory *(T (Red): Harvard   414 Washington St, 617-354-4996   Dir (10 min walk): exit T, R on Massachusetts Ave- becomes Harvard St, L on Quincy St, R on Kirkland St- becomes Washington)*
<u>Indian</u>: Contrary to its name, this Indian take-out spot churns out more than just kebabs, offering a number of freshly-baked breads, samosas, and meat and fish entrees. While on the pricier side for the setting (most dishes $14-20), you can get a filling kebab entrée with soup and rice for $7 at lunch.

El Guapo *(T (Red): Davis   704 Broadway, 617-591-1200   Dir: exit T to College Ave, R on College to Powderhouse Sq, R on Broadway)*
Mexican: A discount for students spices up this standard Mexican fare, as does the colorful, upbeat setting and 15 flavors of margaritas. Appetizers like nachos, queso fundido, and grilled Aztec pizza are half-price from 4-6pm, M-F. Hours: 3pm-1am M-Th, 11-1am F-Su; food served until midnight.

Tu Y Yo Mexican Fonda *(T (Red): Davis   858 Broadway, 617-623-5411   Dir: exit T to College Ave, R on College to Powderhouse Sq, L on Broadway)*
Mexican: Amidst a slew of local "Tex-Mex" eateries, Tu Y Yo's authentic Mexican fare stands apart, as does its friendly service and warm, festive atmosphere.

Dial a Pizza *(T (Red): Harvard   147 Beacon St, 617-868-6100   Dir (10 min walk): exit T, R on Massachusetts Ave, becomes Harvard St, L on Quincy St, R on Kirkland St, L on Beacon)*
Pizza: The pizza isn't exactly gourmet, but it does have some interesting varieties among the 50 toppings offered. With a $5 pick-up special for a large cheese pie, you really can't complain.

The Neighborhood *(T (Red): Harvard   25 Bow St, 617-628-2151   Dir: exit T, take 86 bus to Union Sq, follow Somerville Ave N to where it meets Warren Ave and Bow)*
Portuguese: At this breakfast/ brunch spot, unusual yet delicious food (e.g. banana-mango pancakes) comes in generous portions on the cheap. Lounge on the outdoor patio during warmer months. Open 7am-4pm daily.

**RedBones *(T (Red): Davis   55 Chester St, 617-628-2200   Dir: exit T to Holland St, R on Holland, cross Davis Sq to Elm St, R on Chester)*
Southern, Barbecue: Not for vegetarians or the faint of heart. Known for its slow cooking and southern flavor, Redbones is a must for barbecue lovers. Long waits can be passed quickly at Underbones, the bar on the basement floor. Before 4 pm, an all-you-can-eat buffet includes meats and sides for $8.99 M-Th and $9.99 F-Sa. Most plates $8-14. Late-night menu served until 12:30am.

Rudy's Café and Tequila Bar *(T (Red): Davis   248 Holland St, 617-623-9201   Dir: exit T to Holland St, L on Holland)*

Tex-Mex: The main Teele Square hangout, this decently-priced venue keeps it simple with hot eats and cold drinks. With 10 draft beers and 37 tequilas at the ready, who knows if people are actually coming for the food. Open until 1am Fridays and Saturdays with food served until midnight.

Great Thai Chef *(T (Red): Harvard   255 Washington St, 617-625-9296   Dir: exit T, take 86 bus to Union Sq, E on Somerville Ave, L on Prospect St, L on Washington)*
Thai: Generous portions, attentive service, and reasonable prices draw lovers of well-spiced Thai cuisine to this cozy, relaxed spot.

South End

**Picco *(T (Orange): Back Bay   513 Tremont St, 617-927-0066 Dir: exit T S on Dartmouth St, L on Tremont)*
American/Italian: This unique, chic-but-cheap spot is known for its pizza and ice cream and perfect for a pig-out that won't make your stomach hurt afterwards. Pizzas are creatively crowned with fresh, high-quality toppings such as spinach, goat cheese, and roasted red peppers. The roasted garlic and mushroom pizza is savory and light. (Small: $9.25, Large: $16.25) To finish, grab a scoop or two of homemade ice cream.

Bob's Southern Bistro *(T (Orange): Mass Ave   604 Columbus Ave, 617-536-6204   Dir: exit S on Mass Ave, R on Columbus)*
Bistro: The term "soul food" will take on a whole new meaning as you listen to live jazz (Th-Sa) while eating Louisiana-style Cajun dishes like Cajun crab cakes ($8) and Creole jambalaya ($14). A bistro that seems to have been plucked straight from the South, Bob's is a rare find this side of the Mason-Dixon Line.

Francesca's Espresso Bar *(T (Orange): Back Bay   564 Tremont St, 617-482-9026   Dir: exit T S on Dartmouth, L on Tremont)*
Café: Skip a meal and jump start your heart with a double espresso, or enjoy one another's company as you work your way through one of many specialty sandwiches ($5-8) in this spacious and brightly decorated café.

Joe V's *(T (Orange): Back Bay   315 Shawmut Ave, 617-338-5638 Dir: exit T S on Dartmouth, L on Shawmut)*

<u>Italian</u>: A low-lit, casually cool couple's spot with sleek, modern lines. This quaint Italian restaurant—relatively unknown to those outside the S End—serves cheap thin-crust pizza but their pastas are better. Entrées range from the $12.50 gnocchi (with delicious vodka cream sauce) to the $20 lobster ravioli.

**Red Fez *(T (Sliver): Washington St and E Berkeley   1222 Washington St, 617-338-6060   Dir: walk S on Washington St)*
<u>Middle Eastern/ Moroccan</u>: This authentic international restaurant is the perfect place to enjoy a savory Sunday brunch. Try the Syrian Egg Roll (onions, mushrooms, tomatoes, scrambled eggs and Kasseri cheese rolled in Syrian bread) for $9. Out for an evening date? The live jazz from 9pm-12am Tu and Su nights is just the icing on the Tiramisu (try theirs!) at this quaint S End date spot. Bonus: a great patio dining spot when the weather's nice.

Franklin Cafe *(T (Silver): Union Park St   278 Shawmut Ave, 617-350-0010   Dir: exit T, L on Union, R on Shawmut)*
<u>Modern American</u>: This small, hipster-stocked café is a local favorite but they don't take reservations and there is typically a wait for one of the nine tables. The décor is chic and the food is flavorful, inventive, and well-priced, ranging from $7-19. Try the Garlic-Grilled Calamari ($8).

State Street Area/ Financial District

**Black Rhino *(T (Orange): State   21 Broad St, 617-263-0101   Dir: exit T E on State St, R on Broad St)*
<u>American Bar</u>: Sit down to $7-11 entrées served on white tablecloths in the dimly-lit dining room, head upstairs to the rooftop deck for a drink and heavy flirting, or relax in the courtyard and watch people enter.

Elephant & Castle *(T (Blue): State St   161 Devonshire St, 617-350-9977   Dir: exit T and walk down Devonshire St)*
<u>English Pub</u>: You can steer clear of awkward mid-date silences at this cool interactive pub that boasts "Trivia Tuesdays," "Live Music Fridays" (both start at 6:30pm), and "Scary Karaoke Saturdays" (8pm). Bring a date, grab a beer, and join in the fun.

The Place *(T (Blue): Aquarium   2 Broad St, 617-523-2081 Dir: exit T W on State St, L on Broad St)*
<u>Nightclub</u>: A rowdy hangout popular with local twentysomethings, complete with DJ's, dancing, comedy nights, and half-price appetizers 6-9pm Th-F. Check out their website at *www.theplaceboston.com* for upcoming events.

Cheap Specials

Allston/Brighton

**Beantown Dogs *(T (Green B): Harvard Ave   166 Brighton Ave, 617-783-3647   Dir: exit T N on Harvard, L on Brighton)*
American: Packed with student specials, this tiny neighborhood shop bedecks its walls with photos of Boston sports teams, but their dogs are far superior (in taste and price) to the Fenway Frank. Select your meat of choice (veggie, turkey, chicken, all beef, kosher, and more) and pick from some 50 creative á la carte toppings that are just 25¢ each.

**The Paradise Lounge *(T (Green B): Pleasant St   969 Commonwealth Ave, 617-562-8814   Dir: exit T W on Commonwealth Ave)* American/Asian: A chic lounge attached to an urban music venue that is also great for after work/school snacks. From 5-8pm, all menu items are $5. Late night specials (10pm-1am) include $1 cheeseburgers with the purchase of a drink, and a free pizza with the purchase of a Miller High Life pitcher.

Angora Café *(T (Green B): Babcock St   1024 Commonwealth Ave, 617-232-1757   Dir: exit T onto Commonwealth Ave)*
Health Food/Lebanese: A great place to grab a salad, wrap, or low-carb sandwich between classes, Angora caters to the fast food prone, health conscious crowd. Pair soup or a side salad with half a sandwich for under $6, or a salad and a slice of pizza for just over $4. If you have room for dessert, try one of their custom frozen yogurts.

Cookin' Café & Grill *(T (Green B): Packard's Corner   1096 Commonwealth Ave, 617-566-4144   Dir: exit T onto Commonwealth Ave)* Italian: This laid-back neighborhood stop serves up six different daily breakfast and dinner specials that are perfect for large groups. Try two large pizzas or two roll-ups and a large fries for $13. Carb counters and carnivores will find plenty of salad, sandwich, and dinner options for under $8.

Little Pizza King *(T (Green B): Washington St   379 Washington St, 617-787-7800   Dir: exit T NW on Washington, L onto Washington St after hill)* <u>Italian/American</u>: This Greek pizza shop is best known for its quick delivery. Order up one of their daily combination specials, such as Monday's two large cheese pizzas for $13, or opt for a large one-topping pizza and Greek salad for $10. FREE delivery with $7 purchase. Hours: M-W 11am-11pm, Th-Sa 11am-12pm, Su noon-11pm.

La Mamma Pizzeria *(T (Green B): Harvard Ave   190A Brighton Ave, 617-783-1661   Dir: exit T N on Harvard, L on Brighton)* <u>Italian</u>: A tiny authentic Italian pizza shop with exceptionally speedy late-night delivery (until 3am), reasonable prices, and generous toppings. Try a large sausage pizza for a mere $7.

Sunset Cantina *(T (Green B): BU West   916 Commonwealth Ave, 617-731-8646)* <u>Mexican/American</u>: The sister of Allston's Sunset Grill has the same laid-back ambiance and Mexican food as the Grill but bodes a different set of specials, which all night owls prone to getting the munchies must capitalize on. Their "midnight madness" buffet of nachos, wings, quesadillas, and more runs from 12-1am Su-Tu and is FREE with the purchase of two alcoholic beverages.

Our House *(T (Green B): Harvard Ave   1277 Commonwealth Ave, 617-782-3228   Dir: exit T W on Commonwealth Ave)* <u>Pub Grub</u>: The "Cheers" of Brighton, this eclectic subterranean bar boasts some of the best specials in the area, offering two-for-one appetizers and burgers before 7pm weekdays. Borrow a board game from the staff and relax with a friend on one of many comfortable couches.

Whitehorse Tavern *(T (Green B): Harvard Ave   116 Brighton Ave, 617-254-6633   Dir: exit T N on Harvard, R on Brighton)* <u>Pub Grub</u>: A large, casual restaurant by day and a bare-bones bar by night, the affectionately-deemed "White Ho" has great specials, a fun atmosphere, and a multitude of activities (trivia, pool, darts) that have made it a veritable Allston all-star. Students and professionals alike flock to "The Ho" all day Su-Tu for their food specials, which include $3 Burger/Sandwich with fries and $3 wing platters (10 pieces).

**Sunset Grill and Tap *(T (Green B): Harvard Ave   130 Brighton Ave, 617-254-1331   Dir: exit T N on Harvard, R on Brighton)*
Tex-Mex: The fast and friendly service makes this popular Tex-Mex spot ideal for grabbing a quick drink and dinner, but the cool atmosphere and blaring classic rock will make you want to stay all night. The beer selection is exceptional (112 on tap, 380 microbrews and exotic imports) and the appetizers are the perfect complement to whatever game is playing on the TVs around the bar. Go Tuesdays for two-for-one dinner specials.

Back Bay

Bhindi Bazaar *(T (Green B/C/D): Hynes   95 Mass Ave, 617-450-0660   Dir: exit T to Mass Ave, R on Mass Ave)*
Indian: This quiet and cozy restaurant bedecked in deep colors, sports just the hint of trendy-chic it needs to blend into Back Bay without sacrificing its cultural appeal. Go for the lunch buffet held daily 11:30am-3pm for $7.50.

Kashmir *(T (Green B/C/D): Hynes   279 Newbury St, 617-536-1695 Dir: exit T to Newbury, R on Newbury)*
Indian: A comfortable banquet hall accented with the smells and spices of India, Kashmir's authentic appetizers and entrées will be enough to make you sweat with anticipation. Daily lunch buffet 11:30am-3pm for $9.

Globe Bar and Café *(T (Green): Copley   565 Boylston St, 617-778-6993   Dir: exit T onto Boylston and take a R (E))*
Pub Grub: A slew of TVs, a bar big enough to house weekly crowds that overflow on the weekends, and quality food like burgers, fish and chips, shrimp, and a selection of soups make the Globe Bar and Café a draw for twentysomethings. High-end drinks like martinis and frozen cocktails are $7 or less—a steal by Back Bay standards. Lobster dinners run between $14-20, depending upon market price, and are served with a choice of four sides.

**Whiskey's (T (Green B/C/D): Hynes   885 Boylston St, 617-262-5551   Dir: exit T to Mass Ave, L on Mass Ave, L on Boylston)
<u>Pub Grub</u>: If you're looking for a place to meet up, hook up, or fill up, Whiskey's can help. They cater to the droves of single students who flock here for the loud music, rowdy atmosphere, and reasonably priced food and drinks. Highlights: 10¢ wings at the bar Su-Th, 4-11pm. Ladies receive FREE appetizers Sundays 7-11pm. Summer specials include a $21 twin lobster dinner complete with fries and coleslaw.

**Cactus Club (T (Green B/C/D): Hynes   939 Boylston St, 617-236-0200   Dir: exit T to Mass Ave, L on Mass Ave, L on Boylston)
<u>Tex-Mex</u>: A great place to sip on the house specialty, margaritas, or chow down on heaping platefuls of nachos. Half-price appetizers M-Th 4-6pm

**The Pour House (T (Green): Copley   907 Boylston St, 617-236-1767   Dir: exit T W (L) onto Boylston)
<u>Pub Grub</u>: Dine on typical pub food and daily specials such as $2.50 chicken sandwiches Wednesday nights; half-price Mexican food Th 6-10pm; and half-price burgers Sa 6-10pm.

Brookline

Best Cellars (T (Green C): Coolidge Corner   1327 Beacon St, 617-232-4100   Dir: exit T onto Beacon St)
<u>Wine Shop:</u> Wine shopping's made easy. Most Saturdays between 2-4pm, Best Cellars offers free food—cooked by a professional chef—and wine to its customers. They also have daily wine tastings (5-8pm weekdays, 2pm weekends) so if you are not yet a wino, maybe it's time to become one.

Sichuan Garden (T (Green D): Brookline Village   295 Washington St, 617-734-1870   Dir: head S from Brookline Pl and take R on Washington St)
<u>Chinese</u>: If you're looking to add a little spice to your life, Sichuan Garden is the place to go (as evidenced by the largely Asian clientele). Weekday lunch specials include a three-course meal for $6.

Indian Café (T (Green C): Tappan Street   1665 Beacon St, 617-277-1752   Dir: exit T and head E on Beacon St)

Indian: Indian Café has entrées on the more expensive side ($10+), but an affordable buffet on Sa and Su ($10).

Cambridge

Sidney's Grille *(T (Red): Central   20 Sidney St, 617-494-0011 Dir: walk SE on Mass Ave OR from Harvard take the No. 1 bus)*
American (New): The swanky house-restaurant of the Hotel at MIT serves up expensive but delicious cuisine in the comfortable, chic interior, or in their 8,000 sq ft roof garden during summer. $2 appetizers available midweek 5-6:30pm

The Tavern in the Square *(T (Red): Central   720 Mass Ave, 617-868-8800   Dir: exit T NW onto Mass Ave)*
American (new): With its carefully dimmed lighting, big screen TVs, and floor-to-ceiling windows facing busy Mass Ave, Tavern in the Square is the newest upscale-but-relaxed addition to the area. The mid-20s crowd comes for an after-work drink, stays for dinner, and hangs until the wee hours. While not cheap (entrées $12-17, mixed drinks $4.75-$7), Tavern offers a different drink and food special each week. Plus, you can always grab a PBR for $3.
www.thetavernandwish.com

Rangzen Tibetan Restaurant *(T (Red): Central   24 Pearl St, 617-354-8881   Dir: exit T SE on Mass Ave, R on Pearl)*
Tibetan: A quiet and calm respite from the area's hustle and bustle. Relax with some hot tea, soup, and a meaty—or totally vegan—entrée. $8 lunch buffet 11:30am-3pm daily except for Su. Lunch entrées hover around $8, dinner $12.

Bukowski's Taven *(T (Red): Harvard   1281 Cambridge St, 617-497-7077 Dir: from Harvard Station, take the #69 bus to Inman Sq or walk 10 min E on Cambridge St)*
American (classic): The Cambridge outpost of this dive bar (the original is in Back Bay) whose real draw are their famous "buck burgers," just $1.69 weekdays before 8pm.

Uno's Chicago Grill *(T (Red): Harvard   22 JFK St, 617-497-1530 Dir: exit T onto JFK, walk 1 block towards river)*
Italian: Specials abound at this famed chain including half-priced appetizers during happy hour, Su-F 3-7pm and 10pm-12am plus all

you can eat pizza, pasta, and salad on Tuesdays for $8; buckets of rolling rock (five bottles) for $10 every night; and 14oz beers $2. Warning: Specials change frequently.

Grendels's Den *(T (Red): Harvard   89 Winthrop St, 617-491-1160 Dir: exit T onto JFK St, R onto Winthrop)*
Pub Grub: At this cozy Harvardian pub situated underneath Upstairs On The Square, you'll find a pleasant, relaxed atmosphere and a great deal: Purchase a $3 drink and everything on the menu is half-price between 5-7:30pm every night, and 9-11:30pm Su-Th. As most offerings are regularly $5-8, think $6 for a meal and a drink.

Bengal Café *(T (Red): Porter Square   2263 Mass Ave, 617-492-1944 Dir: exit T, walk down Mass Ave 1mi towards Davis Sq OR take the 77 bus down Mass Ave from Harvard Station)*
Bengali: Delicious, authentic Bengali cuisine (think fish and vegetarian curries) in a quaint, beautiful setting. A filling buffet is served daily until 3pm ($6 on weekdays, $8 on weekends). A students ID gets you 10% off the regular menu at all times.

Chinatown/Theater District

Rock Bottom Brewery *(T (Green): Boylston   16 Hudson St, 617-742-2739 Dir: exit T S on Tremont St, R on Stuart)*
American: This roomy restaurant and brewpub is a great place to meet before a night out. Choose from a myriad of beers brewed onsite and from a menu of upscale barroom eats that includes a great salad selection. For lunch, order one of their specialty burgers—the Hickory or Mushroom Swiss are your best bets.

**King Fung Garden *(T (Orange): NE Med Center   74 Kneeland St, 617-357-5262   Dir: exit T N on Washington St, R on Kneeland)*
Chinese: A hole-in-the-wall Chinatown spot made famous by its delicious Peking Duck (rumors say it's a favorite of several Boston chefs). Call 24 hours in advance to order it and bring a couple of friends to enjoy the veritable duck feast; it's $30 but feeds four and includes duck soup and duck stir-fry with pancakes. Bonus: This restaurant is BYOB, so feel free to tote your alcoholic beverage of choice to complement the meal.

Downtown Crossing/South Station Area

Coogan's Bluff Restaurant *(T (Blue): Aquarium   151 Milk St, 617-451-7415   Dir: exit T S on Atlantic Ave, R on Milk St)*
American: It's a little-known fact that this bar/club's food is marked by their own creatively gourmet flair. Stop in for lunch and check out their specials; if none catch your eye, try the unique and flavorful grilled salmon BLT ($9).

360 Ultra Lounge *(T (Orange): State   33 Batterymarch St, 617-695-9333 Dir: exit T, R on Congress, L on Milk, R on Batterymarch)*
American: True to its name, this bar/club is diverse and sophisticated. However, that doesn't mean they're too cool to offer FREE appetizers from 5-7pm, M-F. Bonus: Drinks are cheap and the bar is stocked with baskets of party mix.

Peking Tom's Longtang Lounge *(T (Orange): Downtown Crossing 25 Kingston St, 617-482-6282   Dir: exit T S on Summer St, R on Kingston)* Chinese: This Asian-infused lounge is a great place to relax after work or a long night out on the town. They have a special late-night menu until 1am. Try the Kung Pao Chicken Lettuce Wraps for a guilt-free, post-booze pig out.

Jose McIntyre's *(T (Blue): Aquarium   160 Milk St, 617-451-9460 Dir: exit T S on Atlantic Ave, R on Milk St)*
Irish/Mexican: The 3.5 bars specialize in huge (60oz) margaritas: They're cheap already and even cheaper when you split one...which you'll have to do if you want to walk out of there. Half-priced appetizers (try the nachos!) weekdays from 4-7pm.

Fenway

**Bertucci's *(T (Green): Kenmore   533 Commonwealth Ave, 617-236-1030   Dir: exit T, walk downtown E on Commonwealth Ave)*
Pizzeria: This Italian chain restaurant undoubtedly has one of the best lunch specials in the area. For $7-$10, choose pizza, pasta, or panini—each of which comes with unlimited salad and rolls (with a savory garlic-infused dipping oil).

**Crossroads *(T (Green): Kenmore   495 Beacon St, 617-262-7371*
Dir: exit T, walk downtown E via Beacon St)
<u>Pub Grub</u>: Only blocks from Fenway, this Irish bar is the ultimate place
to meet before the game for cheap finger food. Get a FREE pizza with
a pitcher on Wednesday nights and FREE wings with your drinks on
Thursday nights. The food—as well as dart games with the regulars—
might even make you forget about the game.

North End

G'Vanni's Ristorante *(T (Green/Orange): Haymarket   2 Prince St,*
617-720-3663   Dir: exit T, follow walkway to North End, R on Cross
St, L on Hanover St, R on Prince)
<u>Italian</u>: This friendly and casual eatery is just around the corner from
Paul Revere's house, offering affordable lunch combinations daily to
serve as the perfect fuel for hiking the freedom trail. The best special
is the panini, served with a choice of pasta or fries and ranging in price
from $7 (for the cold cut panini) to $10 (for the chicken club panini).

Piccola Venezia *(T (Green/Orange): Haymarket   263 Hanover St,*
617-523-3888   Dir: exit T, follow walkway to North End, R on Cross
St, L on Hanover)
<u>Italian</u>: Take advantage of an array of lunch specials (most notably the
pasta specials): tortellini, baked ziti, or ravioli for $6, or
sausage/chicken ziti with broccoli: $7.

Pushcart Café & Pizzeria *(T (Green/Orange): Haymarket   115*
Salem St, 617-523-8123   Dir: exit T, follow walkway to North End, R
on Cross St, L on Salem)
<u>Italian</u>: An inviting pizzeria blanketed with flat screen TVs around a
bar, making it a great place for watching games. To draw the Monday
night game crowds, Pushcart offers FREE slices of pizza with the
purchase of an alcoholic drink. Otherwise, pies are $7 for a 16-incher.

Somerville

**The Independent Restaurant and Bar *(T (Red): Harvard   75 Union Sq, 617-440-6021   Dir: exit T, take 86 bus to Union Sq, E on Somerville Ave past Stone Ave)*
<u>American</u>: Amid the ethnic offerings of Union Square, the Independent offers straightforward American fare. A lively spot with a quasi-intellectual vibe, the Independent keeps it light with Texas Hold'em tournaments on Mondays, Movie Nights on Tuesdays (if the Sox aren't playing!), and cheese tastings on the first Wednesday of the month. For Sox games, get FREE hotdogs during the first inning (and wash them down with $2.50 pints of PBR available all night). www.theindo.com.

**RedBones *(T (Red): Davis   55 Chester St, 617-628-2200   Dir: exit T to Holland St, R on Holland, cross Davis Sq to Elm St, R on Chester)* <u>Southern</u>: Not for vegetarians or the faint of heart. Known for its slow cooking and southern flavor, Redbones is a must for barbecue lovers. Long waits can be passed quickly at Underbones, the bar on the basement floor. Before 4 pm, an all-you-can-eat buffet includes meats and sides for $8.99 M-Th and $9.99 F-Sa. Most plates $8-14. Late-night menu served until 12:30am.

South End

Jae's Cafe and Grill *(T (Orange): Mass Ave   520 Columbus Ave, 617-421-9405   Dir: exit T S on Mass Ave, L on Columbus)*
<u>Asian</u>: A double-decker restaurant featuring an authentic Japanese sushi bar and countless fresh Pan-Asian favorites like Pad Thai and marinated steak and salmon. Lunch specials under $10 M-Sa 11:30am-4pm.

Nashoba Brook Bakery *(T (Orange): Back Bay   288 Columbus Ave, 617-236-0777   Dir: exit T S on Dartmouth, L on Columbus)*
<u>French/American</u>: This sun-filled pastry shop—proof that not all hipster spots are edgy and brooding—is perfect for a Saturday morning cup of coffee with a side of their special: a calorie-filled but delicious French pastry. If you're in the mood for lunch, have the staff make you a fresh sandwich. Try the tuna salad made with celery, red onions, and red peppers, for $7.50.

South End Formaggio *(T (Silver): Union Park St   268 Shawmut Ave, 617-350-6996   Dir: walk N on Union St, R on Shawmut)*
<u>Gourmet Market</u>: Think Whole Foods but cheaper. Buy prepared pastas by the pound, order up a pressed sandwich, select a salad, or simply grab a block of fancy cheese, fresh bread, and a bottle of wine.

State Street Area/ Financial District

Sissy K's *(T (Blue): Aquarium   6 Commercial St, 617-248-6511 Dir: exit T W on State St, R on Commercial St)*
<u>Bar/Club:</u> This popular double-decker college bar/club—with its dance floor, stage, $1 Bud Light drafts, and karaoke Su-Th—claims it's the "place to be," and they just might be right. Although it can get crowded Th-F nights, there is rarely a cover, and the place serves two-for-one appetizers every night from 10pm-1am.

Black Rose *(T (Green): Government Center   160 State St, 617-742-2286   Dir: exit T, walk straight E on Court/State St .2 mi)*
<u>Irish Pub</u>: One of the city's most beloved Irish pubs serves homemade American renditions of traditional Celtic dishes like clam chowder, fish and chips, Shepherd's pie, and corned beef all for under $10 a dish. Check in weekly for specials!

**McFadden's Restaurant & Saloon *(T (Green): Gov't Center   148 State St, 617-227-5100   Dir: exit T, walk straight E on Court/State St .2 mi)* <u>Pub Grub</u>: This bar/club is known for its nighttime festivities, but show up a little earlier for casual dining and great specials such as Thursday's steak tips with rice ($9), Friday's fish and chips ($10), or Saturday's burger and beer ($9). Normal entrée prices are $7-12. You can work off the calories on the dance floor.

Dockside Restaurant & Bar *(T (Blue): Aquarium   183 State St, 617-723-7050   Dir: exit T W on State St)*
<u>Sports Bar:</u> An engaging sports bar with good people, cheap beer, and classic bar cuisine. Hit up their 10¢ wings M-F from 5-10pm and wash it all down with a $2 Molson. Being thrifty never tasted so good.

Worth A Splurge

Allston/Brighton

Grasshopper *(No T nearby) 1 N Beacon St, 617-254-8883)*
Asian/Vegan: One of the few exclusively-vegan restaurants in the area, Grasshopper is stocked with creative noodle and root vegetable options ($9-13). Dine guilt-free with the convincing-but-faux, beef-style Seitan Medallions with Black Pepper and Garlic. While the interior is pretty bland, the food is anything but.

**Café Brazil *(No T nearby) 421 Cambridge St, 617-789-5980)*
Brazilian: Murals of Brazil's coastline cover the walls of this attractive restaurant whose meat-heavy menu of authentic Brazilian cuisine has garnered great reviews for years. Entrées range from $11 to $18, but the extra few dollars are well spent, as you'll find plates heaping with rice and beans. Feeling adventurous? Try the Rabad, a simmered blend of oxtail and vegetables ($15). It is fantastic.

**Tonic *(T (Green B): Griggs St   1316 Commonwealth Ave, 617-566-6699)* Upscale bar food: A stylish and chic metropolitan lounge and eatery that serves as a haven to students and young professionals. The sleek, oval bar is lined with flat-screen TVs. Low-hanging red lights and retro seating give the venue an ultra-cool Manhattan feel. Appetizers, such as the onion blossom and crab cakes, are large and do not exceed $10. For dinner, try the Creole Jambalaya ($15) or get a classic burger ($8) before working off the meal on the dance floor downstairs.

Back Bay

Blue Cat Café *(T (Green B/C/D): Hynes 94 Massachusetts Ave, 617-247-9922 Dir: exit T to Mass Ave, R on Mass Ave)*
<u>American</u>: This is a cool place to get drinks with a friend, listen to Jazz, and grab a bite. Stylish steel seating, plush, spacious booths and a grand piano greet patrons as they enter. A plethora of colorful martini specialties enhance the modern décor.

Scoozi *(T (Green): Copley 237 Newbury St, 617-247-8847 Dir: exit T east (R) onto Boylston, L on Dartmouth St, L on Newbury)*
<u>Italian</u>: Come for pasta ($12-15), salad ($5-9), or just to watch the fashion parade that is Newbury Street from the patio of this prime viewing spot.

**Vinny T's *(T (Green): Copley 867 Boylston St, 617-262-6699 Dir: exit T west (L) on Boylston St)*
<u>Italian</u>: Walking into this Vinny T's is like walking into a scene from the Godfather, but instead of getting whacked, you'll just get full. Huge portions of reasonably priced, exquisite Italian favorites never disappoint. Order two dishes for a group of three or split an appetizer and an entrée between two people. Sign up for their email list and receive digital discounts.

Osushi *(T (Green): Copley 10 Huntington Ave, 617-266-2788 Dir: exit T east (R) onto Boylston, R (S) on Dartmouth St, R on Huntington)*
<u>Sushi</u>: Diners talk excitedly over Osushi's many creative sake and reasonably priced maki options in the urban, candle-lit, red and black-clad ultramodern décor.

Beacon Hill

Artu *(T (Red): Charles/MGH 89 Charles St, 617- 227-9023)*
<u>Italian</u>: This subterranean establishment shares a likeness with the original Artu in the North End, offering the same bold flavors in a classy, comfortable setting but without the noisy tourists, (patrons here are mostly older couples). Entrées run $12-24 with most falling in the middle of that range. Lunch and dinner specials change every day.

Savenor's *(T (Red): Charles/MGH   160 Charles St, 617-723-6328)*
<u>Specialty Food Mart:</u> A great place for fine meats, cheeses, and gourmet prepared foods.

Brookline

Indian Café *(T (Green C): Tappan Street   1665 Beacon St,   617-277-1752   Dir: exit T and take R on Beacon St)*
<u>Indian</u>: An extensive menu of interesting dishes such as Shahi Bhindi (okra cooked with onions, tomatoes, herbs, and spices, garnished with fresh coriander $12) and Beef Saag (beef cubes cooked with spinach and spices $12) will keep you interested and asking for more. Just keep an eye on the prices, as this is one place where it is easy to run up a large bill.

**Matt Murphy's Pub *(T (Green D): Brookline Village   14 Harvard St, 617-232-0188   Dir: head S from Brookline Pl, take R on Harvard St and continue down a block)*
<u>Irish</u>: This tiny pub has what ales you. Patrons of all ages crowd into this cozy, authentic Irish pub, but no matter who is drinking, the crowd is friendly. It may take some time to get a table, but the incredible meals at reasonable prices are well worth the extra bar time. Be friendly to the bartender as he's in charge of seating. Meat lovers, treat yourselves to Guinness-braised roast duck or a juicy T-bone.   Entrées $12-17.

**Zaftigs Delicatessen *(T (Green C): Coolidge Corner   335 Harvard St, 617-975-0075   Dir: exit T and walk N on Harvard St)*
<u>Jewish Deli</u>: With a menu as diverse as Zaftig's, you're going to need some time to order. The trendy, high-energy atmosphere makes this place perfect for a date or family dinner. Try the French toast or one of the other outstanding breakfast items. Almost everything on the menu falls under $10, only problem is you'll want everything on the menu.

The Upper Crust *(T (Green C): Coolidge Corner   286 Harvard St, 617-734-4900   Dir: exit T and head N on Harvard St)*
<u>Pizzeria</u>: With a myriad of interesting toppings to put atop the thin crusts and chunky sauces, this place is heralded by locals as the best around. Pies (18") start at $13. Tip: Call in your order on weekends, as waits may take up to an hour.

Village Smokehouse *(T (Green D): Brookline Village   6 Harvard Sq, 617-566-3782   Dir: head S from Bookline Pl and turn R on Harvard)*
<u>Texas Barbecue</u>: No sooner than you enter the restaurant are your eyes and ears transfixed by the sights and smells of sizzling meats on the huge grill situated in plain view—this venue is not suitable for vegetarians. Friendly service and a large seating area works well for groups. Highlights: fall-off-the-bone ribs; half-priced meals at lunch.

Cambridge

The Enormous Room *(T (Red): Central   567 Mass Ave, 617-491-5550   Dir: exit T S on Mass Ave towards MIT)*
<u>Lounge</u>: The only elitist establishment in Central Sq, this sleek and comfy lounge sits behind an unmarked door next to Central Kitchen. Inside, grad students and young professionals relax with Enormous Plates—an array of appetizers ($14) and cocktails. Live DJs spin a mix of jungle, reggae, hip hop, house, and classic funk every night until 2am. There is a $3 cover after 10pm.

Central Kitchen *(T (Red): Central   567 Mass Ave, 617-491-5599 Dir: exit T onto Mass Ave)*
<u>Mediterranean</u>: A trendy bistro with Mediterranean flair, Central Kitchen's copper tables, blue-tile bar, and hardwood floors give it a modern yet rustic feel. The restaurant's excellent wine list draws some yuppies, but the spot remains classy and cool. Entrées $17-25

Pepper Sky's Thai Sensation *(T (Red): Central   20 Pearl Street, 617-492-2541   Dir: exit T SE on Mass Ave, R on Pearl)*
<u>Thai</u>: Although the décor lacks the usual "authentic" Asian touches most Thai restaurants are adorned with, it certainly doesn't lack authenticity in its recipes. On the menu, you'll find all your usual favorites prepared extremely well and to your liking. Most dinner entrées hover around $12 but a few dishes fall under $9. Shave a few dollars off to determine lunch prices. Note: This place closes between lunch and dinner (3-5pm).

Bombay Club (T (Red): Harvard   57 JFK St, 617-661-8100 Dir: exit T onto JFK, Bombay Club is upstairs)
<u>Indian</u>: Delicious, authentic Indian cuisine in a simplistic, quiet atmosphere—some nights you can practically hear a pin drop. Go on a

weekday 11:30am-3pm for a 10-course, all-you-can-eat buffet for $8/person.

**Grafton Street Pub & Grill *(T (Red): Harvard   1230 Mass Ave, 617-497-0400   Dir: exit T onto Mass Ave, walk 1/4 mi towards Central Sq)*
<u>Irish Pub</u>: Cozy up in one of their huge round booths in winter or lounge by the open floor-to-ceiling windows in summer. Either way, Grafton is fantastic for a boisterous group or an intimate date. Despite the fact that it's always bustling with young professionals, this spacious pub rarely feels cramped. The trendy menu ranges from elaborate pizzas ($8+) to creative fish and meat dishes ($16-21).

**East Coast Grill & Raw Bar *(T (Red): Harvard   1271 Cambridge St, 617-491-6568   Dir: from Harvard Station, take the #69 bus to Inman Sq, or walk 10 min E on Cambridge St)*
<u>Seafood</u>: With its friendly service, upbeat atmosphere, and fantastic food, East Coast Grill attracts seafood connoisseurs and barbecue lovers alike, young and old. The restaurant lacks the pretentiousness of downtown spots and although it's always packed, it remains laid-back. Sit at one of the many tables or grab a stool at the bar and round out the best seafood meal in Boston with their delicious cornbread or a tropical drink.

Pho Lemon *(T (Red): Kendall   228 Broadway, 617-441-8813 Dir: exit T onto Broadway and head W)*
<u>Vietnamese</u>: Pho Lemon serves up authentic, affordable Vietnamese food, but the sparsely decorated dining room makes it a better takeout spot.

Chinatown/Theater District

Jumbo Seafood *(T (Orange): NE Med Center   7 Hudson St, 617-542-2823   Dir: exit T N on Washington St, R on Kneeland, L on Hudson)*
<u>Chinese</u>: This casual restaurant decorated with aquariums swimming with your soon-to-be dinner gives off a strange initial vibe but serves delicious food. Try their giant clams or steamed oysters on the half shell and you'll quickly stop feeling sorry for the little guys. Entrées range from $8-24 on the eight-page menu.

PF Chang's China Bistro *(T (Green): Arlington   8 Park Plaza, 617-573-0821   Dir: exit T E on Boylston St, R on Charles St, R on Park Plaza)*
Chinese/American: This popular franchised eatery serves Westernized Asian cuisine at reasonable prices (dinner entrées range between $9-14). Try the delicious Cantonese Shrimp or Mango Chicken or keep it healthy with vegetarian and gluten-free dishes. Call ahead of time to get on the waiting list as this place is always packed...there is a reason it is traded on the New York Stock Exchange.

Ginza *(T (Orange): NE Med Center   16 Hudson St, 617-338-2261   Dir: exit T N on Washington St, R on Kneeland St, L on Hudson)*
Japanese: The first Japanese restaurant ever in Chinatown, Ginza offers sushi, tempura, noodle, and meat dishes. It gets a little pricey around dinner (entrées $14-21) so you're better off stopping in for lunch (11:30am-2:30pm) for some Kiji-Don chicken or Shrimp Tempura.

Suishaya *(T (Orange): Chinatown   2 Tyler St, 617-423-3848   Dir: exit T S on Washington St, L on Beach St, R on Tyler)*
Korean: One of the only good Korean restaurants in the area, Suishaya boasts great service and excellent sushi as well as traditional Korean house specials. Especially delicious is the Bulgoki ($14)—strips of prime beef soaked in marinade and served on a sizzling platter. Whether you are a vegan, carnivore, or seafood glutton, you'll find something agreeable on their huge menu of entrées (average $10-14).

Downtown

The Big Easy Bar *(T (Green): Boylston 1 Boylston Pl, 617-351-7000)*
The theme is Mardi Gras every weekend at this bar and night club. The strong drinks, two tiers of dance floors (think Bourbon St balconies), and general debauchery consistently draw a crowd. FREE admission before 10pm if you sign up on their website; $8 cover if you're too lazy/ late.

Felt *(T (Orange): Chinatown   533 Washington St, 617-350-5555   Dir: exit T N on Washington St)* There's no getting around it, this place is expensive. However, given the fact it is huge, swanky, full of pool tables, three levels, ultra-modern, and ultra-cool, Felt is undoubtedly worth the splurge.

Gypsy Bar *(T (Green): Boylston St   116 Boylston St, 617-482-7799)*
Gypsy Bar is just as hip, trendy, and New York chic as its predecessor
Pravda, with a maze of lavishly-decorated rooms that match the well-
dressed set of people who lounge in them. Young professionals, and
college students who hope to pass for young professionals, come here
to see and be seen. This place is not cheap, but we thought it was
worth including—so be prepared to shell out big for drinks and at the
door ($10 cover charge after 10pm).

Liquor Store *(T (Green): Boylston   25 Boylston Pl   617- 357-6800)*
For just a $5 cover charge, you can drink beer out of a paper bag, ride
a mechanical bull, and mingle with some of Boston's most dedicated
partiers at this late-night hotspot. Open 9pm-2am F and S.

Downtown Crossing/South Station Area

Last Hurrah Bar and Grille *(T (Green): Government Center   60
School St, 617-227-8600   Dir: exit T, walk with traffic S on Tremont,
L on School St: inside Omni Parker House)*
American: The playful atmosphere, friendly service, and impressive
seafood-infused salads are what ultimately make this grille worth the
splurge. Try their crab cakes ($13) followed by the Beefsteak Tomato
and Shrimp Salad ($13) and discover what completely content feels
like.

**New England Aquarium Whale Watch Tours *(T (Blue):
Aquarium   Central Wharf, 617-973-5281)* Take a relaxing, 3-4 hour
boat tour of the Boston Harbor and beyond while naturalists point out
wildlife along the way. The whale watch may be quiet (and wet), but
spotting the whales is completely worth the ticket price. Prices: $29
adult; $26 college/60+yrs; $23 12-18yrs; $20 under 11. For
schedules: *www.neaq.org/visit/wwatch/hours.html.*

Fenway

Canestaro Restaurant and Pizzeria *(T (Green): Kenmore   16
Peterborough St, 617-266-8997   Dir: exit T, walk away from city W
on Brookline, L on Yawkey, L on Perborough)*
Italian: A charming family-style Italian restaurant with a friendly and
attractive ambiance, delicious pasta dishes, and a diverse menu.

Cooks remain faithful to Northern Italian recipes, culture, and tradition in their preparation of all the restaurant's specialties, such as the savory Cappelini Margherita: a generous portion of angel hair in a white wine, tomato, garlic and basil sauce ($12). Gourmet sandwiches run between $7-10.

Jamaica Plain

Centre St. Café *(T (Orange): Green Street   669A Centre St, 617-524-9217   Dir: exit T, walk (N) up Green .4 mi, L on Centre St, or avoid the T and take #39 bus)*
Eclectic: If you're a vegetarian looking for a healthy, worthwhile meal in Boston, this is the place to go. Carnivores don't fret; there is plenty for you as well including a great brunch with innovative dishes like Cuban scrambled eggs. Fresh-squeezed juices and organic ingredients yield a health-conscious crowd and long waits for groups on weekend mornings. Dishes $8-18

Jake's Boss BBQ *(T (Orange): Green Street   3492 Washington St, 617-983-3701   Dir: exit T and walk S on Washington St 3 blocks)*
BBQ: Get out your bibs, your napkins, and your appetites because Jake's is going to have you gorging like a pig at a trough, Texas-style. Vegetarians are not welcome, unless they're willing to fall off the wagon for a night.

North End

Al Dente Ristorante *(T (Green/Orange): Haymarket   109 Salem St, 617-523-0990   Dir: exit T, follow walkway to North End, R on Cross St, L on Salem)*
Italian: This snug, candle-lit restaurant is great for a filling dinner and features an open kitchen, allowing patrons to watch their meals being prepared. Order the bruschetta ($7), Puttanesca ($12), or another one of the freshly-made pasta dishes.

Bella Vista Ristorante *(T (Green/Orange): Haymarket   288 Hanover St, 617-367-4999   Dir: exit T, follow walkway to North End, R on Cross St, L on Hanover)*

Italian: Comfortably classy and deliciously affordable, Bella Vista is praised for its family-style atmosphere. Try the Lobster Fra Diavolo ($13) and be sure to order the Tiramisu ($4) for dessert. The food is hit or miss depending on the night but is usually good, especially for the price.

La Famiglia Giorgio *(T (Green/Orange): Haymarket   112 Salem St, 617-367-6711   Dir: exit T, follow walkway to North End, R on Cross St, L on Salem)*
Italian: A Roman-style restaurant featuring traditional Italian classics, seafood, and over 18 vegetarian dishes. Especially delicious are the fresh shrimp and scallops, sautéed in a tomato/butter/wine sauce and served with vegetables over linguine ($17). The majority of pasta, pizza, and salad items fall under $12.

Ristorante Saraceno *(T (Green/Orange): Haymarket 286   Hanover St, 617-227-5353   Dir: exit T, follow walkway to North End, R on Cross St, L on Hanover)*
Italian: With its murals and pillars, this Napolitian restaurant conjures the feel of a Tuscan sidewalk café. Heaping pasta dishes like the Linguine Ai Fruitti di Mare (Linguine with seafood) give you the most bang for your buck and plenty of leftovers.

**Antico Forno *(T (Green/Orange): Haymarket   93 Salem St, 617-723-6733   Dir: exit T, follow walkway to North End, R on Cross St, L on Salem)*
Mediterranean: With floors covered in sawdust and Tuscan painting-adorned walls, this Mediterranean restaurant's Old Italy feel and brick-oven pizza (Antico Forno means "old stove") is worth the extra few dollars. Try the Carciofi e Porcini pizza topped with imported Italian mushrooms ($11).

Somerville

**Evoo *(T (Red): Harvard   118 Beacon St, 617-661-3866   Dir (10 min walk): exit T, R on Massachusetts Ave, becomes Harvard St, L on Quincy St, R on Kirkland St, R on Beacon)*
American (New): The name is an acronym for Extra Virgin Olive Oil, and that's the only thing you can count on finding at Evoo as the funky, inventive New American menu changes with the seasons.

Sample everything—all of their offerings are fantastic, fresh, and fun—and stay awhile to enjoy the modern venue's quiet, laid-back attitude.

Orleans *(T (Red): Davis   65 Holland St, 617-591-2100   Dir: exit T to Holland St, L on Holland)*
American (new): The cozy lounge—complete with couches, ample window space, and a big-screen TV—is an ideal setting to enjoy designer cocktails or one of 20 beers on tap. Dinner fare is hearty though uninventive. Bar open until midnight.

Gargoyles on the Square *(T (Red): Davis   219 Elm St, 617-776-5300   Dir: exit T to Holland St, R on Holland, cross Davis Sq to Elm)*
American, French: This neighborhood bistro is worth the cost of a special night. For a low-key evening, pair the imported beers with the creative bar fare like $7 crispy fried ravioli *or* $8 jalapeno, onion, and cheddar corn dogs. Live jazz on Sunday nights.

Zoe's Chinese Restaurant *(T (Red): Porter   289 Beacon St, 617-864-6265   Dir (10 min walk): exit T, R on Somerville Ave, R on Beacon)*
Chinese: Delicious, authentic Chinese food (the proof is in the mostly-Chinese clientele) in a pleasant, clean, and friendly environment. Well worth the trip, but with FREE delivery, you don't even have to make it.

Diva Indian Bistro *(T (Red): Davis   246 Elm St, Davis 617- 629-4963   Dir: exit T to Holland St, R on Holland, cross Davis Sq to Elm)*
Indian: While the service can be hit or miss, the dishes are always on point. Diva boasts an endless selection of Indian cuisine and a sleek, modern décor. Split the two-person "Royal Dinner for two" (about $34), for a 10-course sampling of the restaurant's best.

**Antonia's *(T (Red): Davis   37 Davis Sq, 617-623-6700   Dir: exit T to Holland St, R on Holland to Davis Sq)*
Italian: A little piece of the North End right in Davis; this bistro offers some classic Italian comfort food. Cozy, quaint, and romantic, Antonia's offers a prime view of the Square.

Out of the Blue *(T (Red): Davis   382 Highland Ave, 617-776-5020   Dir: exit T to College Ave, L on Highland)*
Seafood: The place for Seafood connoisseurs who want the freshest catch but don't care about décor. Out of the Blue is cute and small but slightly cafeteria-esque.

South End

Equator *(T (Orange): Mass Ave   1721 Washington St, 617-536-6386 Dir: exit T S on Mass Ave, L on Washington)*
Thai: Thought to be located right where the city's actual "equator" may in fact be, this family-owned Thai restaurant is stocked with a variety of authentic options and great service.

**Giacomo's *(T (Orange): Mass Ave   431 Columbus Ave, 617-536-5723   Dir: exit T S on Mass Ave, L on Columbus)*
Italian: This old fashioned Tuscan restaurant is hands-down the best-known Italian spot in the S End (and nearly as busy as its N End location), so be sure to make reservations (especially on weekends). Choose from generously cut salmon, sirloin steak, or opt for the "create your own pasta" where diners can choose from various noodles, sauces, and seafood for a personally-customized dish. Most entrees: $12-20.

Jae's Cafe and Grill *(T (Orange): Mass Ave   520 Columbus Ave, 617-421-9405   Dir: exit T S on Mass Ave, L on Columbus)*
Asian: A double-decker restaurant featuring an authentic Japanese sushi bar and countless fresh Pan-Asian favorites like Pad Thai and marinated steak and salmon. The lower level has a barroom vibe, while the upper level has a calm, dinner-time feel. Take your pick and follow their motto: "Eat at Jae's: Live Forever," (we don't get it either, but the food is great).

**Pho Republique *(T (Orange): Back Bay   1415 Washington St, 617-262-0005   Dir: exit T S to Dartmouth St which turns into W Dedham St, L on Washington)*
Modern Asian: This trendy ethnic restaurant's bright and stylish décor alone will make you want to stay for a while. Try the vegetarian Rangoon spring rolls ($8.50), or for a few extra dollars opt for a bowl of Pho (fresh rice noodles and aromatic broth with chicken, beef, shrimp or tofu); it's Vietnam's national dish and the eatery's specialty.

**Piattini Wine Café *(T (Orange): Back Bay   162 Columbus Ave, 617-423-2021   Dir: exit T S on Dartmouth, L on Columbus)*
Italian: Everyone can feel like a connoisseur at this cute wine bar offering hot and cold meals ranging from sandwiches ($9) to seafood

linguine ($23). You may feel cooler at the sister location on Newbury St, but this location is more spacious and less crowded. Note: Piattini translates to "small plate" so don't come here if you're a famished linebacker.

Stella *(T (Orange): Mass Ave   1525 Washington St, 617-247-7747·*
Dir: exit T S on Mass Ave, L on Washington)
American Italian: A bright, airy, sophisticated eatery with a huge wraparound patio serving Italian comfort foods like fettuccine Alfredo and gourmet thin-crust pizza to a crowd composed largely of twentysomething couples. Bonus: Food is served nightly until 1:30am (for those who, amidst their drunken stumble home, seek something more refined than burgers and fries).

State Street Area/Financial District

**Boston Sail Loft *(T (Blue): Aquarium   80 Atlantic Ave, 617-227-7280   Dir: exit N on Atlantic Ave)*
American/Caribbean: With its ideal location and small-town feel, the Sail Loft will continually surprise you with its plentiful portions of savory seafood (steamed, fried, or broiled) and harbor views. Waitresses are friendly and know locals by name. Entrées $8-12

Legal Sea Foods *(T (Blue): Aquarium   255 State St, 617-227-3115*
Dir: exit T, head E on State St to Long Wharf)
American: This waterfront location featuring outdoor dining and views of the Boston Harbor is one of the best spots for this classic NE seafood chain. Forget the expensive entrées and fill up on their award winning chowders and appetizers instead.

**The Living Room *(T (Blue): Aquarium   101 Atlantic Ave, 617-723-5101   Dir: exit T N on Atlantic Ave)*
Lounge: This lounge is furnished with plush, inviting couches, polished coffee tables, and wood stoves, reminiscent of a nicely furnished basement/living room combo. Take a break from standing and being bumped at the bar by sitting down and ordering one of their creative martinis, such as The Strawberry—a sugar-rimmed glass filled with a blend of Stoli Strawberry, daiquiri mix, and lime juice (they're $10, but unlike most Boston bars, you won't have to power-drink to keep from getting crowd-rage).

Where to Bring Your Parents/Guests

Allston/Brighton

Allston and Brighton may be home to cozy hole-in-the-wall bars, convenient late-night delivery, and eateries that are easy on the wallet, but let's face it: These aren't exactly the glamorous places you want to show off to your guests. So don't be lazy: Grab a cab or jump on the T and head downtown where the meals are better and the atmosphere is a bit more enticing.

Back Bay

The Cheesecake Factory *(T (Green E): Prudential   115 Huntington Ave, 617-399-7777   Dir: exit T, R on Huntington)*
American: With an enormous menu that includes everything from burgers to Pad Thai, you'd be hard pressed not to find something that interests you here. Great service, great food, and a great atmosphere have made The Cheesecake Factory famous throughout the country. Don't leave without trying one of their 33 types of famed cheesecakes.

Sonsie *(T (Green B/C/D): Hynes   327 Newbury St, 617-351-2500 Dir: exit T to Newbury St, R on Newbury)*
American: With servings from tomato soup with crabmeat to grilled lamb chops with bacon mozzarella, Sonsie aims its sights at more sophisticated taste buds. Don't be surprised to see famous faces sipping martinis or espressos here. Naturally, such trendiness comes at a high price—entrées range from $9-29 with most falling on the higher end of that scale.

**Vox Populi *(T (Green): Copley   755 Boylston St, 617-424-8300 Dir: exit T W (L) onto Boylston)*

American: An older, professional crowd fills the bar as martinis and mixed drinks are consumed over appetizers. The soft dining room colors, wood-adorned walls, and modern lighting create a very chic environment. Make sure you have your guests try the Asparagus Milanese $10, the Vox burger, or one of the superb but pricey entrées like the Garlicky Clams and Linguini ($19). This place has the best steak and eggs in town ($12).

Casa Romero *(T (Green B/C/D): Hynes   30 Gloucester St, 617-536-4341 Dir: exit T to Newbury St, R on Newbury, L on Gloucester)*
Mexican: Walking into Casa Romero is like walking through a transporter to Mexico, but the décor is secondary to mouth-watering dishes such as stuffed squid, pork tenderloin, and vegetarian enchiladas.

Dick's Last Resort *(T (Green): Copley   55 Huntington Ave, 617-267-8080   Dir: exit T, R on Boylston St, R on Dartmouth St, R on Huntington)*
Seafood/BBQ: Dick's provides great BBQ and seafood in sawdust-on-the-floor style. A huge draw for bachelorette parties, Dick's is always full of smiling, laughing patrons. Don't be put off by the attitudes of the staff, it's intentional and part of the place's charm. So bring your thick skin, a good sense of humor, and let them be Dick's.

Beacon Hill

Scollay Square *(T (Green/Red): Park St   150 Bowdoin St, 617- 742-4900   Dir: exit T, walk straight, L on Park St, R on Beacon St, L on Bowdoin)*
American (New): This classy 1920s-themed spot looks as highly secured as the pentagon from the outside with its dark walls and the posted notice regarding its strict dress code. Once inside however, it's surprisingly relaxed, serving upscale American favorites and seafood entrées for $18-30 (lunch ~ $12).

The Hungry I *(T (Red): Charles/MGH   71 1/2 Charles St, 617- 227-3524)* French: A seemingly ordinary brownstone is home to one of the premier restaurants in Beacon Hill: the low-lit, antique-filled Hungry I. This romantic, cozy, and elegant space has long been known for its charm and flavor, though not for its thrift—most entrées approach

$30. Hidden from view of passerby is a courtyard that is used in nice weather.

Ristorante Toscano (T (Red): Charles/MGH   41 Charles St, 617-723-4090) <u>Italian</u>: This intimate space is decorated with rustic Tuscan charm—antique maps and trinkets adorn the exposed brick walls—offering up an elaborate menu of Northern Italian cuisine (i.e. no Americanized Italian).

Torch (T (Red): Charles/MGH   26 Charles St, 617- 723-5939) <u>New American, Mediterranean</u>: Elegant copper paneling serving as a backdrop for the tables, coupled with romantic low lighting and pricey plates (be prepared to spend at least $16 per entrée), give this swanky spot a very New York feel.

Brookline

The Fireplace (T (Green C): Washington St   1634 Beacon St, 617-975-1900   Dir: exit T onto Beacon)
<u>American</u>: Although there is limited room around the actual fireplace, the restaurant still maintains warmth and personality. This stylish, sophisticated hotspot puts out a wide array of delicious meals and sports a packed bar on the weekends.

**The Elephant Walk (T (Green C): St Mary's St   900 Beacon St, 617-247-1500   Dir: exit T onto Beacon St)
<u>French-Cambodian</u>: Consistently good reviews, exotic food choices, and an upscale albeit simple décor make The Elephant Walk a wonderful and original place for a night out. Make sure to take notice of the elephant décor; they are supposed to bring good luck. Most entrées fall between $16-24 on a menu suitable for carnivores and vegetarians alike.

Ginza (T (Green C): St. Mary's Street   1002 Beacon St, 617-566-9688   Dir: exit T onto Beacon)
<u>Japanese</u>: Sit in the simple, elegant Japanese décor and enjoy the abundance of sushi choices, incredibly fresh fish, and a huge selection of sake (20). While not as chic or modern as Fugakyu, Ginza remains one of Boston's best sushi dens. Tip: Get a reservation for weekend nights.

Café St. Petersburg *(T (Green D): Brookline Village   236 Washington St, 617-277-7100   Dir: head S from Brookline Pl, R on Washington St)*
<u>Russian</u>: Don't let the tuxedoed waiters scare you; these Russians know how to party. Authentic dishes of borscht and blini with smoked salmon will crowd your table but don't even think about leaving without sampling one of the many types of vodka this café has to offer...it's just the Russian way.

Cambridge

Harvest *(T (Red): Harvard   44 Brattle St, 617-868-2255   Dir: exit T S on JFK St, R onto Brattle St, R again to stay on Brattle)*
<u>American (new)</u>: Softly-lit walls adorned with paintings of pastoral scenes, a beautiful outdoor patio, and an eclectic menu that caters to what's in season makes Harvest suitable for families and dates seeking exquisite, inventive food and impeccable service (entrées $24-33; three course prix-fix $48).

Upstairs on the Square *(T (Red): Harvard   91 Winthrop St, 617-864-1933   Dir: exit T S onto JFK St, R on Winthrop)*
<u>American (new)</u>: Formerly called Upstairs at the Hasty Pudding, this gourmet restaurant may have lost its name but not its reputation as the best (and perhaps the priciest) restaurant in Cambridge and one of the top in Boston. The food and Alice-in-Wonderland décor make for an unforgettable combination. Try the charcoaled lamb sirloin with Japanese eggplant and sugarcane roasted tomatoes ($34) or the butter-poached lobster with Andalusian gazpacho and bruléed aioli ($42).

Sandrine's Bistro *(T (Red): Harvard   8 Holyoke St, 617-497-5300   Dir: exit T onto Mass Ave, R on Holyoke)*
<u>French</u>: The Square's premier bistro serves up classic French cuisine in an elegant but simple setting reminiscent of the French countryside. For intimacy, opt for the cozy, low-lit seating in the downstairs room. Entrées $16-30.

Chinatown/Theater District

**Finale *(T (Green): Arlington   1 Columbus Ave, 617-423-3184 Dir: exit station S on Arlington and turn L on Columbus)*
French/American: A luxurious after-dinner spot where dessert is a *really* big deal (the light fare on the dinner menu is considered a mere prelude to the "main course": dessert). Try the Crème Brulee or Chocolate Euphoria and you won't need to ask why it costs so much.

Davio's Nern Italian Steakhouse *(T (Green) Arlington   75 Arlington St, 617-357-4810 Dir: exit T S on Arlington)*
Italian: A spacious fine-dining spot offering over 300 wines, traditional Italian favorites, and unique gourmet spins on decidedly non-gourmet comfort foods (think glorified macaroni-and-cheese made with white truffle oil: $8). You can never go wrong with the Angel Hair Pomodoro ($15) and the veal tenderloin ($33) nearly melts in your mouth.

Shabu-Zen *(T (Orange): Chinatown   16 Tyler St, 617-292-8828 Dir: exit T S on Washington St, L on Beach St, R on Tyler St)*
Japanese: This fine-dining spot serves incredibly fresh Shabu-Shabu: plates stocked with meats, vegetables, a side of jasmine rice, udon noodles, or vermicelli, and an eclectic selection of dipping sauces. Try the Surf and Turf, a seafood platter with beef, chicken, pork, or lamb ($17).

Bonfire (in the Park Plaza Hotel) *(T (Green): Arlington   64 Arlington St, 617-262-3473 Dir: exit T S on Arlington)*
Steakhouse: The décor is rich, dark, and Gothic-esque inside the carnivorously blood-red dining room, but the food at this fusion steakhouse is to-die-for. Here, at local culinary sensation Todd English's most upscale restaurant, you get what you pay for so be prepared for a very steep bill (figure $45 per person).

Downtown

No. 9 Park *(T (Red): Park St   9 Park St, 617-742-9991)*
American (New): The classic décor of this restaurant is as straightforward as the name, but the food isn't—No. 9 is continually voted as serving some of the finest and most inspired dishes in Boston. Be prepared to shell out (make your guests shell out) for a

taste of Chef Barbara Lynch's cuisine, as most entrées are in the $30-40 range.

Downtown Crossing/South Station Area

West Street Grille *(T (Green): Park St   15 West St, 617-423-0300*
Dir: exit T, walk with traffic (S) on Tremont, L on West)
<u>Modern American</u>: A hip, contemporary grill prone to an older crowd with entrées ranging from $20 to $30. They have great pasta and fish dishes such as the Eggplant and Portobello Lasagna or their "famous" Grilled Yellow Fin Tuna.

Fenway

Elephant Walk *(T (Green): Kenmore   900 Beacon St, 617-247-1500*
Dir: exit T, walk away from city (W) on Beacon)
<u>Cambodian</u>: If you want to impress your guests and show off your knowledge of exotic foods, bring them here. While pricey, Elephant Walk serves extremely unique and flavorful Cambodian/French fusion meals. Three and four course fixed price meals are available for $30 and $40, respectively.

**Great Bay *(T (Green): Kenmore   500 Commonwealth Ave, 617-532-5300   Dir: exit T, walk downtown (E) on Commonwealth Ave)*
<u>Seafood</u>: A hip approach to fine dining with celebrated "conspicuously excellent seafood." The lighting and décor mimic underwater ambiance, the bar is huge, and the fish is the crème de la crème of Boston's already-renowned seafood selection. Order the Dayboat Sea Scallops ($28) or Cousin Mark's Dayboat Lobster ($44) and play VIP for a night.

Jamaica Plain

JP Seafood *(T (Orange): Green Street   730 Centre St, 617-983-5177*
Dir: exit T, walk W on Green and turn L on Centre St)
<u>Japanese</u>: A local hotspot for young professionals and seafood lovers, JP Seafood's extensive list of sushi choices reads like a who's who of

the fish world. Colorful creations and maki rolls served on a sailboat turn a seemingly simple meal into a worthwhile dining experience.

Ban Chiang House *(T (Orange): Green Street   707 Centre St, 617-522-2299   Dir: exit T, walk W on Green St .3 mi, L on Centre St, or avoid the T and take #39 bus)*
Thai: A comfortable place for a small group, Ban Chiang House dishes out traditional Thai cuisine. Mild dishes of pad thai and curry are characteristic of this low-key, family oriented restaurant with most entrées costing between $10-15.

North End

5 North Square *(T (Green/Orange): Haymarket   5 North Square, 617-720-1050   Dir: exit T, follow walkway to North End, R on Cross St, L on Hanover St, R on Prince St, R on Garden Court St)*
Italian: Quaint, fine dining in a building that looks like a bed and breakfast. Impress the parents with some of Boston's finest seafood dishes and Italian classics. The décor is like a shabby-chic wedding reception, but the food is excellent. Entrees run $15-22.

Bacco Ristorante & Bar *(T (Green/Orange): Haymarket   107 Salem St, 617-624-0454   Dir: exit T, follow walkway to North End, R on Cross St, L on Salem)*
Italian: An inventive and refreshing take on traditional North End dining, this modern double-level bar and restaurant is filled with the casually chic every weekend. Either the creative Sweet Potato Gnocchi ($22) or the Herb-Crusted Monkfish ($24) will leave you completely satisfied, but not so much that you won't be craving one of the downstairs bar's famous martinis. Make your reservations online at http://baccoboston.com.

**Giacomo's Restaurant *(T (Green/Orange): Haymarket   355 Hanover Street, 617-523-9026   Dir: exit T, follow walkway to North End, R on Cross St, L on Hanover)*
Italian: Savor a night of timeless Italian classics at this tiny, family eatery renown for sporting a constant line at the door (Giacomo's does not accept reservations). Don't fret though; the food is worth waiting for and it is fun to watch the staff dash around the place. Dive into simple Italian dishes (Chicken Parmigiana, Shrimp Scampi) honed to perfection, or stick strictly to seafood; either way, you can't go wrong.

Plan on desert at Mike's pastries or elsewhere as Giacomo's doesn't serve any. CASH ONLY

Somerville

**Dali *(T (Red): Harvard   415 Washington St, 617-661-3254 Dir (10 min walk): exit T, R on Mass Ave - becomes Harvard St, L on Quincy St, R on Kirkland St - becomes Washington)*
<u>Spanish</u>: Beautiful, flavorful, and never dull, this restaurant is worth going to simply for the visual experience, to say nothing of the food. Dimly-lit and romantic while still vibrant and fun, Dali is perfect for dates, friends, or families that want exotic, exquisite cuisine in a colorful setting.

**The Elephant Walk *(T (Red): Porter   2067 Mass Ave, 617-492-6900   Dir: exit T onto Mass Ave, walk N towards Davis, follow for 3/4 mi to Russell St)*
<u>Cambodian</u>: A fusion of Cambodian and French cuisine, the flavors of the Elephant walk are easy to enjoy but difficult to describe, with countless delicious menu offerings from which to choose. With a warm, open interior (think high ceilings, exposed bricks walls, and copper hues) and attentive staff, the restaurant yields a loyal following. Entrées $17-28.

**Sabur *(T (Red): Davis   212 Holland St, 617-776-7890   Dir: exit T to Holland St, L on Holland)*
<u>Mediterranean</u>: At Sabur, "Mediterranean" is used as a catchall for the eclectic cuisine—a fusion of Turkish, North African, and Bosnian. Reasonable prices, a simple but inviting décor, flavorful dishes, and impeccable service grant Sabur a loyal following. The space is great for dates, families, or big groups. Try the slow-roasted lamb, which the server will remove from the hearth before your eyes. Bar open until 1am; occasional live music.

South End

Aquitaine *(T (Orange): Back Bay   569 Tremont St, 617-424-8577 Dir: exit T S on Dartmouth, L on Tremont)*
<u>French</u>: Unleash your subtly-chic Parisian side for the evening at this dressy, French bistro-inspired fine dining spot. Entrées like lamb confit and seared tuna steak are guilt-free and delicious.

**B&G Oysters Ltd. *(T (Orange): Back Bay   550 Tremont St, 617-423-0550   Dir: exit T S on Dartmouth, L on Tremont)*
<u>American</u>: This top-of-the-line seafood place is very expensive (most entrées $24), small, and has a limited menu, but the lobster bisque and clam chowder are some of Boston's best. Equally noteworthy are the seared scallops and fried clams. Watch for stars as B&G is one of the city's notorious celebrity hangouts.

Caffe Umbra *(T (Orange): Back Bay   1395 Washington St, 617-867-0707   Dir: exit T S on Dartmouth, L on Washington)*
<u>French/Italian</u>: A trendy eatery prone to an older crowd with a great wine list and inventive country French-style entrées that are worth their hefty price tag ($14-23). Regardless of your choice for dinner, you must try their signature sticky toffee pudding ($9) served with vanilla bean ice cream and warm toffee sauce.

Sibling Rivalry *(T (Orange): Back Bay   525 Tremont St, 617-338-5338   Dir: exit T S on Dartmouth and turn L on Tremont)*
<u>New American</u>: Bob and David Kinkead, the brothers who own this posh/hip restaurant in the ritzy Atelier 505 building, each cook using their own unique touches to form the aptly named restaurant's split menu. Particularly delicious is David's Roasted Halibut ($25), but Bob's Nantucket Bay Scallops are equally tempting. (Hey, we had to be fair.)

Equator *(T (Orange): Mass Ave   1721 Washington St, 617-536-6386   Dir: exit T S on Mass Ave, L on Washington)*
<u>Thai</u>: Thought to be located right where the city's actual "equator" may in fact be, this family-owned Thai restaurant is stocked with a variety of authentic options and great service. Start with the Coconut-Chicken Soup ($4.50), and try the house specialty Avocado Shrimp ($19) for your entrée; it's worth the few extra dollars!

State Street Area/Financial District

**Barking Crab *(T (Blue) Aquarium   88 Sleeper St, 617-426-2722   Dir: exit T S on Atlantic Ave, L on Seaport Blvd, L on Sleeper)*
<u>American</u>: A sawdust-on-the-floor type of crab and lobster shack situated on the edge of the Harbor with fantastic skyline views of Boston and a fantastic summertime happy hour. Cozy up to your

friends, coworkers, or total strangers on the long benches and get
ready to crack and drink your way to seafood heaven. Try the king
crab legs ($22) or opt for the more inexpensive "famous" fish and
chips ($12).

Intrigue *(T (Blue): Aquarium   70 Rowes Wharf, 617-856-7744 Dir:
exit T S on Atlantic Ave, L into Rowes Wharf)*
American: Escape the hustle and bustle of the city and sample the
fresh grilled tuna or swordfish (entrées are in the $20-$30 range) on
this restaurant's perfect terrace with comfortable chairs and
spectacular views of the water.

Oceana (At the Marriot) *(T (Blue): Aquarium   296 State St, 617-
227-0800   Dir: exit T E on State St)*
American: With its live jazz 8pm-12am F-Sa and a seasonal outdoor
terrace, the food at this harbor-side casual seafood restaurant could
be mediocre and it would still be worth going to. As it turns out, the
food is great: Try the generous portions of Mako Shark or Swordfish
(all entrées under $30).

The Vault *(T (Green): Government Center   105 Water St, 617-292-
3355   Dir: exit T SE on State St, R on Devonshire, L on Water St)*
American: Contrary to popular belief, this self-proclaimed "classic
Boston bar" also specializes in fine dining, offering mouth-watering
plates like Pasta Primavera ($13) and Shrimp Newport ($22). The
Vault derives its name from the fact it replaced a bank.

Union Oyster House *(T (Orange/Green): Haymarket   41 Union St,
617-227-2750   Dir: exit T S on Congress St, L on Hanover St, R on
Union)* Seafood: Indulge in seafood and history at this Boston
landmark (it's the oldest restaurant in Boston, open since 1826). Try
the famous Union Special Lobster—a savory medium baked lobster
topped with NE seafood stuffing (Market price)—and of course the
Union Grilled Oysters on the half shell ($11)... this place has been open
for so long for a reason!

Midnight Munchies

Allston/Brighton

**The Paradise Lounge *(T (Green B): Pleasant St   969 Commonwealth Ave, 617-562-8814   Dir: exit T W on Comm Ave)*
<u>American/Asian</u>: A chic lounge attached to an urban music venue that is also great for after-hours snacks. Late night specials (10pm-1am) include $1 cheeseburgers with the purchase of a drink and a FREE pizza with the purchase of a Miller pitcher.

Redneck's *(T (Green B): Harvard Ave   140 Brighton Ave, 617-782-9444   Dir: exit T N on Harvard, end at Brighton)*
<u>BBQ</u>: When the bars close, expect Redneck's to be packed but don't fret, it's worth the wait. Grab a roast beef sandwich and some chili-cheese fries, or split a pizza and enjoy the camaraderie of the drunk and hungry until 3am.

La Mamma Pizzeria *(T (Green B): Harvard Ave   190A Brighton Ave, 617-783-1661   Dir: exit T N on Harvard, L on Brighton)*
<u>Italian</u>: A tiny authentic Italian pizza shop with exceptionally speedy late-night delivery (until 3 am), reasonable prices, and generous toppings. Try a large sausage pizza for a mere $7.

Back Bay

Deville Restaurant and Lounge (T (Green B/C/D): Hynes   10 Scotia St, 617-266-2695   Dir: exit T to Mass Ave, L on Mass Ave, L on Boylston, R on Dalton St, R on Scotia)
<u>American</u>: Attached to the popular bowling alley, Kings, this restaurant keeps patrons entertained and well fed while they wait for a lane. Begin with the fried calamari ($8), move on to pizza ($10-13), and

end with Boston Cream Pie or chocolate cake for dessert ($6 each). Nachos and pizza served until 1am every night of the week, full menu served until 12am.

Parish Café *(T (Green): Arlington   361 Boylston St, 617-247-4777 Dir: exit T west (L) to Boylston St)*
<u>American</u>: A full menu of American favorites from hamburgers to Turkey sandwiches is served daily until 1am.

Sonsie *(T (Green B/C/D): Hynes   327 Newbury St, 617-351-2500 Dir: exit T to Newbury St, R on Newbury)*
<u>American</u>: Serves a full menu of upscale entrées ($9-29 with most falling on the higher end of this range) until 12am every night, and pizza until 12:30am F and Sa nights. See Places to Take Parents or Guests.

Golden Temple *(T (Green C): Washington Square   1651 Beacon St, 617-277-9722   Dir: exit T, restaurant visible from station)*
<u>Chinese</u>: Delicious dishes of traditional Chinese food served into the wee hours of the morning. Open: Su-Th 11:30am-1am, F-Sa 11:30am-2am.

Kaya *(T (Green): Copley   581 Boylston St, 617-236-5858   Dir: exit T east (R) on Boylston St)*
<u>Korean/Japanese</u>: A selection of sushi, soup, and noodle dishes such as Bibim Naeng Myum—fine noodles tossed with homemade chili sauce—attracts growling stomachs daily until 2am.

Dick's Last Resort *(T (Green): Copley   55 Huntington Ave, 617-267-8080   Dir: exit T, R on Boylston St, R on Dartmouth St, R on Huntington)*
<u>Seafood/BBQ</u>: Dick's provides great BBQ and seafood in sawdust-on-the-floor style served until 1am F and Sa.

Gyuhama *(T (Green): Copley   827 Boylston St, 617-437-0188   Dir: exit T to Boylston St, L (W) on Boylston, 3 blocks down)*
<u>Sushi</u>: Late night sushi every night until 2am will make Gyuhama your after hours rendezvous spot.

Beacon Hill

7-11 *(T (Red): Charles/MGH   66 Charles St, 617-720-3588)*
Convenience Store: In true Charles St style, even the 7-11 looks and feels classy—gentle calligraphy replaces the usual tacky logo—but the stop still maintains its low prices and late hours (open until 2am every night).

Venice Ristorante *(T (Red): Charles/MGH   204 Cambridge St, 617-227-2094 Dir: exit T E onto Cambridge St)*
Italian: Venice Ristorante may not look like much from the outside, but it's all that you could ask for in a pizza and sub stop: warm, friendly, cheap, and open late (until 12:30am weeknights, 2am weekends).

Brookline

Golden Temple *(T (Green C): Washington Square   1651 Beacon St, 617-277-9722   Dir: exit T, restaurant visible from station)*
Chinese: Delicious dishes of traditional Chinese food served into the wee hours of the morning. Open: Su-Th 11:30am-1am, F-Sa 11:30am-2am.

Cambridge

The Hong Kong *(T (Red): Harvard   1236 Mass Ave, 617-864-5311 Dir: exit T onto Mass Ave, walk towards Central Sq)*
Chinese: After downing scorpion bowls and dancing up a storm on the third floor, head downstairs with your new friends to round out the night with egg rolls, crab rangoons, and fortune cookies. Open Su-Th until 2am, F-Sa until 2:30am.

7-11 *(70 JFK St, corner of JFK and Mt Auburn)* If you're really stuck, there's always 7-11's 24 hour-a-day offerings such as chips, donuts, slushies, and microwave macaroni and cheese.

Pinnochio's Pizza & Subs *(T (Red): Harvard   74 Winthrop St, 617-876-4897   Dir: exit T onto JFK St, L on Winthrop)*

<u>Pizza:</u> The freshly made, deep-dish Sicilian slices and sub bread are always perfect (see cheap eats). Open until 1am every night and sometimes later when they've got extra slices to get rid of.

Felipe's *(T (Red): Harvard   83 Mt Auburn St, 617-354-9944   Dir: exit T onto JFK, L on Mt. Auburn)*
<u>Mexican:</u> If it's late and nowhere else is open, it's a good bet that Felipe's is. This burrito stop will often stay past its regular hours to accommodate particular Harvard events or a busy night. Open Su-W until 1am, Th-Sa until 2am if crowded.

Pizza Ring *(617-864-1800)* Delivers pizza until 1am Su-Th, 2am F-Sa.

Chinatown/Theater District

Bennigan's *(T (Green): Arlington   191 Stuart St, 617-227-3754 Dir: exit T S on Arlington St, L on Stuart)*
<u>American:</u> This casual eatery serves $8-$12 dishes of pasta and seafood until 12:30am Su-Th, and 1:30am F-Sa. It's the perfect place to stop in for a quick bite when the evening comes to an early end.

Grand Chau Chow Restaurant *(T (Orange): Chinatown   52 Beach St, 617-426-6266   Dir: exit T S on Washington St, L on Beach St)*
<u>Chinese:</u> The cooks don't quit until 2:30 or 3:30am daily at this Chinese restaurant. Grab some chop suey ($5) or sesame chicken ($8) and enjoy your culinary justification for late bedtimes.

**News Cafe *(T (Orange): NE Med Center   150 Kneeland St, 617-426-6397   Dir: exit T N on Washington St, R on Kneeland)*
<u>Eclectic:</u> In the city that definitely sleeps, hit up the News Café, open until 4am Tu-Th and 5am F-Su (closed M). The eclectic menu is stocked with random goodies like omelets, sushi, and calamari. Eat in the trendy TV and leather-adorned bar or in the more casual dining area. If you plan on being out late, you may want to start here—News makes the best espresso martini in town. After two, you'll be bounding through Chinatown on your way to the clubs.

Downtown

Parish Café *(T (Green): Arlington   361 Boylston St, 617-247-4777*
Dir: exit T to Boylston St, L (W) at top of stairs)
<u>American:</u> A full menu of American favorites from hamburgers and
french fries to turkey sandwiches is served daily until 1am.

North End

**Bova's Bakery *(T (Green/Orange): Haymarket   134 Salem St,*
617-523-5601   Dir: exit T, follow walkway to North End, R on Cross
St, L on Salem)
<u>Bakery:</u> This place is truly a hidden treasure of bliss. Allow yourself to
be lured in by the smell of freshly baked breads and pastries and you'll
soon be starving—good thing a hard working family keeps it open 24-
hours-a-day and sells a myriad of super cheap sandwiches and baked
delights.

**Cafe Paradiso *(T (Green/Orange): Haymarket   255 Hanover St,*
617-742-1768   Dir: exit T, follow walkway to North End, R on Cross
St, L on Hanover)
<u>Café</u>: Everything you could ask for in a local neighborhood café:
coffee, cocktails, and cheap, traditional food packed into a quaint,
eclectically-decorated space (there is a bicycle hanging from the
ceiling). Try the unique Torta Rustica (eggplant parmigiana-style
pouch filled with vegetables and cheese) for a mere $6 or one of their
signature salads or sandwiches. Open daily until 2am.

Corner Café *(T (Green/Orange): North Station   87 Prince St, 617-*
523-8997   Dir: exit T NE on Causeway St, R on Prince)
<u>Pub Grub</u>: This small, dark, and rowdy neighborhood pit stop offers a
variety of cheap eats ranking from franks and beans to chicken
parmigiana (all for under $8). Order a $10 pitcher or $3 bottle of Red
Hook with your sausages—highly recommended by the local clientele—
and enjoy views of passing foot traffic until 2am.

Somerville

**RedBones *(T (Red): Davis   55 Chester St, 617-628-2200   Dir: exit T to Holland St, R on Holland, cross Davis Sq to Elm St, R on Chester)*
<u>Southern, Barbecue</u>: Not for vegetarians or the faint of heart. Known for its slow cooking and southern flavor, Redbones is a must for barbecue lovers. Long waits can be passed quickly at Underbones, the bar on the basement floor. Most plates $8 - $14. Late-night menu served until 12:30am.

South End

Stella *(T (Orange): Mass Ave   1525 Washington St, 617-247-7747 Dir: exit T S on Mass Ave, L on Washington)*
<u>American Italian</u>: A bright, airy, sophisticated eatery with a huge wraparound patio serving Italian comfort foods like fettuccine Alfredo and gourmet thin-crust pizza to twentysomething couples daily until 1:30am.

Anchovie's *(T (Green E): Prudential   433 Columbus Ave, 617-266-5088   Dir: exit T, walk S on W Newton St, L on Columbus)*
<u>Italian</u>: Huge portions, late-night dining (open until 1am), low prices, and a low-key, unassuming environment make Anchovie's a hit across just about every demographic imaginable. Don't let this restaurant/bar's late-night status fool you into thinking it's just another greasy spoon. If you can get a table (there is always a wait), try the pasta topped with fresh clams.

Franklin Café *(T (Silver): Union Park St   278 Shawmut Ave, 617-350-0010   Dir: exit T, L on Union, R on Shawmut)*
<u>Modern American</u>: Serves up a gourmet assortment of cuisines off a menu laden with seafood dishes until 1:30am. Pop in for a fish taco ($8) or linger over tempura soft shell crab ($19).

Badass Brunches

BEST DEALS

Centre St. Café *(T (Orange): Green Street   669A Centre St, 617-524-9217   Dir: exit T, walk (N) up Green .4 mi, L on Centre St, or avoid the T and take #39 bus)* A great brunch with innovative dishes like Cuban scrambled eggs. Fresh-squeezed juices and organic ingredients yield a health-conscious crowd and long waits for groups on weekend mornings.

Charley's *(T (Green C/D/E): Hynes   284 Newbury St, 617-266-3000 Dir: exit T onto Newbury St and make a R)*
American: Two eggs, hash browns, bacon, toast, coffee, and a complimentary cocktail (mimosa, screwdriver, or Bloody Mary) for $8 on Newbury St; need we say more?

**Charlie's Sandwich Shoppe *(T (Orange): Mass Ave   492 Columbus Ave, 617-536-7669   Dir: exit T S on Mass Ave, L on Columbus)* An old-school joint that's been serving up huge breakfasts and their signature turkey hash since 1927. Sit at the counter and catch the chaos around the grill, or relax in a booth as you dine on heaping portions of any greasy American favorite you can dream up at Boston's famed breakfast institution (served all day).

**Eagle's Deli *(T (Green C): Cleveland Circle 1918 Beacon St, 617-731-3232   Dir: exit T E on Beacon St)*
American: This popular Boston College brunch spot and burger joint was rated one of the top ten places "to pig out" in the US by the Travel Channel. Short order cooks rush to meet demand at this no-frills godsend. Be nice to the grill master and you'll get your order faster.

**Sorella's *(T (Orange): Stony Brook   388 Centre St, 617-524-2016 Dir: exit T, head W on Boylston St .3 mi, R on Centre St, or avoid the T and take the #39 bus to Centre St)*

<u>Diner</u>: The best breakfast place around, but be careful not to sleep through their hours (6:30am-2pm) and expect about a 20-30 minute wait on weekends. Oversized omelets and creative pancake options will make your mouth water as the plates go by.

**South Street Diner (T (Orange): NE Med Center   178 Kneeland St, 617-350-0028   Dir: exit T N on Washington St, R on Kneeland) Try the stack of chocolate-chip pancakes for $5.50. Not a morning person? Burgers and most sandwiches don't exceed $6.

**Zaftigs Delicatessen (T (Green C): Coolidge Corner   335 Harvard St, 617-975-0075   Dir: exit T and walk N on Harvard St) With a menu as diverse as Zaftig's, you're going to need some time to order. The trendy, high-energy atmosphere makes this place perfect for a date, family outing, or post-celebration refueling. Try the French toast or one of the other outstanding breakfast items.

UPSCALE

**East Coast Grill & Raw Bar (T (Red): Harvard   1271 Cambridge St, 617-491-6568   Dir: from Harvard Station, take the #69 bus to Inman Sq, or walk 10 min E on Cambridge St) The menu for Sunday brunch includes corn bread-crusted French toast, traditional egg breakfasts with a hint of Mexican, and a do-it-yourself Bloody Mary bar.

**Vox Populi (T (Green): Copley   755 Boylston St, 617-424-8300 Dir: exit T W (L) onto Boylston) An older, professional crowd is drawn here by the soft dining room colors, wood-adorned walls, and chic, modern lighting. This place has the best steak and eggs in town ($12): a thick, juicy, perfectly cooked filet mignon and two eggs. Add a cup of coffee and a newspaper and you're in leisure heaven.

Under 21

Allston/Brighton

Paradise Rock Club *(T (Green B): Pleasant St   969 Commonwealth Ave, 617-562-8800   Dir: exit T W on Comm Ave)* This legendary rock club hosts several 18 and over concerts a week. The venue is open and spacious, but the low stage makes performances intimate. Arrive early as shows get packed quickly. Prices vary.

**Sculler's Jazz Club (At the Doubletree Hotel)
(T (Green B): BU West   400 Soldier's Field Rd, 617-562-4111   Dir: cross the BU bridge and walk 1 mile W on Soldiers' Field Rd) A fashionable 200-seat jazz venue with gorgeous views of the Boston skyline and Charles River. The venue's mahogany walls, theatrical lighting, and large windows make the $14-28 ticket price tag well worth it.

Beacon Hill

Cheers Beacon Hill *(T (Red): Charles/MGH   84 Beacon St, 617-227-0111   Dir: exit T onto Charles St, head S towards Public Garden)* This Boston landmark whose façade was featured on the famed sitcom is generally so packed with tourists that no one's going to know your name. Nonetheless, to many it's worth the overpriced bar food just to get to say you've been there. Be warned, the inside of the bar is completely different than the set used for the show.

Cambridge

**The Middle East *(T (Red): Central   472 Mass Ave, 617-864-3278   Dir: exit T onto Mass Ave, walk SE towards MIT)* This small, Middle Eastern restaurant in the heart of Central Square is actually a front for Cambridge's premier alternative music venue.

Avalon (Live Music, Dancing) *(T (Green): Kenmore   15 Lansdowne St, 617-262-2424   Dir: exit T, walk away from city (W) on Brookline Ave, L on Lansdowne)* This flashy club is one of the city's largest and best techno venues (though music genres vary by night). Go on one of the "Avaland" club nights to dance to beats spun by some of the world's best DJs, or go early for a live show. Avalon also features Boston's largest and longest running gay night, every Sunday—it's great for techno lovers, people watchers, and guys who want their drinks bought for them. While Avalon is by no means cheap (between the cover charge, coat check price, and outlandish drink prices), it is one of Boston's best clubs and should be experienced. Nearly all of Avalon's live shows and club nights are 18 and over.

Bill's Bar & Lounge *(T (Green): Kenmore   5 Lansdowne St, 617-421-9678   Dir: exit T, walk away from city (W) on Brookline Ave, L on Lansdowne)* Sunday nights are 18+ at this no frills, mostly student bar offering "fun without pretense." Dance to the bar's diverse music selection (hip-hop/reggae/salsa/top 40) or watch a game on the large-screen TVs that line the bar. Live bands play every night; there's usually a $10 cover.

**Jake Ivory's Piano Bar *(T (Green): Kenmore   9 Lansdowne St, 617-247-1222   Dir: exit T, walk away from city on Brookline Ave (W), L on Lansdowne)* This live, piano-fueled, albeit bare-boned nightclub gets rowdy! Dueling pianists play ANY song requested (they boast knowledge of 100,000 songs). Jake Ivory's is 19+ <u>Thursday night only</u>, proving that you don't have to be wasted to enjoy dancing, good people, and great music (though of course it helps). $10 under 21, $4 otherwise; open Th-Sa only.

Who's On First? *(T (Green): Kenmore   19 Yawkey Way, 617-247-3353   Dir: exit T, walk away from city (W), L on Yawkey)* A popular sports bar and dance club, Who's on First is a haven to a diverse crowd of families and game-goers by day, students and young professionals by night. Packed on game days, the bar compensates for its minimal elbow room and blasting music with $1 test tube shots and $2 drafts. 18+ Th-Sa nights.

Jillian's *(T (Green): Kenmore   145 Ibswich St, 617-369-9400
Dir: exit T, walk away from city (W) on Brookline Ave, L on Lansdowne
St, L on Ibswich)* This gigantic, three story sports bar and pool hall
lives up to its "eat, drink, play" axiom. It houses a Vegas-style lounge
with ping pong tables, large-screen TVs, pool tables, an arcade, and a
bowling alley. With so many things to do, a date couldn't possibly go
awry.

Jamaica Plain

The Milky Way *(T (Orange): Jackson Square   403 Centre St, 617-
524-3740   Dir: exit T, walk S on Alpert, R on Centre .3 mi, or avoid
the T and take the #39 bus)* Concerts, candlepin bowling, and pool
make the Milky Way a unique crossroads for all types of partiers. Rent
a lane for $25 per hour for up to six bowlers (includes shoes) instead
of paying by game. Lane reservations are accepted. Hours: 6pm-1am
daily; Under 21 admitted before 9pm.

Somerville

Jimmy Tingle's Off Broadway *(T (Red): Davis   255 Elm St, 617-
591-1616   Dir: exit T to Holland St, R on Holland, cross Davis Sq to
Elm)* This theatre has quite a range of performances; comedy
dominates, but music, poetry, and children's programs are also
popular. Check out *www.jtoffbroadway.com* for shows/times as well as
"dinner and a show" discounts at local restaurants.

Sacco's Bowl Haven *(T (Red): Davis   45 Day St, 617-776-0552
Dir: exit T to Holland St, R on Holland to Davis Sq, R on Day)*
Candlepin bowling, pool tables, and beer (if you have an ID). Though
slightly run down, Sacco's is the place for some good old-fashioned
fun. Games $2.50 before 5, $2.75 after, $1.50 shoe rental.

Somerville Theater *(T (Red): Davis   55 Davis Square, 617-625-
4088   Dir: exit T to College Ave, L on College to Davis Sq)* The historic
Somerville Theater, built in 1918, is home to performing arts as well
as to first-rate movies that have already been around the block
(shown here generally after 1 month of release). Cost: $4 weekday
matinees, $6.50 evenings and weekends. Check for shows and show-
times at *www.somervilletheatreonline.com*.

Dance Venues

Disclaimer: We've included the following list of places to dance just in case you wanted to loosen up the grips on your dollar bills for a night and shake off some stress.   While few of these venues are cheap, they are all very cool, popular night spots with dance floors. Enjoy.

An Tua Nua *(T (Green B/C/D): Kenmore Square   835 Beacon St., 617-262-2121   Dir: exit T, R on Beacon St)* A popular hangout for BU students and Sox fans who come for cheap beers and a friendly, flirty dance floor.

Aria *(T (Green): Boylston   246 Tremont St, 617-338-7080   Dir: exit T and walk with traffic (S) on Tremont)* Hip-hop, Latin, and techno liven up this swanky club. Pre-gaming is highly recommended, as the drinks run steep. Open Th-Sa, 10:30pm to 2 am. Dress to impress as the place sports a serious attitude.

Atlas *(T (Green): Kenmore   145 Ipswich St, 617-437-0300   Dir: exit T onto Comm Ave, L on Brookline Ave, L on Lansdowne St, L on Ipswich)* A young crowd frequents this casually hip scene. The club is located under Jillian's and is open Th-Sa for dinner, drinks, and dancing. Cover charges may be negotiated with cleavage.

**Avalon *(T (Green): Kenmore   15 Lansdowne St, 617-262-2424 Dir: exit T, walk away from city (W) on Brookline Ave, L on Lansdowne)* This is one of the city's largest clubs and best concert venues. Music genres vary by night but nearly all of Avalon's live shows and club nights are 18 and over. Dress to impress but prepare to sweat on the large but crowded dance floor. Head to the balcony for a reprieve from the heat and for people watching.

Axis *(T (Green): Kenmore   15 Lansdowne St, 617-262-2437   Dir: exit T onto Comm Ave, L on Brookline Ave, L on Lansdowne St)* Two floors offer a funky, industrial feel. Axis is 19 and older weeknights (including

Fridays), which draws a large college crowd. A great flirting spot for any sexual preference: Mondays offer a drag show; Fridays are a hit with techno downstairs and 80s upstairs; Sunday is amateur strip night beginning at 11pm.

The Big Easy *(T (Green): Boylston   1 Boylston Place, 617-351-7000 Dir: exit T, R on Boylston)* A chill spot for drinks and dancing. Live bands and DJs downstairs; bar upstairs.

Dad's Beantown Diner *(T (Green): Hynes   911 Boylston St, 617-296-3237   Dir: exit T S (L) on Mass Ave, L on Boylston)* From the outside, Dad's looks like an average diner, but don't be discouraged; the place is a major meat market. Venture in for $3 margaritas and daiquiris, dancing, flirting, and cute waitresses.

The Hong Kong *(T (Blue/ Orange): State   65 Chatham St, 617-227-2226   Dir: exit T E on State St, L on Chatham)* The two floors of this club divide the crowd: Downstairs runs on the preppier, younger side; upstairs, a multiethnic crowd enjoys an urban dance scene. Both levels feature generally drunken masses. Have your group chip in on a Scorpion Bowl to get a bang for your buck (and we mean bang — these drinks are strong!).

Johnny D's *(T (Red): Davis   17 Holland St, 617-776-2004   Dir: exit T, cross Davis Sq)* Live music and low cover charges (usually under $10) make this unpretentious bar a blast any night of the week. We particularly recommend Sundays: Start with the Blues Jam (4:30-8:30pm) and stick around for Salsa (9pm-12am). Take advantage of FREE lessons as the band warms up.

The Kells *(T (Green B): Harvard   161 Brighton Ave, 617-782-9082 Dir: exit T N on Harvard Ave, R on Brighton Ave)* This college bar balances any good party night with a room for dancing and a room for drinking. The hip-hop dance floor gets you moving, while a quieter spot with plush booths and fancy drink menus gives your feet a rest.

Mojitos *(T (Red/ Green): Park   48 Winter St, 617-988-8123   Dir: exit T on Winter St)* A largely international crowd dances to Salsa and Merengue; FREE dance lessons for novices Th-Sa nights.

**The Roxy *(T (Green): Boylston   279 Tremont St, 617-338-7699 Dir: exit T and walk with traffic (S) on Tremont St)* While this huge, converted 1920s ballroom will satisfy your craving for a hardcore club—great music plays to a large, swanky crowd—it will also drain your bank account. Be prepared to take a hit before you even start buying your $10 drinks with the $15-20 cover charge. As Boston's premier club, they can get away with it. Thursdays are 18+, while Fridays and Saturdays attract an older, better dressed clientele.

Ryles *(T (Red): Central   212 Hampshire St, 617-876-9330 Dir: exit T N on Prospect St, L on Hampshire St)* Live jazz, a small dance floor, and small café tables make the first floor perfect for dancers and those who prefer to chill and nurse a drink. Venture upstairs on Thursdays for salsa dancing and Saturdays for swing dancing (lessons available for early birds).

Sissy K's *(T (Blue/ Orange): State   4 Commercial St, 617-248-6511 Dir: exit T and walk E (against traffic) on State St, L on Commercial St)* Two levels of dancing, one with live music. Cheap drinks and a good-sized crowd make this Faneuil Hall destination ideal for a flirtatious outing any night of the week.

Tonic *(T (Green B): Harvard   1316 Commonwealth Ave 617-566-6699   Dir: exit T W on Comm Ave away from city)* Seventy-foot ceilings and top shelf alcohol aren't the only steep things you'll find at Tonic. Still, the bar is high on class and packs a well-dressed, young crowd. Better than average bar food and six well-positioned flat-screen TVs make it ideal for watching sports but if you're not into that, get your dance on downstairs.

Trinity (T (Blue/ Orange): State   61 Chatham St, 617-367-6172 *Dir: exit T, walk against traffic (E) on State St, L on Chatham)* A good compromise for groups with dancers and the reluctant guys who end up holding the dancers' purses. This multi-floor, low-key Irish Pub offers Guinness, darts, live music, and close quarters dancing in the basement.

Who's on First *(T (Green): Kenmore   19 Yawkey Way, 617-247-3353   Dir: exit T onto Comm Ave, L on Brookline Ave, L on Yawkey Way)* The crowd and dress varies at this perpetually busy sportsbar and nightclub from ultra chill to super primped but everyone ends up drunk and dancing. Thursdays, the 18 and older crowd takes advantage of low covers (FREE for gals before 10:30pm), $1 shots, and $2 drafts.

Gay & Lesbian Nightlife

Axis *(T (Green B/C/D): Kenmore   15 Lansdowne St, 617-262-2437
Dir: exit T onto Comm Ave, L on Brookline Ave, L on Lansdowne St)*
Mondays from 10pm-2am, this young (19+) crowd enjoys lively music
and a drag show; $7 cover charge.

Avalon (Sunday Nights), see page 148

Chaps *(T (Green): Boylston   100 Warrenton St, 617-695-9500   Dir:
exit T S (with traffic) on Tremont St, R on Stuart St, L on Warrenton)*
Wednesday from 10pm-2am, and Sunday from 5pm-2am, join Chaps'
"Go-Go Boys" as they dance to tribal beats and Latin house. This is the
place to find Boston's Latino men. $6-8 cover; FREE before 7 pm.

Club Café *(T (Green): Arlington   209 Columbus Ave, 617-536-0966
Dir: exit T S (L) onto Arlington St, R on Columbus)* This bistro, bar,
and lounge features some cheap eats, designer martinis, and one of
Boston's most popular gay (mostly) and lesbian hot spots; no cover.

Dyke Night at Toast *(T (Red): Harvard   70 Union Sq, 617-623-9211
Dir: exit T, take #86 bus to Union Sq)* Every Friday night is ladies'
night at this Somerville club. From 5:30-9 pm, the evening warms up
with Dykotomy, an after-work party. From 9pm to 2am, retro and 80s
music sets the tone for Dyke Night's lively dance floor; $5 cover.

Embassy *(T (Green): Kenmore   36 Lansdowne St, 617-536-2100
Dir: exit T onto Comm Ave, L on Brookline Ave, L on Lansdowne)* Live
"The Glamorous Life" every Thursday at this hip-hop and Top 40s club.
This place is trendy with an attitude, so dress to impress; $10 cover.

Machine *(T (Green): Kenmore   1256 Boylston St, 617-266-2986   Dir:
exit T onto Comm Ave, L on Brookline St, L Yawkey Way, L Boylston
St)* A popular, mostly male club offering techno, dancing, billiards,
several bars, and attractive bartenders. Open Th- Su; $5 cover charge.

Milky Way Lounge *(T (#39 Bus): Centre Street   401 Centre St, 617-524-3740)* Sunday nights are for ladies only and feature live entertainment, which varies from drag bingo to jazz bands; $6 cover.

The Modern *(T (Green B/C/D): Kenmore   36 Lansdowne St, 617-536-2100   Dir: exit T onto Comm Ave, L on Brookline Ave, L on Lansdown)* Thursday nights at The Modern—the more low-key space below Embassy—well-manicured and dressed girls 19+ party from 10pm–2am. Cover is $10; $5 with a printed coupon from www.lesbiannightlife.com.

Midway Café *(T (Orange): Green St   3496 Washington St, 617 524-9038   Dir: exit T and walk towards Brookside Ave, R on Washington St)* A great dive bar for cheap drinks and flirting, with Thursdays being particularly lively for ladies. "Women's Dance Night" features classic rock, hip-hop, and outbursts of "Queeraoke." Bring your costume and wig, or borrow one from the club's collection of props. Open 9pm-2am; no cover charge.

Paradise *(T (Green B/C/D): Hynes   180 Massachusetts Ave, 617-494-0700   Dir: exit T S on Mass Ave)* Every night until 2am, this two-level bar offers live male dancers upstairs and a dance club downstairs. Expect a slightly older crowd, attractive guys, and a sketchy but fun atmosphere; no cover charge.

Pink @ Club ID *(T (Green B/C/D): Kenmore   13 Lansdowne St   Dir: exit T onto Comm Ave, L on Brookline Ave, L on Lansdowne)* Every Saturday night is lesbian night. You'll sometimes find $4 drink specials; you'll always find a packed crowd and a $10 cover.

Ramrod *(T (Green): Kenmore Square   1254 Boylston St, 617-266-2986   Dir: exit T onto Comm Ave, L on Brookline Ave, L on Yawkey Way, L on Boylston St)* Open all week from noon to 2am, Ramrod attracts mostly men. This is not the spot for a low-key night. On weekends, one room is devoted exclusively to guests wearing leather and those going shirtless...or both; $5 cover.

Felt *(T (Green): Boylston   533 Washington St, 4th Floor   Dir: exit T, L (SE) on Boylston St, L on Washington)* Hip-hop and Top 40s music plays for ladies only on Thursday nights, 9pm-2am. This pool hall/lounge tries to be a swanky hotspot, but most people show up in jeans and casual ware; $5 cover charge.

Cheap Entertainment

Allston/Brighton

**Charles River Canoe & Kayak Center *(T (Red): Harvard Soldier's Field Rd, 617-965-5110   Follow JFK Street toward the river, cross river and immediately follow bike path to right. Walk one mile, pass under the Eliot Bridge. Green-roofed kiosk is 200 yards past the bridge)* Beat the sticky city heat and rent a canoe (for $14-18/hour) so you can race your friends down the Charles. Note: You have to pass a written test in order to go, so make sure to pick up a boating safety sheet and brush up on it first. Opens in early May; call for up-to-date times and hours.

Harper's Ferry *(T (Green B): Harvard Ave   156 Brighton Ave, 617-254-9743   Dir: exit T N on Harvard Ave, L on Brighton Ave)* Formerly a blues club, this live music venue has been around since 1974 and features both local and national headliners. Low covers, cheap beer, and some of the best live music in Boston continue to pack this Allston classic with patrons.

The Kells *(T (Green B): Harvard Ave   161 Brighton Ave, 617-782-9082   Dir: exit T N on Harvard Ave, L on Brighton Ave)* Show off your vocal talents at the bar's acoustic open mic night every Tuesday, or get a team together and work your beer pong skills at their Monday night beirut tournament. Either way, The Kells is one of the few venues where the guys can slam beers at the bar while the girls get down and dirty on the dance floor.

Back Bay

Boston Institute of Contemporary Art *(T (Green B/C/D): Hynes 955 Boylston St, 617-266-5152   Dir: exit T to Mass Ave, L on Mass Ave, L on Boylston)* The ICA in Boston proudly houses popular and innovative rotating exhibits by contemporary artists. With a history dating back to 1936, this museum has received well-deserved national recognition for its displays but not for the space it houses them in. Price: $7 for adults, $5 for students. FREE for members and children under 12 at all times, and for anyone Thursdays after 5pm. Hours: T, W, F 12-5pm; Th 12-9pm; Sa-Su 11am-5pm.

Brookline

Coolidge Corner Theatre *(T (Green C): Coolidge Corner   290 Harvard St, 617-734-2500   Dir: exit T and walk N on Harvard)* This is not your average movie theatre; this Art Deco cinema specializes in independent and international films, documentaries, revivals of old classics, as well as first-run movies and the occasional live speaker. Prices: Adults $9, Under 12 and over 60 $6; Matinees $7. Note: Event prices vary.

Cambridge

Busch-Reisinger Museum *(T (Red): Harvard   Located inside the Fogg; Open M-Sa 10am-5pm, Sun 1-5pm)* Houses the art of Central and Northern Europe with a heavy emphasis on German works. The collection spans from medieval to modern works, including expressionist and abstract paintings. Tours included in admission price of Fogg Museum and take place M-F at 1pm when Harvard University is in session.

Cambridge Historical Society Tours *(T (Red): Harvard   159 Brattle St, 617-547-4252 Dir: exit T S onto JFK St, R on Brattle, R again to stay on Brattle, walk 1/2 mi)* Three hour walking tours of historic, mansion-lined Brattle St and other parts of Cambridge for $5 from April to mid-October, T and Th 2-5pm.

Charles Riverboat Tours *(T (Green): Lechmere, or take 69 bus from Harvard Sq   100 Cambridgeside Place, 617-621-3001 Tours leave from Dock outside Cambridgeside Galleria)* Take a 60 minute cruise along the Charles River for $10 and learn about its bridges, the Esplanade, Beacon Hill, and the John Hancock Tower. In June, July, and August tours run daily every 75 minutes between 10am and 4:15pm. April, May, and September tours only run

on weekends. **Sunset Cruises** are also available for $12/person.
Cocktails may be purchased during the 75 minute aquatic adventure,
which departs at 5:30pm and 7pm.

Fogg Art Museum *(T (Red): Harvard   32 Quincy St, 617-495-9400
Dir: exit T E on Mass Ave, L on Quincy St   Hours: M-Sa 10am-5pm,
Su 1-5pm)* The Fogg maintains a stunning and well-rounded collection
of work, including one of the country's most impressive collections of
Impressionist and post-Impressionist works. The art spans from the
Middle Ages to the present day and includes well-knowns like Degas
and Picasso, as well as exhibitions in printmaking and photography.
The museum's beautiful architecture features a large indoor courtyard.
Cost: $7.50 earns admission to the Fogg as well as the **Busch-
Reisinger** and **Sackler Museums**; $6 for student ID holders and
those over 65. FREE for Harvard students and for the general public
Saturdays until noon. General tours every day at 11am:
www.artmuseums.harvard.edu/fogg/.

Harvard Museum of Natural History *(T (Red): Harvard   24 Oxford
St, 617-495-3045   Dir: exit T E onto Mass Ave, L on Quincy St, L on
Kirkland St, R on Oxford   Hours: 9am-5pm daily)* The Museum of
Natural History is not just one museum but a collection of many—
containing the Botanical Museum, Museum of Comparative Zoology,
Mineralogical and Geological Museums, and the Peabody Museum of
Archaeology and Ethnology. $7.50 general admission, $6 for students
and those over 65, FREE for Harvard ID holders and everyone on W 3-
5pm and Su 9am-12pm. *www.hmnh.harvard.edu*

Longfellow House Historical Site *(T (Red): Harvard   105 Brattle
St, 617-876-4491   Dir: exit T S onto FK, R on Brattle St, walk 1 mile)*
The former home of famed poet Henry Wadsworth Longfellow is a
beautiful architectural and National Park Service site decorated with
original pieces from the 18th and 19th centuries. It is only open to the
public June-Sept (sometimes through October; call in advance) W-Su
10am-4:30pm. Admission is by guided tour only for $3 at 10:30am,
11:30am, 1pm, 2pm, 3pm, and 4pm. Year-round, you can visit by
booking a group tour in advance (12 or more people).

Sackler Museum *(T (Red): Harvard   485 Broadway, 617-495-9400
Dir: exit T E onto Mass Ave, L on Quincy St, follow to Broadway
Hours: M-Sa 10am-5pm, Sun 1-5pm)* Ancient, classical pre-
Colombian, Islamic, Indian, and Asian art collections with an emphasis

on anthropological artifacts. Highlights include a collection of ancient weapons, Buddhist sculptures, and calligraphy.

Downtown

Loew's Theaters (Boston Common) *(T (Green): Boylston   175 Tremont St, 800-326-3264   Dir: exit T and walk against traffic (N) on Tremont)* This popular movie theater's convenient location and multiple theaters make it a rainy day no-brainer. If the weather's nice, walk through the Boston Common during your post-movie discussion. $9.75 adults; $6.50 children and seniors.

Fenway

Boston Conservatory *(T (Green D): Fenway   8 Fenway, 617-912-9222   Dir: exit T to Mass Ave, L onto Mass Ave, R on Boylston St, L on Charlesgate East)* This accredited institute for music, dance, and theatre is an inexpensive alternative to a Symphony Hall performance. Conservatory students put on over 200 performances a year. The venues vary (from Symphony Hall to St. Cecilia's Church), as do ticket prices, but the performances are consistently ovation inducing.

Fenway Park Tours *(T (Green D): Fenway   4 Yawkey Way, 617-236-6666   Dir: exit T, walk away from city (W) on Brookline, L on Yawkey)* Whether you're a Sox fan or not, this tour provides a cheap ($12) backstage look at the beloved ballpark's press box, broadcast booth, hall of fame, dugout, and field. Tours leave from the Souvenir Store across Yawkey Way hourly, seven days a week (9am-4pm), or 3 hours before game time.

**Isabella Stewart Gardner Museum *(T (Green E): Longwood 280 Fenway, 617-566-1401   Dir: exit T NW on Longwood Ave past MassArt, R on Palace Rd, R on Louis Prang St   Hours: 11-5)* Three floors of galleries surround a beautiful garden courtyard. View one of the city's finest collections of art housed in a three-story house that surrounds a beautiful garden courtyard and remains virtually unchanged since Isabella Stewart Gardner's death in 1924. Admission is cheap ($5 with a college I.D.; $10 for adults) and the collections of paintings, sculpture, tapestries, and furniture are stunning.

Jamaica Plain

Franklin Park Zoo *(T (Orange): Forest Hills 1 Franklin Park Rd, 617-541-LION Dir: Take #16 bus from T station to Franklin Park Zoo stop)* Giraffes, zebras, gorillas, lions, leopards, kangaroos, and hippos, as well as a petting zoo. From June 11 to Sept 15, visitors may encounter 1,000 species of butterflies in flight in a special exhibit within the 72-acre Franklin Park Zoo. Admission: $9.50 adults; $5 children 2-12, FREE under 2. Special: half-price admission the first Saturday of every month. Hours: Apr-Sept 10am-5pm M-F, 10am-6pm Sa-Su; Oct-Mar 10am-4pm daily. FREE Parking.

The Milky Way *(T (Orange): Jackson Square 403 Centre St, 617-524-3740 Dir: exit T, walk S on Alpert, R on Centre .3 mi, or avoid the T and take the #39 bus)* Concerts, candlepin bowling, and pool make the Milky Way a unique crossroads for all types of partiers. But no matter who's looking to have fun, they will all find that this JP favorite is high on energy, low on price. Rent a lane for $25 per hour for up to six bowlers (includes shoes) instead of paying by game. Lane reservations are accepted. Hours: 6pm-1am daily; Under 21 admitted before 9pm.

**The Samuel Adams Brewery *(T (Orange): Green St 30 Germania St, 617-368-5080 Dir: exit T, walk E on Green St (Glen Rd), L on Brookside Ave for 4 blocks, R on Germania)* You may not believe it, but this tour is FREE and lasts about an hour. The only thing asked of you is a $2 donation for local charities and those over 21 may sample the various Sam derivatives.

North End

**New England Aquarium Whale Watch Tours *(T (Blue): Aquarium 1 Central Wharf, 617-973-5200 Dir: Exit T, head E onto Long Wharf)* A serene alternative to an aquarium visit; for $32, take a relaxed 3-4 hour boat tour of the Boston Harbor and beyond while naturalists point out wildlife along the way. The whale watch may be quiet, wet, and slightly expensive, but spotting an 80 foot humpback whale is an experience that's worth the splurge. Check their website (www.neaq.org/visit/wwatch/hours.php) or call for the schedule. Whale sightings are guaranteed.

Paul Revere House *(T (Green/Orange): Haymarket   19 North Square, 617-523-1676   Dir: exit T, follow walkway to North End, R on Cross St, L on Hanover St, R on Prince St, R on Garden Court St Hours: Nov 1-Apr 14 9:30am-4:15pm (closed M Jan-Mar), Apr 15-Oct 31 9:30am-5:15pm)* Built in 1677, the Revere House is the last 17th century building still standing in Boston. Get a taste of the city's history in a tour of the home of one of Boston's most famous residents. The house/museum costs $3 for adults and $2.50 for students and seniors.

**Puopolo Park / Langone Park / Mirabella Pool
(T (Green/Orange): North Station   475 R. Commercial St, 617-635-4920 x2213 or x3446 www.cityofboston.gov/bcyf   Dir: exit T NE on Causeway St, cross Joe Tecce Way/99, road curves to become Commercial) Play a game of basketball, bocce ball, or baseball; lounge by the pool; or just stroll along the harbor at this scenic park with views of the Bunker Hill Bridge, Navy Yard, and USS Constitution. Cost for pool use: $10 for Boston residents; children under five are FREE.   Soak up some sun, smell the ocean, and watch the ships sail by in this urban oasis.   Pool hours: 11am-7pm, July 1st - Sept

South End

Rough & Tumble Theatre at the Calderwood Pavilion for the Arts (Boston Center for the Arts) *(T (Orange): Back Bay   527 Tremont St, 617-933-8600   Dir: exit station S on Dartmouth and turn L on Tremont)* This consortium of nonprofit theatre companies offers over 40 productions annually, ranging from comedy to drama to musicals. Matinees (2pm), and evening shows (8pm) generally range from $15-20.

State Street Area/Financial District

Boston By Foot *(617-367-2345   Dir: call or visit website to find out where to meet your guide www.bostonbyfoot.com)* Think you know Boston? Pick a region and take a 90-minute walking tour with an experienced guide and get the inside edge on both familiar and hidden attractions. Tours include: Beacon Hill, North End, Underground Boston, Literary Landmarks, and Victorian Back Bay. Tours cost $10.

Free Entertainment

Allston/Brighton

Boston Public Library: Honan-Allston Branch *((Car needed) 300 N Harvard St, 617-787-6313   Hours: M 12-8, Tu 10-6, W 12-8, Th 10-6, F-Sa 9-5)* This library has a huge book collection and more than 100 newspapers and magazines. Get a library card, grab one of the available multimedia stations and enjoy a CD, book on tape, video, or just curl up with a book...all for FREE!

Back Bay

Charles River Esplanade *(T (Green B): BU Central   Dir: exit T, cross Marsh Plaza and cross the bridge over Storrow Dr)* Enjoy the beauty of the Charles River FREE of charge. Run, walk, rollerblade, or bike on the tree-lined, paved paths. Chill out on the various docks, swing in the kiddie parks, or simply soak in some sun in front of the hatch shell (a riverside venue where the Boston Pops frequently play FREE summer shows).

City View *(T (Green B): Summit Ave)* Walk about .3 miles to the top of Summit Ave and enjoy a spectacular panoramic view of the Boston skyline. This grassy little vista serves as a perfect picnic spot during the day and a great romantic spot at night. Pack a blanket and a bottle of wine for a superb cheap date.

Copley Society of Art *(T (Green): Copley   158 Newbury St, 617-536-5049   Dir: exit T, R (E) on Boylston St, L on Dartmouth St, L on Newbury)* The Copley Society of Art displays rotating amateur and professional art exhibits from realist and abstract painters, photographers, sculptors, and printmakers. Hours: Tu-Sa 10:30am-5:30pm. FREE.

Kidder Smith Gallery *(T (Green): Copley   131 Newbury St, 617-424-6900   Dir: exit T, R (E) on Boylston St, L on Dartmouth, R on Newbury)* The Kidder Smith Gallery features experienced contemporary (i.e. modern), abstract, and representational artists and photographers. The art is housed in a beautiful space and samples of the collection can be found on its website: *http://kiddersmithgallery.com/site/*. Hours: M-Sa 11am-5:30pm. FREE.

Brookline

Armory Playground *(T (Green C): Hawes St   Dir: exit T, park is across st)* Hit aces on the tennis courts, homeruns on the softball fields, or build castles in the sandboxes. Armory Playground is a convenient place for pick-up games or to watch some of the local high school sporting events.

**Brookline Booksmith *(T (Green C): Coolidge Corner   279 Harvard St, 617-566-6660   Dir: exit T and head N on Harvard St)* Come listen to readings from new and seasoned authors or just to pick up the latest best-seller. This bookstore is one of the hottest places to showcase up-and-coming writers.

Chestnut Hill Reservoir *(T (Green C): Cleveland Circle   Dir: exit T and follow Beacon St to Reservoir)* "The Res" as it is known to locals is filled with those who come to jog or walk the quiet, scenic paths around the 125 acre reservoir.

The Children's Book Shop *(T (Green D): Brookline Village   237 Washington St, 617-734-7323   Dir: exit T, R on Station St, R on Washington St)* Explore old favorites like the *Velveteen Rabbit* or check out the newest adventures of Harry Potter. No matter how long you've been around, there's something for every age.

Cypress St. Playground *(T (Green D): Brookline Village   Dir: exit T, take L on Davis Ave and continue on across Cyprus St)* A large green space just outside the center of the city that is perfect for Frisbee, dog walking, and picnics.

Waldstein Playground *(T (Green C): Dean Road   Dir: exit T and walk S down Dean Rd)* Play on the jungle gym, shoot some hoops, hit around a tennis ball, watch a little league baseball game, get some sun, or bring your dog to meet and greet others—many locals come to frolic with their pets.

Cambridge

Fresh Pond Reservoir *(T (Red): Harvard   Dir: take the #72 or #74 bus down Huron Ave until it intersects Fresh Pond Parkway)* A couple of miles away from Harvard Square sits a beautiful pond with a 2.5 mile path around it—a haven for joggers, bikers, and dog-walkers. Road races occur here every Saturday year-round at 10am and begin by the lower parking lot.

Harvard University Historical Tours *(T (Red): Harvard   1350 Mass Ave, 617-495-1573 Dir: exit T, turn to face Mass Ave, R into Holyoke Center- a glassed-in corridor next to Au Bon Pain)* Take an informative and fun tour of the nation's oldest university for FREE. During school sessions, tours leave M-F 10am and 2pm, Sa at 2pm. Summer hours: M-Sa 10am, 11:15am, 2pm, 3:15pm. No signup is necessary, just show up in the Information Center at any tour time.

Harvard-Smithsonian Center for Astrophysics *(T (Red): Harvard   60 Garden St, 617-495-7461   Dir: exit T N onto Mass Ave towards Porter Sq, L on Garden--15 min walk)* Houses temporary exhibits on astrophysics and planetary sciences. During observatory nights (doors open at 7:30pm and the programs begin at 8pm on the third Th of each month) watch a film, hear a lecture, and observe stars from telescopes on the roof for FREE. *http://cfa-www.harvard.edu/*

JFK Park, Charles River *(T (Red): Harvard   Dir: exit T, L on JFK, follow .3 miles to JFK on your right)* The Charles River stretches for miles, but this particular riverside spot is the classic Harvard section you see in the movies where rowers pass beneath the Weeks Footbridge. A dirt path alongside the water and a cement one up by the road are perfect for jogging; a stretch of lawn between the river and road provides a spot to tan or throw a football in the spring and summer.

Mount Auburn Cemetery *(T (Red): Harvard   580 Mt Auburn St, 617-547-7105   Dir: from the Harvard Square Station take the #71 or #73 bus 2 mi down Mt Auburn St; the cemetery will be on your L)* It may sound morbid to go walking in a cemetery but the 175 acres of landscaped grounds and beautiful sculptures shouldn't be missed. The cemetery boasts a number of famous headstones from Isabella Stuart Gardener to Henry Wadsworth Longfellow and was the first landscaped burial ground in the U.S. Its design inspired many modern parks. FREE.

Semitic Museum *(T (Red): Harvard   6 Divinity Ave, 617-495-4631 Dir: exit T E onto Mass Ave, L on Quincy St, bear R onto Divinity Hours: M-F 10am-4pm, Su 1-4pm)* Exhibits of archaeological finds from the Near East including Ancient Israel, Iraq, Egypt, and Cyprus all for FREE.

List Visual Arts Center (MIT) *(T (Red): Kendall   20 Ames St, Building E15, 617-253-4680   Dir: exit T W on Main St, L on ames Hours: 12-6pm Tu-Th, Sa, and Su; Friday 12-8pm)* LVAC shows are of very modern art, including everything from video to Internet art. Exhibitions change three times per year and are FREE but a $5 donation is suggested.

Downtown

Boston Common and the Public Gardens
The 50 acre Boston Common has quite a history that dates back to 1634, making it the oldest public park in the U.S. Over the past three and a half centuries, the Common has been host to a multitude of events ranging from military encampments to public hangings to grazing cattle. Today, Boston's main green is the perfect place to picnic, walk, or read a book. Stretch out on a patch of grass, take shade under a tree, or take a tour of the many statues that dot the sprawling area. Inside the Common you'll find the **Frog Pond**, which in winter becomes a small ice-skating rink where you can rent skates and cruise to cheesy tunes. In summer, Shakespeare in the Park takes over the back corner of the Common, with FREE shows a few times a week.

Attached to the Common is the 25 acre **Public Gardens**, filled with flower gardens, manicured lawns, and winding paths. The Public Garden is the site of children's book *Make Way for Ducklings*, as well as the home of the famous park bench from Good Will Hunting. Take a ride in the man-powered **Swan Boats** and feel like a kid again (except for the inescapable fact that it's a very small pond). Grab an ice cream or lemonade, sit under a weeping willow by the water, and enjoy the beauty of your picturesque surroundings in the heart of downtown.

The Freedom Trail disappoints some tourists initially—it's pretty much a red line of paint drawn down the road—but as a Boston attraction it shouldn't be missed. Two and a half miles long, the trail connects 16 historic sites from the Boston Common just outside the Park St station to the ship "Old Ironsides," the USS Constitution. Follow the (red) brick road past the famous **Old Granary Burial Ground**, the graveyard where John Hancock lies, and check out the hundreds-of-years old headstones (perfect for grave-rubbings.) Also peek into **King's Chapel**, built in the 1750s but with a congregation that first met in the 1680s. Ninety-minute tours begin at the Visitor Center at 15 State St and leave at regular intervals in the spring, summer, and fall, weather permitting. Call 617-242-5642 or 617-242-5689 for schedule or group reservations.

Walking Tours of the Freedom Trail *(T (Orange): State St   15 State St, 617-242-5642   Dir: Exit T to State St, will see Visitors' Center)* If you think you know everything there is to know about Boston, you probably don't. Follow a good span of the notorious double-brick path and visit such Boston sights as the Common, Statehouse, King's Chapel, Faneuil Hall, and Old North Church. Tours are 3 miles long, last 90 minutes, cover some 16 sites, are guided by employees of the National Park Service, and are completely FREE. Call for daily schedule and reservations.

Haymarket *(T (Green): Haymarket   Dir: exit T S on Congress towards Faneuil Hall, L on Hanover St, R on Blackstone St)* While the most notable thing about Haymarket is the way it smells, this urban farmers' market shouldn't be missed. Shoppers pack the narrow isles of discounted fresh fruit, vegetables, meat, and seafood on Fridays and Saturdays from dawn until dusk turning the area into a noisy, bustling mess.

Tourist Information Center *(T (Green): Park   148 Tremont St Dir: exit T, turn R on adjacent Tremont St)* While most in-the-know Boston residents turn their noses up at the idea of visiting a Tourist Info Center, this one's worth going to. It holds a wealth of pamphlets detailing everything from Boston Harbor Island cruises (Thompson's

Island is a must-see) to listings of all the FREE events on the Boston Common.

Jamaica Plain

The Arnold Arboretum *(T (Orange): Forest Hills   125 Arborway, 617-524-1718   Dir: exit T, head W on N South St 1 block)* The 265-acre Arnold Arboretum is composed of a wide variety of exotic and domestic flora used for education, research, and aesthetic enjoyment. Learn about flowers, plants, and trees as you walk the grounds. Regardless of the time of year or the weather, there is always something to see and enjoy. Call ahead for times for FREE hour-long walking tours. The Arboretum is open sunrise to sunset and is completely FREE.

Jamaica Pond *(T (Green E): Health Street   Jamaicaway and Perkins St   Dir: exit T to R, walk S on S. Huntington, R on Centre St)* Stocked yearly with trout, salmon, pickerel, bass, hornpout, and perch, Jamaica Pond is a prime fishing spot during warmer months. Fresh, clear water, abundant wildlife, and footpaths surrounding Jamaica Pond create a beautiful backdrop for a morning, afternoon, or evening walk or run in the park.

North End

Old North Church *(T (Green/Orange): Haymarket   193 Salem St, 617-523-6676   Dir: exit T, follow walkway to North End, R on Cross St, L on Salem   Hours: 9am-5pm M-Sa, 12:30-5pm Su)* This gorgeous Georgian-style building built in 1723 is still an active Episcopal church and perfectly demonstrates Boston's unique conjunction of history and art. Take a FREE tour of the church where Paul Revere hung two lanterns to signal the beginning of the British invasion at Lexington.

**Puopolo Park / Langone Park / Mirabella Pool
(T (Green/Orange): North Station   475 R. Commercial St, 617-635-4920 x2213 or x3446 www.cityofboston.gov/bcyf   Dir: exit T NE on Causeway St, cross Joe Tecce Way/99, road curves to become Commercial) Play a game of basketball, bocce ball, or baseball; lounge by the pool; or just stroll along the harbor at this scenic park with

views of the Bunker Hill Bridge, Navy Yard, and USS Constitution. Cost for pool use: $10 for Boston residents; children under five are FREE.   Soak up some sun, smell the ocean, and watch the ships sail by in this urban oasis.   Pool hours: 11am-7pm, July 1st - Sept

The Wine Bottega *(T (Green/Orange): Haymarket   341 Hanover St, 617-227-6607   Dir: exit T, follow walkway to North End, R on Cross St, L on Hanover)* This exceptional wine store—reminiscent of an aristocrat's wine cellar—lists their selections by flavor, meal, and price. Attend a FREE wine tasting Fridays 5-8pm, or call in your order for FREE local delivery to your door.

Somerville

Mystic River Reservation *(2-2149 Mystic Valley Pkwy, Somerville, 617-727-5380   Dir: Commuter rail to W. Medford or Wedgemere stations for access to Mystic Lakes; Orange line to Wellington Station for access to Mystic River; Bus lines to Medford Square for access to bike path)* The publicly-owned banks of the Mystic River—flowing through Medford, Somerville, and Everett—are a great place to run, bike, picnic or stroll.   There are a number of trails, athletic fields, and tennis courts scattered throughout the area as well as spots that offer sailing, swimming, and boating.
http://www.mass.gov/dcr/parks/metroboston/mystic.htm

Prospect Hill Park *(T (Red): Harvard   Dir: exit T, take 86 bus to Union Sq, E on Somerville Ave, L on Stone Ave, R on Prospect Hill Pkwy)* Just up the street from Union Square lies Prospect Hill Park, a small park containing the Prospect Hill Tower, an old Revolutionary War era fort and the site of the raising of the first American Flag. While you can't enter the fort, you can walk on its ramparts and get a great skyline view of Boston.

Somerville Museum *(T (Red): Davis   1 Westwood Rd, 617-666-9810 Dir: exit T, #88 bus toward Lechmere, exit at Benton Rd, R on Benton, L on Westwood   Hours: 2-7pm Th, 2-5pm F, and 12-5pm Sa)* Apart from exhibitions in the visual arts, the space hosts historical exhibitions, musical events, and talks by scholars, activists, and artists.   FREE but a donation is suggested.

Tufts Campus and Tour *(T (Red): Davis   518 Bendetson Hall, Tufts University 617-627-3170   Dir: exit T to College Ave, take the #94 or #96 bus or walk 15 min along College Ave to campus)* Take a stroll around the Tufts campus on your own or go on a student-led tour, offered daily year-round (times change depending on the season, so check their website beforehand: http://admissions.tufts.edu/visit.htm#Campus%20Tours)

Tufts University Gallery *(T (Red): Davis   Aidekman Arts Center, Talbot Ave, 617-627-3518   Dir: exit T to College Ave, take the #94 or #96 bus or walk 15 min along College Ave to the Tufts campus, L on Talbot)* FREE and open to the public, the Gallery contains contemporary art, a sculpture court, video and film screenings, and everything in between. MFA students showcase their thesis work here as well. Open T-Su, 11am–5pm and Th until 8pm. http://www.tufts.edu/as/gallery/

Vinal Avenue Community Growing Center *(T (Red): Harvard, 22 Vinal Ave, 617-666-2969   Dir: exit T, take 86 bus to Union Sq, follow Somerville Ave N to Bow St, continue on Bow, slight L on Summer St, R on Vinal)* Meant to be an oasis within the city, the Growing Center contains an arboretum (lots of plants), nursery (lot of baby trees), and an amphitheater for performances. www.thegrowingcenter.org

South End

Bromfield Gallery *(T (Orange): Back Bay   450 Harrison Ave, 617-451-3605   Dir: exit T S (L) on Dartmouth St, L on Harrison)* Boston's oldest artist-run gallery, Bromfield is host to paintings, drawings, photographs, prints, digital media, ceramics and sculptures. Hours: W-Sa 12-5pm. FREE.

Kingston Gallery *(T (Orange): Back Bay   450 Harrison Ave, 617-423-4113   Dir: exit T S (L) on Dartmouth St, L on Harrison)* The Bromfield Gallery's neighbor, an artist-run gallery featuring interesting and eclectic pieces by emerging Boston artists. The gallery also sponsors *New Art*, an annual national juried exhibition. Hours: Tu-Sa 12-5pm. FREE

South End Open Market *(T (Orange): Back Bay   540 Harrison Ave Dir: exit T S on Dartmouth St until it turns into W Dedham, L on*

Harrison) Starting late spring and continuing every Sunday through Nov. 28th from 10am-4pm, this open-air farmers' market draws vendors selling everything from produce to art to handbags.

Wally's Café *(T (Orange): Mass Ave   427 Mass Ave, 617-424-1408 Dir: exit T S on Mass Ave)* Visit this consistently-packed bar and club founded in 1947 that has live music (Latin, swing, jazz, etc.) nearly every night. The bands may not be well known, but shows are always a no-cover-charge blast!

Where to Buy Cheap Clothes

Allston/Brighton

Brighton Congregational Thrift Shop *(T (Green B): Washington St 404 Washington St, 617-254-4046   Dir: exit T N on Washington, L at base of Hill onto Washington)* This thrift shop is located in the Brighton Congregational Church and is open on Wednesdays and Saturdays from 10am-2pm.

Hadassah Bargain Spot *(T (Green B): Packard's Corner   1123 Commonwealth Ave, 617-254-8300 Hours: Su-M 10-6, T-TH 10-5, F 10-3)* Secondhand clothes, books, furniture, etc. all on the cheap.

**Urban Renewals *(T (Green B): Harvard Ave   122 Brighton Ave, 617-783-8387   Dir: exit T N on Harvard, R on Brighton   Hours: M-Sa 10-6)* Many good deals may be found at this cramped little thrift store.

Back Bay

Second Time Around *(T (Green B/C/D): Hynes   252 Newbury St, 617- 266-1113   Dir: exit T to Newbury St, R on Newbury)* If you're looking to buy or sell designer clothing, Second Time Around is the place for you. This high-end consignment shop carries the hottest brand names in women's fashion for a huge price reduction. After all, no one else will know it wasn't brand new. A second store at 176 Newbury Street carries brand names for both men and women. Hours: M-F 11am-7pm, Sa 10am-7pm, Su 12-6pm.

Brookline

Cafi Society *(T (Green D): Brookline Village   131 Cypress St, 617-738-7186   Dir: head S from T station, take R on Washington St and L on Cypress)* With vintage jeans, shirts, dresses, and accessories, Cafi Society keeps the fashions of old in style today.

Mint Julep *(T (Green C): Coolidge Corner   1302 Beacon St, 617-232-3600)* Trendy, young clothing options for nightlife or everyday wear at prices sure to please your pocketbooks.

Cambridge

Burlington Coat Factory *(T (Red): Porter   37 White St, 617-354-7314   Dir: exit T and cross Mass Ave into Porter Square shopping center; located below the Shaw's supermarket)*

Garment District *(T (Red): Kendall   200 Broadway St, 617-876-9795   Dir: exit T onto Main St, cut through the Marriott hotel or walk around it to get onto Broadway, L on Broadway, follow for 4 blocks)* On the pricey side for used clothes but visiting is an adventure in and of itself. Go during Halloween for their amazing costumes and ridiculous displays.

H&M *(Cambridgeside Galleria) (T (Green): Lechmere   100 Cambridgeside Place OR from Harvard, take #69 Bus to Lechmere Dir: from Lechmere, follow Land Blvd into Galleria)* THE place to go for cheap, trendy clothing for men and women.

Old Navy *(Cambridgeside Galleria) (T (Green): Lechmere OR from Harvard, take #69 Bus to Lechmere   100 Cambridgeside Place, 617-577-0070   Dir: from Lechmere, follow Land Blvd into Galleria)*

Oona's *(T (Red): Harvard   1210 Mass Ave, 617-491-2654   Dir: exit T onto Mass Ave, walk 3/4 mi SE towards Central Sq)* Fun, funky used clothing and a great place to find a Halloween costume.

Planet Aid *(T (Red): Harvard   30 JFK St, 617-354-6413   Dir: exit T onto JFK St)* Enjoy guilt-free shopping at this non-profit, second-hand clothing emporium that donates its profits to charity.

Tello's *(T (Red): Central   596 Mass Ave, 617-876-9704   Dir: exit T onto Mass Ave)* Ghetto-fabulous clothing, including some great clubbing wear, at prices that make it fun to play around.

TJ Maxx *(T (Red): Alewife   198 Alewife Brook Pkwy, 617-492-8500 Dir: follow Alewife Brook Pkwy, cross bridge to Fresh Pond Shopping Center)*

Downtown Crossing/ South Station Area

DSW Shoe Warehouse *(T (Green): Park St   385 Washington St, 617-556-0052   Dir: exit T, cross Tremont St, walk down Winter St, L on Washington)* This palace of shoes is a woman's fantasy come true...rows upon rows of brand name high heels at huge discounts. Men's shoes are available too. Hours: M-Sa 10am-8pm, Su: 11am-6pm.

Filene's Basement (T (Green): Park   426 Washington St, Dir: exit T, cross Tremont St, walk down Winter St, L on Washington) A bastion of deals on the latest clothing styles that's also a Boston landmark. The store gets crowded weekends and around holidays but that's because it's worth the wait for the savvy shopper.

H&M *(T (Green): Park St   350 Washington St, 617-482-7081   Dir: exit T, cross Tremont St, walk down Winter St, L on Washington)* A chain department store selling discount clothing that, while not of the greatest quality, still exhibits the latest fashion trends. Hours: M-Sa 10am-8pm, Su 11am-7pm.

Marshalls *(T (Green): Park St   350 Washington St, 617-338-6205 Dir: exit T, cross Tremont St, walk down Winter St, L on Washington*) A well-known, discount department store selling basic clothing and great fashion finds for the tenacious bargain hunter. Hours: M-Sa 9am-7:30pm, Su 11am-6pm.

Tello's *(T (Green): Park St   449 Washington St, 617-482-0058   Dir: exit T, cross Tremont St, walk down Winter St, R on Washington)* A Massachusetts-based retailer featuring stylish clothes and shoes for men and women at reasonable prices. Hours: M-Sa 9am-7:30pm, Su 11am-6pm.

TJ Maxx *(T (Green): Park St   350 Washington St, 617-695-2424 Dir: exit T, cross Tremont St, walk down Winter St, L on Washington)* A well-known, discount department store selling everything from jewelry to kitchenware. Hours: M-Sa 9am-7:30pm, Su 11am-6pm.

Somerville

AJ Wright *(Accessible only by car   176 Somerville Ave, 617-623-5599)* Discount women's and men's clothing.

Black & Blues *(T (Red): Davis   89 Holland, 617-628-0046   Dir: exit T to Holland St, L on Holland)* Quality brands at affordable prices.

Dots *(Accessible only by car   Twin City Plaza, 22 McGrath Highway, 617-628-6277)* Trendy and fun women's fashions for less.

Good Will *(T (Red): Davis   230 Elm St, 617-628-3618   Dir: exit T to Holland St, R on Holland, cross Davis Sq to Elm)* Goodwill sells donated clothing to raise money for the less fortunate. What better way to justify a shopping spree!

Target *(Accessible only by car   180 Somerville Ave, 617-776-4036)* Think upscale Wal-Mart.

DISCOUNT JEWELRY

Freedman Jewelers *(T (Green): Park St   333 Washington St, Suite 408, 617-227-4294   Dir: exit T N on Tremont St, R on Bromfield St, L on Washington St   Hours: M-F 9:30-5:30, Th 9:30-7, Sa 9-4)* For 61 years, the family-owned and run Freedman Jewelers has been offering discounted, high quality jewelry in the heart of downtown Boston. Since the owners save money by manufacturing many pieces themselves, Freedman's can pass along savings of up to 50% to their customers. This service also affords customers the opportunity to have Freedman's customize pieces at significant discounts. All jewelry comes with a money back guarantee if you're not completely satisfied. This bastion of exceptional customer service was recognized as Boston's "Best Jeweler" by WHDH Channel 7 News and we easily concur. www.freedmandiamonds.com

Where to Buy Cheap Furniture

Generally speaking, the three best places to find cheap furniture around Boston are along Rt 9, which becomes Huntington Avenue, on Harvard Avenue in Brighton/Allston, and at the IKEA in Stoughton, MA (781-344-IKEA)—about 30 minutes from Boston.   We've listed other places below.

However, you can find everything super cheap, albeit in varying degrees of used, on www.Craigslist.org. Since so many people are constantly moving in and out of apartments and dorms in Boston, amazing deals may be found by those in a rush to move out on Craigslist.org.

Allston/Brighton

BostonWood *(T (Green B): Packard's Corner   1117 Commonwealth Ave, 617-783-0274   Dir: exit T W on Comm Ave   Hours: M-F 10-7, Sa 10-6, Su 12-5)* A great place to find discounted quality furniture.

CORT Clearance Center *((no T nearby) 155 N Beacon St, 617-254-5455   Hours: M-F 9-6, Sa 10-5)* CORT rents furniture out, which is often a nice alternative to buying if you know your stay is temporary, and houses a clearance center for its second-hand merchandise. Here you can find great deals on used furniture and living room sets.

Model Hardware *(T Green B): Harvard Ave   22 Harvard Ave, 617-782-5131   Dir: exit T N on Harvard   Hours: M-F 7:30-6, Sa 8-5, Su 11-5)* Don't let the name fool you, this hardware store is stocked mostly with cheap furniture, lights, fixtures, and anything else one would need for their first apartment.

Back Bay

Cort Furniture Rental *(T (Green): Boylston   98 Boylston St, 617-542-8383   Dir: exit T, R (W) on Boylston)* Great deals on used furniture.

Economy True Value Hardware *(T (Green B/C/D): Hynes   219 Mass Ave,   617-536-4280   Dir: exit T to Mass Ave, R on Mass Ave, walk 4 blocks)* Half hardware store/half furniture store, Economy is a good place to go for chairs, end tables, lamps, blinds, curtains, and other miscellaneous decorating items.

Montage *(T (Green): Arlington   75 Arlington St, 617-451-9400   Dir: exit T to Boylston St, R (W) on Boylston, R (S) on Arlington)* Upscale furniture at reasonable prices.

Brookline

Bowl and Board *(T (Green C): Coolidge Corner 1354 Beacon St, 617-566-4726)* Selling home accessories, Bowl and Board has great deals on furniture items as well as decorative options for the home, apartment, or dorm.

Economy Hardware and Home Center *(T (Green C): St. Mary's Street   1012 Beacon St, 617-277-8811)* Looking for basic home needs such as paint, nails, and screws? Economy has it along with basic chairs, stools, and anything else you might need to pull together your home design.

Pier 1 Imports *(T (Green C): Coolidge Corner   1351 Beacon St, 617-232-9627)* This well-known chain has a wide selection of goods to make your living space more livable. Although a bit upscale and pricier, good deals may be spotted by a keen eye.

Cambridge

Buckaroo's *(T (Red): Harvard   1297 Cambridge St, Inman Sq. Dir: exit T and take #69 bus down Cambridge St)* Funky room accessories on the cheap.

Jamaica Plain

**Boomerangs *(T (Orange): Green St   716 Centre St, 617-524 5120   Dir: exit T, walk W on Green St .3 mi, L on Centre St)* Boomerangs has an eclectic selection of cheap goods from throw rugs to chests to chairs. Proceeds from sales support the AIDS Action Committee, a nonprofit working to stop HIV transmission.

Cobwebs *(T (Orange): Green St   703 Centre St, 617-983-0154   Dir: exit T, walk W on Green St .3 mi, L on Centre St)* This store, specializing in older fashions and antiques, verges on the pricier side, but with a good eye you can spot the occasional deal.

Gumshoe *(T (Orange): Forest Hills   40 South St, 617-522-5066 Dir: exit T, R (W) on Arborway, R on South St)* A small vintage store with a selection that spans the decades. Call ahead to make sure it is open.

Somerville

Porter Square Furniture *(T (Red): Porter   95 Elm St, 617- 625-9744   Dir: Cut across parking lot of Porter Sq shopping center, L on Elm)* Cheap new and used furniture.

South End

Labhome *(T (Silver): Union Park St   63 Wareham St, 617-482-7772 Dir: take Union St S, R on Harrison St, L on Malden St, bare R onto Wareham)* Like to decorate your house or apartment but don't want to be a Crate & Barrel cutout? This place is your solution to disillusion with standard decorating procedures.

Dating Tips

1) Stick to having drinks or coffee for a first date. That way, if the date is going badly, you don't have to eat in awkwardness and can leave quickly without raising suspicions.

2) Find a place to go where the atmosphere or surroundings can become a conversation topic. We've chosen plenty in this guide for you.

3) Try a walking date down Newbury St, along the Charles River, or through the Boston Common and Public Gardens.

4) Keep a draft text message in your phone asking friends to call you immediately with an "emergency" to get you out of bad dates in a hurry while allowing your date to save face.

5) If you are out and want to know if you are being checked out: Look at your watch, wait a second, and check to see if the person you think is checking you out is looking at his/her own watch. It is an unconscious instinct to check the time after we see someone else do it. Yawning works the same way.

6) Surveys have shown that a kiss is not necessary or expected on the first date. Try a kiss just to the side of the lips instead to keep your date guessing whether you are interested. They in turn, will become more interested as they attempt to decipher your body language.

7) Always meet your date at a public place for the first date or two to make sure he isn't a crazy stalker. If he picks you up, he'll not only have you alone in a car, he'll also always know where you live. Need more convincing? Watch *Fatal Attraction* or *Fear*.

8) For online dating, don't give out personal information over email. Simply meet at a public place for your first date. That way, if the person is crazy, he/she can't find you again. It is also better not to use your primary email account for correspondence with new people.

9) Remember that 80 percent of communication is nonverbal, so make sure your body language is saying the same things your mouth is or else your date won't trust you.

10) It is customary for a guy to pay for the first date. However, women should always offer to pay.

11) Never call someone more than twice without them calling you back first. The same is true for email.

For more dating tips,
visit **www.BrokeinBoston.com**

Fast Facts

Humorous:
- 10,000 people are injured by toilets each year in the US
- Montana mountain goats sometimes butt heads with one another so hard their hooves fall off
- Believe it or not, urine's yellow color was once believed to come from gold. Long ago, alchemists attempted to extract gold from pee.

Animal Facts
- When a giraffe is born, it is six feet tall
- The longest recorded flight of a chicken is 13 seconds
- A full grown bear can run as fast as a horse
- It takes 40 minutes to hard boil an ostrich egg
- Bees must collect the nectar from two thousand flowers to make one tablespoonful of honey.
- There are more beetles than any other kind of creature
- A group of ravens is called a murder
- Ninety-nine percent of all lobsters die within a few weeks of hatching. The odds are 10,000 to 1 against any larval lobster living long enough to become your dinner
- Orcas (killer whales) kill sharks by torpedoing up into the shark's stomach, causing the shark to explode.

Environmental
- 25 Billion Styrofoam cups are thrown away in the U.S. each year-- enough to string around the Earth 50 times.
- Starbucks offers a 10 cent discount to coffee drinkers who bring in their reusable mugs. Dunkin Donuts does not.
- It takes three pounds of baitfish to raise one pound of salmon
- 25 percent of all fish caught is discarded (usually dead) due to a lack of market value of applicable harvesting permits
- The world's population is growing by 77 million annually

Health
- Coffee is protective against type 2 diabetes, colon and rectal cancer, and liver disease thanks to high levels of antioxidants.
- Tomatoes, red grapefruit, and watermelon are high in lycopene, a substance that may protect against cancer
- Eating blueberries may help alleviate hemorrhoids
- Kiwis contain more Vitamin C than oranges.
- Pomegranates have the most antioxidants of any fruit

Discoveries
- The microwave was invented after a researcher walked by a radar tube and a chocolate bar melted in his pocket.
- Nerves were discovered by dissecting a dead giant squid that washed up on shore. No giant squid has ever been seen alive.

Outrageous
- From 1898 through 1910, Bayer drug company marketed Heroin as a non-addictive morphine substitute and cough medicine for children
- Before the Vietnam War era, LSD was used experimentally for psychiatric therapy. Psychiatrists often took LSD to better understand schizophrenia.
- 60 percent of surgeries in China are performed using acupuncture as the sole form of anesthetic.
- Some sects of Christianity believe that when Jesus was given a rag of vinegar to drink from at his crucifixion, the rag was soaked with mandrake—a root with strong anesthetic properties referred to a number of times in the Old Testament. The plant is thought to have rendered Christ unconscious and able to withstand the torture he then awoke from once the drug wore off.

Boston Facts
- John Hancock Tower (790 ft) was finished in 1976. Its reflective glass frames kept popping out during construction until engineers found a solution in using single-paned frames in lieu of double-paned glass.

Height of the Prudential Tower	= 750ft
Empire State Building	= 1,250ft
Height of the Sears Tower	= 1,450ft
Tapei 101 (Taiwan)	= 1,671ft

Presidents from MA: John Adams, John Quincy Adams, John F. Kennedy, George H. Bush

Disgusting
- Guinea worms are a parasitic organism that grow inside humans and can reach three feet in length. They affect people mainly in West Africa.
- The Candiru fish is a small, freshwater Amazonian fish that may swim up a human urethra or anus and lodge itself there.

Intellectual
- Psychologists have discovered they can implant false memories in people simply through testing
- over 30,000 people a year are killed by firearms in the US; 56 percent of those deaths were suicides
- Only 25 percent of US citizens possess passports

Technology
- The military has shipped lasers to Iraq to use in roadblocks. These "lasers" are designed to simply inflict intense pain without injury, thus allowing troops to stop those proceeding through a roadblock without killing them. The weapons will also be instrumental for crowd control, replacing rubber bullets as the preferred method of deterrence.
- Moore's Law states that every two years, technologies become twice as fast and half the size.
- The first hard drive available for the Apple II computer had a capacity of 5 MB

Alcohol
- The older a wine is, the less time it needs to breathe. This is because older wines have more time to oxidate (breathe) inside the bottle. Oxidation enhances the flavors in the wine.
- Bacterial spoilage in the cork may make some wines go bad.
- A wine that leaves your mouth feeling dry is known as an astringent wine. A dry wine refers to a wine that is less sweet.
- All bourbons are whiskeys, but not all whiskeys are bourbons. To qualify as bourbon, a whiskey must be produced from 51-79% Indian corn, made in the US, and aged for 2 years.
- When making mixed drinks, always pour the alcohol over ice before adding the mixers. This locks in the flavor of the alcohol by preventing it from volatizing (leaving the glass as a gas).

Recipes

CROWD-PLEASING DRINK RECIPES

Chocolate Martini: Pour three shots of vanilla vodka, one shot of crème de cacao, and half a shot of Godiva chocolate liquor over ice inside a martini shaker, shake well, and pour. Use regular vodka to make less sweet, and only pour two shots of vodka to make it sweeter. If you want a better presentation, add a half or full shot of Bailey's. This will make the drink appear smoother and creamy. For a chocolate orange martini, substitute orange vodka, but leave out the Bailey's if you do.

Regular Martini: You can use vodka or gin, but most prefer the taste of vodka. Pour three shots of vodka and one shot of vermouth over ice. Vermouth comes either sweet or dry. Sweet vermouth will make it "dirtier" and more appealing for those who do not like the taste of vodka unmasked. To make it even dirtier, pour a teaspoon/tablespoon of olive preserve (the juice from the jar) into the mix. The more olive preserve, the saltier it will become. Shake well and pour, straining the ice chunks. Add olives on a small skewer to the drink.

Screwdriver: This one is simple; fill a glass halfway with ice cubes. Fill one quarter of the glass with vodka and the rest with orange juice and stir.

Fuzzy Navel: Same as a screwdriver except you substitute Peach Schnapps for vodka.

Madras: Fill a glass halfway with ice. Fill one quarter of the glass with vodka, one half of the glass with orange juice, and the remainder of the glass with cranberry juice.

Smoky Crystal (Editor's concoction): Fill half of low glass with ice. Fill glass with vodka until ice is covered. Add Frangelico liquor until entire contents BEGIN to brown (about 1/2 shot's worth) and stir. If you have a sweet tooth: substitute vanilla vodka for regular vodka. Note: The better the vodka, the better the taste.

Irish Car Bomb: Drop a shot of Bailey's into a Guinness and chug it all at once. It will taste like butterscotch. This should not be done on a full stomach.

EASY MEALS

Macaroni & Cheese with Broccoli and Chicken:

You will need butter, milk, canned chicken, and a package of frozen broccoli. Grab a box of Kraft macaroni and cheese and follow cooking directions. While water is boiling, empty water out of can of chicken and place dewatered chicken into skillet with a tablespoon of olive oil. Add frozen broccoli to skillet and cook on high flame until chicken is starting to brown and broccoli is no longer frozen. Add both chicken and broccoli to pasta noodles when adding cheese, milk, and butter (as directions say—don't forget to strain water from pasta first!). Stir over very low flame until cheese has spread evenly.

Beef Stew:

Get a can of beef stew. Pick up a bag of carrots and a bag of small potatoes. Chop carrots and potatoes into small pieces and place in pot of boiling water. Drain water after 15 minutes, add can of beef stew, and heat contents for 10 minutes while stirring.

Wasabi-glazed Tilapia:

Pick up one pound of tilapia filets for every two people eating. Buy a container of wasabi powder and a bottle of soy sauce. Add one teaspoon of hot water to one tablespoon of wasabi powder in a small bowl, mix, and let sit for five minutes. Add one tablespoon of soy sauce to bowl and mix. Brush mixture onto one side of tilapia filets and cook in broiler (usually located below the oven) sauce-side up for about six minutes, or until fish becomes flaky and white.

To get fancier, heat one package of spinach with one tablespoon of chopper garlic, one teaspoon of olive oil, and one teaspoon of margarine or butter in a pan over medium heat while mixing until spinach shrinks. (Prep time should only take two to four minutes.) Serve tilapia over spinach.

Tacos:

Pick up some ground turkey (healthy) or beef, a packet of taco seasoning, one large tomato, one packet of shredded taco or mozzarella cheese, one container of salsa, and one packet of taco shells.

Cut up tomatoes into small pieces. Place meat in skillet and cook on medium heat until browning occurs while stirring. Add 1/4 cup of water, taco seasoning, and three tablespoons of salsa. Cook and stir for three minutes until meat is cooked and all seasoning and salsa is mixed in. Scoop meat into taco shells, add cheese and tomatoes.

Chicken Parmesan:

Buy one packet of pre-cooked, low fat Purdue chicken tenders (green package), a bottle of spaghetti sauce, and sliced cheese. Microwave chicken breast for one minute. Pour sauce over chicken and place one slice of cheese over sauce. Microwave for another minute...*BAM!* Can't find these pre-made chicken breasts? Just cook a thin piece of chicken breast in a skillet for about four minutes on one side over a tablespoon of olive oil or Pam, flip, and cook for another two minutes. Add spaghetti sauce and cheese and let cook for another two minutes. You can boil some angel hair pasta in water if you want to serve Chicken over the pasta. Pasta will take about 15 minutes in all to cook. Boil water first, then add pasta and cook for about seven minutes or until pasta sticks to a wall (throw it).

For more easy recipes,
visit **www.BrokeinBoston.com**

Abbreviations & Definitions

** Signifies the Editor's Choice

ABBREVIATIONS

Directions		*Days of the Week*

L = Left   **Rd** = Road   **M** = Monday
R = Right   **St** = Street   **T** = Tuesday
E = East   **Ave** = Avenue   **W** = Wednesday
W = West   **Dr** = Drive   **Th** = Thursday
N = North   **Rt** = Route   **F** = Friday
S = South   **I** = Interstate   **Sa** = Saturday
Dir = Directions   **Su** = Sunday

Places & Things

Comm Ave = Commonwealth Avenue
Govt = Government
Mass Ave = Massachusetts Avenue
Med Ctr = Medical Center
MGH = Massachusetts General Hospital
NE = New England
T = Trolley/subway/metro system
Sq = Square

In this book, when we say "**T (Green B): Harvard**," we mean: Take the Green Line T (subway), B Branch, to the Harvard Avenue T Stop

CATEGORY DEFINITIONS

Cheap Eats
Places where the average entrée cost is under 8 dollars, or where many entrees under $8 are served.

Cheap Drinks
Cheap is a relative term when used with drinks in Boston, but we typically included places where beers were under $4, mix-drinks were reasonably priced ($5-6), or with cheap specialty drinks.

Cool Cheap Date Places
For dinner spots, this category includes places where the average entrée costs between $8-16 but the décor or atmosphere is well-suited for dates. Otherwise, we included romantic or interesting locations and events to take your date to that won't cost much.

Cheap Specials
This category lists the best food and beverage deals in Boston that are offered at specific times of the day, week, month, or year.

Cheap Entertainment
Cheap things to do in and around Boston.

Free Entertainment
Free things to do in and around Boston.

Worth a Splurge
This section includes restaurants that are a bit on the pricey side ($10-15 per entrée for restaurants) but are exceptional in taste and portion size. Bars, clubs, and some other types of entertainment may be included in this category if they just shouldn't be missed.

Where to Bring Parents or Guests
Expensive ($15-30 per entrée) restaurants that rock—so long as you're not paying.

Badass Brunches
Fantastic, cheap brunches.

Midnight Munchies
Restaurants that serve food after midnight (12am).

For additional copies, dating tips, recipes, or to contact the staff, visit:

www.BrokeinBoston.com.

186 Index

188 Index

Editor's Picks

RED LINE SCHEDULE				
		Minutes Between Trains		
WEEKDAY	**First Trip**	**Max Time**	**Rush Hr***	**Last Trip**
LV Alewife	5:24 AM	12	9	12:15 AM
LV Braintree	5:15 AM	12	9	12:18 AM
LV Alewife	5:16 AM	12	9	12:22 AM
LV Ashmont (Mattapan Line)	5:16 AM	12	9	12:30 AM
LV Ashmont	5:16 AM	12	5	1:05 AM
LV Mattapan	5:05 AM	12	5	12:50 AM
SATURDAY				
LV Alewife	5:24 AM	14	14	12:15 AM
LV Braintree	5:15 AM	14	14	12:18 AM
LV Alewife	5:16 AM	14	14	12:22 AM
LV Ashmont (Mattapan Line)	5:16 AM	14	14	12:30 AM
LV Ashmont	5:15 AM	13	8	1:05 AM
LV Mattapan	5:05 AM	13	8	12:50 AM
SUNDAY				
LV Alewife	6:08 AM	16	16	12:14 AM
LV Braintree	6:00 AM	16	16	12:18 AM
LV Alewife	6:00 AM	16	16	12:22 AM
LV Ashmont (Mattapan Line)	6:00 AM	16	16	12:30 AM
LV Ashmont	6:01 AM	12	11	1:05 AM
LV Mattapan	5:51 AM	12	11	12:50 AM

*Morning Rush: 6:30-9:00AM. Evening Rush: 3:30-6:30PM.

GREEN LINE SCHEDULE

WEEKDAY	First Trip	Minutes Between Trains		Last Trip
		Max Time	Rush Hr	
LV Boston Col. (B)	5:01 AM	10	5	12:10 AM
LV Gov't Center (B)	5:34 AM	10	5	12:45 AM
LV Cleveland Cir. (C)	5:01 AM	10	7	12:10 AM
LV North Station (C)	5:36 AM	10	7	12:46 AM
LV Riverside (D)	4:56 AM	10	5	12:05 AM
LV Gov't Center (D)	5:32 AM	10	5	12:45 AM
LV Lechmere (E)	5:01 AM	10	8	12:30 AM
LV Heath St. (E)	5:30 AM	10	8	12:45 AM
SATURDAY				
LV Boston Col. (B)	*4:45 AM	8	6	12:10 AM
LV Gov't Center (B)	5:35 AM	8	6	12:50 AM
LV Cleveland Cir. (C)	4:50 AM	10	8	12:10 AM
LV North Station (C)	5:30 AM	10	8	12:50 AM
LV Riverside (D)	4:55 AM	10	8	12:00 AM
LV Gov't Center (D)	5:32 AM	10	8	12:45 AM
LV Lechmere (E)	5:01 AM	10	7	12:30 AM
LV Heath St. (E)	3:30 AM	10	7	12:45 AM
SUNDAY				
LV Boston Col. (B)	5:20 AM	10	9	12:10 AM
LV Gov't Center (B)	6:06 AM	10	9	12:48 AM
LV Cleveland Cir. (C)	5:30 AM	10	10	12:10 AM
LV North Station (C)	6:06 AM	10	10	12:48 AM
LV Riverside (D)	5:40 AM	10	10	12:00 AM
LV Gov't Center (D)	6:19 AM	10	10	12:45 AM
LV Lechmere (E)	5:35 AM	11	10	12:30 AM
LV Heath St. (E)	6:45 AM	11	10	12:47 AM

*Morning Rush: 6:30-9:00AM. Evening Rush: 3:30-6:30PM.

ORANGE LINE SCHEDULE				
		Minutes Between Trains		
WEEKDAY	**First Trip**	**Max Time**	**Rush Hr**	**Last Trip**
LV Oak Grove	5:16 AM	13	5	12:26 AM
LV Forest Hills	5:16 AM	13	5	12:22 AM
SATURDAY				
LV Oak Grove	5:16 AM	13	10	12:26 AM
LV Forest Hills	5:16 AM	13	10	12:22 AM
SUNDAY				
LV Oak Grove	6:00 AM	14	18	12:17 AM
LV Forest Hills	6:00 AM	14	18	12:22 AM

*Morning Rush: 6:30-9:00AM. Evening Rush: 3:30-6:30PM.

SILVER LINE WATERFRONT SCHEDULE

| WEEKDAY | First Trip | Minutes Between Trains | | Last Trip |
		Max Time	Rush Hr	
LV Silver Line Way	5:28 AM	5	12	12:33 AM
LV South Station	5:35 AM	3	12	12:50 PM
SATURDAY				
LV Silver Line Way	5:28 AM	12	12	12:40 AM
LV South Station	5:35 AM	12	12	12:48 AM
SUNDAY				
LV Silver Line Way	6:04 AM	12	12	12:40 AM
LV South Station	6:12 AM	12	12	12:48 AM

*Morning Rush: 6:30-9:00AM. Evening Rush: 3:30-6:30PM.

SILVER LINE WASHINGTON ST. SCHEDULE

| WEEKDAY | First Trip | Minutes Between Trains | | Last Trip |
		Max Time	Rush Hr	
LV Dudley Station	5:15 AM	12	5	12:48 AM
LV Downtown Crossing	5:30 AM	12	5	1:02 AM
SATURDAY				
LV Dudley Station	5:16 AM	9	6	12:46 AM
LV Downtown Crossing	5:32 AM	9	6	12:58 AM
SUNDAY				
LV Dudley Station	6:00 AM	10	8	12:25 AM
LV Downtown Crossing	6:13 AM	10	8	12:45 AM

BLUE LINE SCHEDULE				
		Minutes Between Trains		
WEEKDAY	**First Trip**	**Max Time**	**Rush Hr**	**Last Trip**
LV Wonderland	5:13 AM	11	4	12:26 AM
LV Orient Heights	5:13 AM	11	4	12:33 AM
LV Gov't Center	5:30 AM	11	4	12:50 AM
SATURDAY				
LV Wonderland	5:25 AM	11	9	12:26 AM
LV Orient Heights	5:13 AM	11	9	12:33 AM
LV Gov't Center	5:31 AM	11	9	12:51 AM
SUNDAY				
LV Wonderland	5:58 AM	14	9	12:26 AM
LV Orient Heights	6:05 AM	14	9	12:33 AM
LV Gov't Center	6:23 AM	14	9	12:51 AM

*Morning Rush: 6:30-9:00AM. Evening Rush: 3:30-6:30PM.

Ocean State Job Lot *(located throughout MA and New England)*
Think of Job Lot as a slightly smaller Wal-Mart that has grown organically from one store to 80 without losing its neighborhood feel or undergoing a corporate transformation. The privately-owned chain sells nearly every type of good imaginable—from cosmetics to cookware—at seemingly surreal prices. By purchasing items in mass quantities, buying out excess inventories, and maintaining a very small markup from cost to retail price, Job Lot fills its stores and gigantic warehouse with virtually any type of merchandise at huge discounts to its customers. So think again before heading off to the mall to pick up that $60 sweater you've been craving: Job Lot may be selling the very same one for $12.99. It's worth the trek.

Nearest location:

Quincy
141 Newport Ave, 617-479-1778
Store Hours: M-Sa 8am-9pm, Su 9am-8pm
Dir: from Bston, take I-93 South to exit 12, R on Gallivan Blvd / MA-203E, R on Neponset Ave / MA-3AS, R onto Newport Ave

Other Locations in MA

Athol	Foxboro	Plymouth
Brockton	Gardner	Quincy
Buzzards	Bay Holyoke	Rockland
Chatham	Hyannis	Seekonk
Chicopee	Kingston	Somerset
Chicopee - Clearance	Marlboro	South Yarmouth
Dennisport	Marshfield	Southbridge
E.Bridgewater	Medway	Southwick
East Springfield	Middleboro	Springfield
Fairhaven	New Bedford	Taunton
Fall River	Norwood	Westboro
Falmouth	Palmer	Westfield

Visit www.oceanstatejoblot.com for more information and to locate a store in CT, ME, NH, or RI.

Christmas Tree Shops *(located throughout MA and New England)*
Don't let the name fool you; this regional chain sells a lot more than seasonal gifts and decorations. Stores are packed with a variety of home-related goods, including furniture, rugs, lighting, tableware, kitchen items, books, and toys to name just a handful. Although recently acquired by Bed, Bath & Beyond, Christmas Tree Shops continue to provide unique, high quality goods for prices ranging from very reasonable to ridiculously cheap. The chain's following seems to border on fanaticism at times, as shoppers head there for fun as much as for necessitates. Regardless of your intent, you'll likely end up buying something cool that wasn't on your shopping list. To showcase its individuality in the chain retail business, many Christmas Tree Shop building designs are both novel and attractive.

Nearest location:

Somerville
177 Middlesex Ave, 617-623-3428
Dir: from Boston, take I-93 North to Rt 28N and take a slight right onto Middlesex Ave

Store Hours:	**Other Locations in MA**
<u>Jan 1 - Oct 28</u>	
M-Sa: 9am – 9pm	Avon
Su: 9AM - 8PM	Falmouth
	Holyoke
<u>Oct 29 - Dec 24</u>	Hyannis
7 days: 8AM - 10PM	Lynnfield
	Natick
<u>Dec 26 - Dec 31</u>	North Attleboro
7 days: 8am – 10pm	North Dartmouth
	Orleans
	Pembroke
	Sagamore
	Shrewsbury
	West Dennis
	West Yarmouth
	Yarmouthport

Visit www.christmastreeshops.com for more information and to locate a store in CT, ME, NH, NJ, NY, RI, or VT.

MBTA Subway Map

LECHMERE
SCIENCE PARK
NORTH STATION
HAYMARKET
← COMMUTER RAIL / AMTRAK
GOVERNMENT CENTER
PARK STREET
BOYLSTON
ARLINGTON
COPLEY
BACK BAY / SOUTH END
COMMUTER RAIL / AMTRAK →
HYNES CONVENTION CENTER / ICA
PRUDENTIAL
SYMPHONY
KENMORE

(T) GREEN LINE

SUBWAY   STREET CAR
RAPID TRANSIT LINES

(P) FOR MBTA POLICE CALL 617-222-1212
(?) FOR CUSTOMER SERVICE & TRAVEL INFORMATION CALL 617-222-3200

NORTHEASTERN
MUSEUM OF FINE ARTS
LONGWOOD MEDICAL AREA
BRIGHAM CIRCLE
FENWOOD RD
MISSION PARK
RIVERWAY
BACK OF THE HILL
HUNTINGTON AVE

BLANDFORD ST
BOSTON UNIVERSITY EAST
BOSTON UNIVERSITY CENTRAL
BOSTON UNIVERSITY WEST
ST PAUL ST
PLEASANT ST
BABCOCK ST
PACKARDS CORNER
HARVARD AVE
GRIGGS ST
ALLSTON ST
WARREN ST
WASHINGTON ST
SUTHERLAND RD
CHISWICK RD
CHESTNUT HILL AVE
SOUTH ST

COMMONWEALTH AVE

BOSTON COLLEGE (B)

ST MARYS ST
HAWES ST
KENT ST
ST PAUL ST
COOLIDGE CORNER
WINCHESTER ST
BRANDON HALL
FAIRBANKS ST
WASHINGTON SQ
TAPPAN ST
DEAN RD
ENGLEWOOD AVE

CLEVELAND CIRCLE (C)

BEACON ST

FENWAY
LONGWOOD
BROOKLINE VILLAGE
BROOKLINE HILLS
BEACONSFIELD
RESERVOIR
CHESTNUT HILL
NEWTON CENTRE
NEWTON HIGHLANDS
ELIOT
WABAN
WOODLAND

RIVERSIDE (D)

HEATH ST / VA MEDICAL CENTER (E)

MBTA Commuter Rail Routes

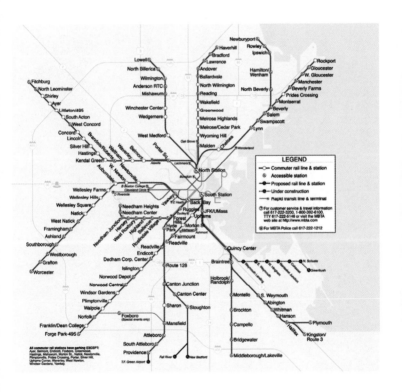

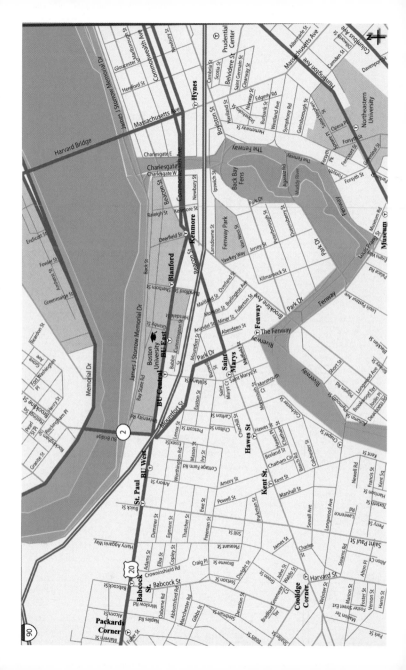

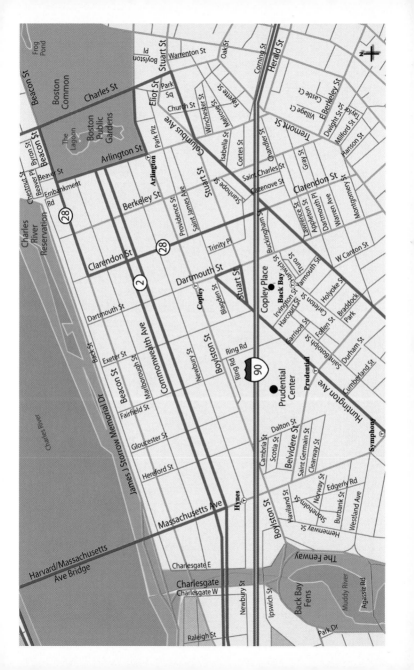

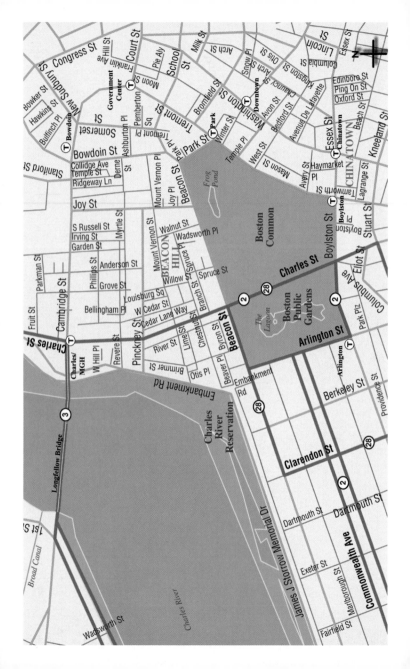

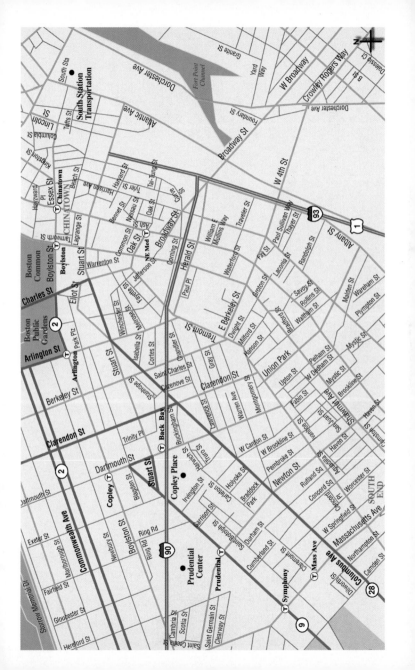

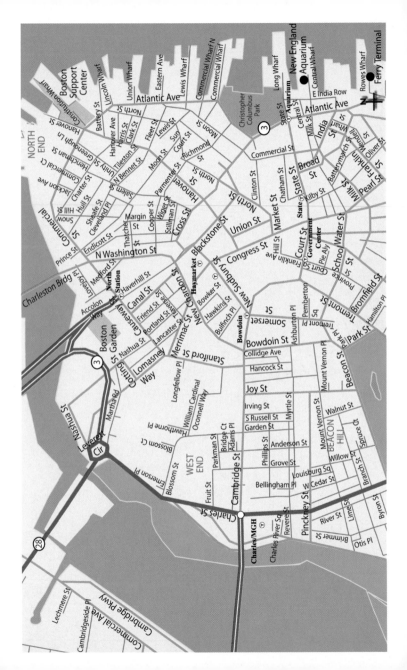

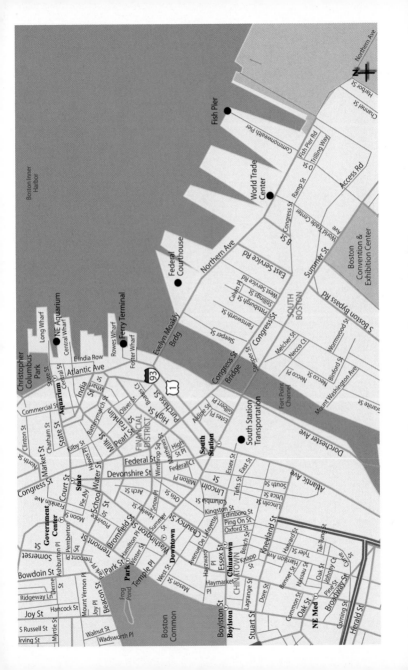

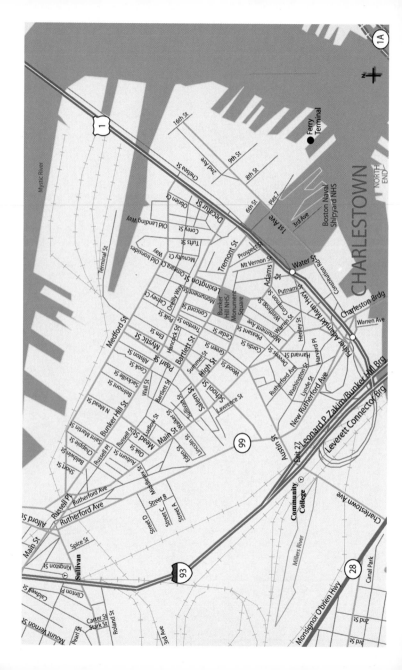

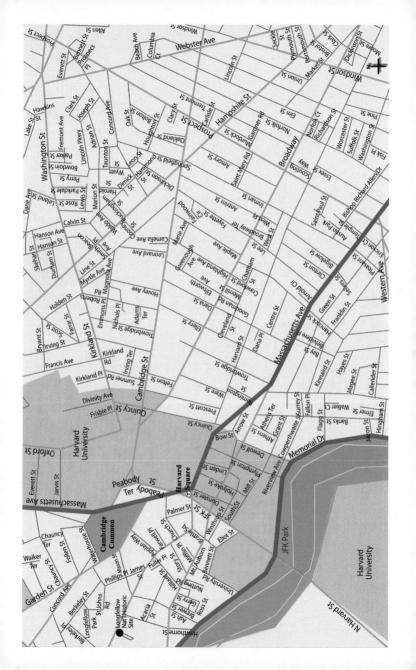

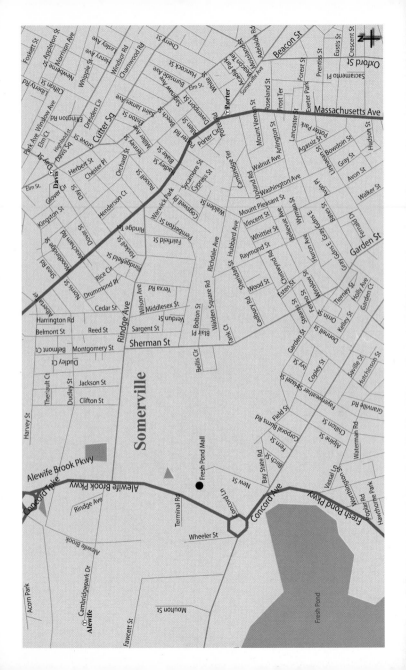